TEEN to TEEN

365 DAILY DEVOTIONS

BY TEEN GUYS FOR TEEN GUYS

COMPILED BY
PATTI M. HUMMEL

B&H
PUBLISHING GROUP
Nashville, Tennessee

INTRODUCTION

As a teen male in today's society, do you question what you see in men that are supposed to be representing God to you? Do you find life difficult to live as a Christian when what the world offers is much more appealing? Is there a battle raging inside your heart and mind that you feel ill-equipped to deal with? Do you wonder about being a husband, father, church, and community leader? Well, don't be discouraged by the wonder and doubts you may be experiencing. Your feelings and your questions are not uncommon. As a matter of fact, there are teens all over the world wondering, doubting, and questioning what is going on in their lives.

Teen-to-Teen: 365 Daily Devotions by Teen Guys for Teen Guys will bless and encourage you as you read from your peers how they are walking through the valleys, how they are praising God when they reach the mountaintops, and how they are abiding in Him as they learn to embrace all of Christ by His abundant grace. This book will aid you as you learn to go to the Word of God and as He teaches you how to live the Christian life consistently and with great joy.

Ephesians 5 and 6 explain that consistency in the Christian life is essential. Be encouraged to listen to the Father heart of God and allow Him to remove the doubt, the questions, and wonder and as Paul reminds us, "Pay careful attention, then, to how you walk not as unwise people but as wise—making the most of the time, because the days are evil. So don't be foolish, but understand what the Lord's will is. And don't get drunk with wine, which leads to reckless actions, but be filled by the Spirit: speaking to one another in psalms, hymns, and spiritual songs, singing and making music from your heart to the Lord, giving thanks always for everything to God the Father in the name of our Lord Jesus Christ, submitting to one another in the fear of Christ" (5:15–21).

My prayer is that every young man who reads these devotional messages will be drawn closer to the Lord God in a deep relationship that will illuminate the world around them with the gospel message of hope that does not disappoint.

Dr. Fred Luter Jr., President, The Southern Baptist Convention
Senior Pastor, Franklin Avenue Baptist Church, New Orleans, LA; husband;
father to a precious daughter and to a son; one of God's mighty men

1

JANUARY

Delight in God's Word

How can a young man keep his way pure?

By keeping Your word.

I have sought You with all my heart;

don't let me wander from Your commands.

I have treasured Your word in my heart

so that I may not sin against You.

LORD, may You be praised;

teach me Your statutes.

With my lips I proclaim all the judgments

from Your mouth. I rejoice in the way revealed by Your decrees as much

as in all riches.

I will meditate on Your precepts

and think about Your ways.

I will delight in Your statutes;

I will not forget Your word.

(Psalm 119:9–16)

PRIORITIZING

"In the beginning God created the heavens and the earth."

—Genesis 1:1

When we look at the story of creation, there are so many important details that it would take years to study the relationships between each and every one. But one of the most prevalent themes is God's sense of order. Everything that He created is absolutely necessary for the next one to follow. Sunlight and water are created before plants, and plants before beasts, so that everything can work the way it is supposed to. This reveals God's value of order and prioritization.

Now for us, prioritizing is usually a very hard task. We rarely take time to plan our actions—and, most importantly, our time—to create the most efficient plan. But we need to realize that without a definite plan and without having guidelines and priorities by which we live, we are wandering hopelessly through life and more than likely won't reach our full potential. Understand that God must come first in everything, lining up the remainder of our priorities with His Will to help us become more like Him. In fact, if we, as Christians, do not have some sense of priority in our lives, then we are living wrong. Though it may come easier to some more than others, God expects us to be able to prioritize and keep Him first. Start by making sure your actions line up with God's will, then list the things you value and spend most of your time on. See what your current priorities are and make sure they match up with what you want them to be.

CODY BRANDON: *17, Old Hickory, TN*
The Fellowship at Two Rivers, Nashville, TN: Mt. Juliet High School, Mt. Juliet, TN

DEALING WITH SINFUL DESIRES

"You took off your former way of life, the old self that is corrupted by deceitful desires; you are being renewed in the spirit of your minds; you put on the new self, the one created according to God's likeness in righteousness and purity of the truth." —*Ephesians 4:22–24*

A disobedient child stuck her hand between the car and the door as it was closing, smashing her hand. That pain will be enough to keep her from doing that again. Sometimes I act like a child, but in my case it pertains to sin. I repeatedly stick my hand in the proverbial door. We have a loving Father who warns us against getting into sin. He tells us how it brings about guilt, sadness, pain, separation, and fear. We decide, however, that we will be fine doing it our way. So we stick our hands into cheating, stealing, sexual sin, disrespect, and just plain ignoring what our heavenly Father has to say about our lives and our choices. God still loves us and forgive us; however, He will not always remove the consequences. You might say, "When I sin, nothing seems to go wrong. Why should I stop?" It often takes months, or even years, to recognize how our choices affect our lives and the lives of others. The consequences of sin aren't always obvious or physical. Fundamentally, sin takes us further from God, causing our spiritual lives to suffer. Jesus offers us help, eternal life, meaning, and purpose. Sin will remain an epidemic until people realize that the only thing that can fill the holes in their hearts that they try to fill with sin is Jesus. I think all of us need to learn to walk closer to and depend more on our Savior every day.

LUKE MERRICK: *15, Springdale, AR*
Immanuel Baptist Church and Shiloh Christian School, Springdale, AR

4

FAMILY

"What is the source of wars and fights among you?
Don't they come from the cravings that are at war within you?
You desire and do not have. You murder and covet and cannot obtain.
You fight and war. You do not have because you do not ask."

—James 4:1–2

If you're like me, sometimes your family can be super annoying. There's always a specific family member that will really get to me for a certain period of time. It seems everything they say or do gets under my skin! So why did God give us our families if all they do is annoy us? You can think about it this way: God gave you your family as a challenge to conquer. He specifically formulated each family member to exhibit qualities that would annoy you. Really! God gave you your family so that you could learn to get along with each type of person in your family. He knew all of the types of people you would encounter throughout your life, and He placed each member of your family in your home so that could help you grow in areas He knows you needed growth. So, rather than trying to get away from your family, why not spend some time with them? Try to overlook it when they do stuff that irritates you, because they will. You can choose whether to allow their behavior to rain on your parade or not! Try to learn to get along with them, knowing that in doing so you are improving the way you will get along with other people for the rest of your life. What we learn at home is the foundation for life when we leave home!

MICAH COOKSEY: *19, McMinnville, OR*
Valley Baptist Church, McMinnville, OR

SOME SIMPLE THINGS

"Mankind, He has told you what is good and what it is the LORD requires of you: to act justly, to love faithfulness, and to walk humbly with your God." —*Micah 6:8*

Sadly, I haven't been a good follower of God's commandments. Jesus died for my sins, and the more I learn from the Bible the more I see that I'm not following God like I should. I can't break free from my sins. Yet, there have been ways out, and there has been progress. Sin can only be overcome through Jesus. I was given good advice when I was younger: deal with the simplest and most manageable sins in your life. Ask God to help you recognize and overcome your sins and see ways to reduce temptation. I used to curse and talk about unwholesome things. Asking for help made me aware that the company I kept was not good. I have to watch those things now. Be mindful of your tongue, slow to speak, and control your thoughts because they influence your life. Let God help you overcome sinful habits. Keep your thoughts focused on God and His Word, asking Him to help you. The results and growth in Him will amaze you. One sin put down can lead to two sins put down, then three, and eventually you can see improvement in your Christian walk. You will have times of increased difficulty and times of failure, but God is there to rescue you from those pits. Surround yourself with good wholesome things and people, so that you may be uplifted. Focus on Jesus and His promises, because He can be trusted to help.

ROBBY D. LAND: *18, Gatlinburg, TN*
First Baptist Church and Gatlinburg-Pittman High School, Gatlinburg, TN

FAVORITISM

"My brothers, do not show favoritism as you hold on to the faith in our glorious Lord Jesus Christ." —*James 2:1*

In this passage we as the church, God's children, are told to not show favoritism. If you read the rest of the chapter, you'll see the author uses the example of a rich man and a poor man. He says that if these two men walk into the church, we shouldn't treat the rich man as if he is better than the poor man. Favoritism can also speak to many scenarios we struggle with. One that most men our age would struggle with is if two girls walked into church one day, and one was beautiful and the other wasn't. We shouldn't completely ignore the one we don't find attractive, focusing on and treating the one that looks good as if she is more of a person than the other one. The common thing in both of these situations is selfishness. Instead of viewing people as equals, as we should, we let their outward appearance or financial status define them. This is an area we struggle with but don't really view as sin. However, James 2:9 says, "But if you show favoritism, you commit sin and are convicted by the law as transgressors." As Christians, we should view people as lost or saved. We shouldn't let things such as money, outward appearance, skin color, gender, or race define how we view people.

CLAY NORMAN: *18, Albany, GA*
Sherwood Baptist Church and Sherwood Christian Academy, Albany, GA

NATURE'S PROCLAMATION (PART 1)

"The heavens declare the glory of God, and the sky proclaims the work of His hands." —*Psalm 19:1*

God's brilliance and creativity shine forth in the entire world around us. I love to surfboard. Whenever I paddle out into the ocean on a surfboard, I get to truly enjoy the sea and the world around me because I can see the glory of our God. Every aspect of nature points directly to the existence of an omnipotent God. For any human to so much as hint that the world somehow changed into its present state by evolution is to degrade the status of an almighty God. In man's heart, he knows that evolution is a theory with no solid foundation in fact. He has invented the theory of evolution so that he may live in a way that pleases him, without ever having to answer for a single sinful act. Although many people put up a façade of believing the theory of evolution, if they truly considered the so-called facts that support evolution, they would see that the only explanation for a beautiful world like ours is that a beautiful God like ours created it for His own good pleasure. For instance, a single cell can have 60,000 proteins, of which there are 100 different configurations. Besides this, there are extremely complex cell types. The chances for the random assembly of a cell are 1 in 104,478,296. This is so far-fetched that it is basically impossible. Only when someone knows the truth about how the earth was created can he truly enjoy its beauty.

LUKE ABENDROTH: *16, Lancaster, MA*
Bethlehem Bible Church and Bethlehem Bible Church Homeschool Co-op, West Boylston, MA

NATURE'S PROCLAMATION (PART 2)

"The heavens declare the glory of God, and the sky proclaims the work of His hands." —*Psalm 19:1*

When surfing early in the morning, the sun shining on my back and the ocean shifting beneath me, I feel the true power of our God. When someone who believes in a Creator sees a sky full of brilliant stars, a waterfall sparkling in the sunlight, or a horse's bulging muscles as it gallops down a beach, he can appreciate the awesome splendor of a sovereign God. In each gnarled oak tree, each flash of lightning, or every roar of thunder the believer in Christ Jesus sees his Creator's own design. Although the only way to truly enjoy nature is by seeing God's handiwork in everything, it is possible, maybe even common, that a man sees the evidence of a Creator in creation but has never heard the name of Jesus. This is why we are called in Matthew 28:18–20 to go out as missionaries into the world and preach the gospel. Without a substitute for our sins there is no hope for salvation. We can do nothing to save ourselves. The only way to be delivered from sin and the eternal punishment of God is to have someone to pay for that sin. Jesus Christ, the Son of God, did that at Calvary. He came down from heaven and lived a perfect life, then was sacrificed on the cross for all believers' sin. On the third day, He defeated death and rose again according to the Scriptures. We should not rest until we are right with a just God. He will deliver us from our sins so that we can enjoy the beauty of heaven.

LUKE ABENDROTH: *16, Lancaster, MA*
Bethlehem Bible Church and Bethlehem Bible Church Homeschool Co-op, West Boylston, MA

LUST

"We too all previously lived among them in our fleshly desires, carrying out the inclinations of our flesh and thoughts, and we were by nature children under wrath as the others were also. But God, who is rich in mercy, because of His great love that He had for us, made us alive with the Messiah even though we were dead in trespasses. You are saved by grace!" —*Ephesians 2:3–5*

Lust is a problem. The Bible tells us that we will struggle with lust. It's hard for boys to stop looking at girls or to stop watching pornography on the computer screen. It's hard for girls to put down the fiery romance books or stop watching romantic movies. Ephesians tells us that, "We all once conducted ourselves in the lusts of our flesh." It is a constant battle being fought in the war against sin and Satan, but God provides hope for us in the war, "even when we were dead in trespasses, [He] made us alive together in Christ." God is here, and He is ready to help us win this battle. Job 31:1 says, "I have made a covenant with my eyes. How then could I look at a young woman?" Matthew 5:29 instructs, "If your right eye causes you to sin, gouge it out and throw it away. For it is better that you lose one of the parts of your body than for your whole body to be thrown in hell." God has a plan for us to win this. Bounce your eyes from looking at that girl and change the channel when the sensual commercial or show comes on. If there is anything that causes you to lust, destroy it! Get rid of the porn sites, put up parental blocks, burn the romance book, and break the romance DVD. God is available in prayer and through His Word to help when the temptation to lust haunts us. Call on Him.

ZACH WATKINS: *16, Henderson, NV*
Highland Hills Baptist Church and Green Valley High School, Henderson, NV

GO!

"Go, therefore, and make disciples of all nations, baptizing them in the name of the Father and of the Son and of the Holy Spirit, teaching them to observe everything I have commanded you. And remember, I am with you always, to the end of the age." —*Matthew 28:19–20*

The Bible has much to say about outreach, as we see in the verse above. Christians have received a calling from God to reach out to the lost and point them toward Him. No matter how badly you've acted, it just matters that you reach out. You can also repent of your ways. Take Paul for example: as Saul he arrested Christians for their beliefs. Then Jesus came to him and told him to knock it off. Saul was blinded but then was healed. Saul who was also called Paul began to evangelize the world, which is amazing, right? We need to develop a relationship with the person who needs God, then invite them to church. What I've discovered is that people are more likely to come with a friend than with a stranger. If they go to church, that's great, keep inviting them. It's important to ask and to be you without putting pressure on them. Using the ABCs of Christianity may help. **A:** Admit that you're a sinner. **B:** Believe that Jesus is God's Son. **C:** Confess your faith in Jesus, your Lord and Savior. The lost need a person to help them find Jesus. They need living encouragement.

TERRELL STRAIN: *13, Spokane, WA*
Airway Heights Baptist Church, Airway Heights, WA; Medical Lake Middle School, Medical Lake, WA

EFFORT

"There is no favoritism with God." —*Romans 2:11*

When I was at a Young Life camp in New York, there was a girl I thought was amazing. I wanted to ask her out, but every time I tried, something would come up or I would get nervous. I decided to take a different approach. Since I have always been able to speak well through music, I thought I would play her a song to get my point across. I went out early by the lake and hid my guitar; then later she and I were at the lake and she sat down on a bench overlooking the lake. I took out my guitar and began to play the first couple lines of "In My Head" by Jason Derulo. And I sang the rest of the song to her. She really loved it, and that was my way of asking her out. I was thinking about this a couple of weeks ago, and I realized I had put a lot of effort into that. I went out early, hid my guitar, learned the song, and got her out there. Then I thought, I have never put that much work into anything having to do with my relationship with God. Now, you are probably thinking, What does asking a girl out have to do with a relationship with God? It really doesn't, but I'm talking about the work I put into asking that girl out in an interesting way. If we all used the same amount of effort in our spiritual relationships, we would be so close to God. In Nehemiah, the people worked hard and put all their effort toward rebuilding the wall in Jerusalem. If we are that diligent in building a relationship with God, it could be like the wall, strong and firm with a sturdy foundation and base.

DANIEL BAEHR: *17, Manassas, VA*
Emmanuel Baptist Church Youth Group and Emmanuel Christian School, Manassas, VA

THINGS WILL GET BETTER!

"We know that all things work together for the good of those who love God: those who are called according to His purpose."

—Romans 8:28

We can think of dozens of times in our lives when things weren't going as well as we thought they should; times when we felt like everyone was against us and we had no one to go to. But there is always someone. God has our whole lives planned out before we are even born, and everything that happens is part of that larger plan He has created. So even though it seems that nothing is under control, it is, just not under our control. Though it may look like a situation will never get better, and nothing good can come of it, something always will whether we realize it or not. My brother, Matthew, is a great example. Diagnosed with leukemia when he was very young, he spent a long time in the hospital undergoing chemotherapy, and it took a toll on his small body. My mother stayed in the hospital with him the whole time, offering encouragement and caring for him as much as she could. My other brother, Jedediah, and I visited him often. Matthew spent the worst times of his life in the hospital and almost died! He was so determined to not let cancer defeat him, and it didn't. He pulled through and has been in remission for years, which he thanks God for. Instead of trying to forget the whole situation, he is a light for others with cancer. He witnesses to people with cancer letting them know that you can beat it and survive. I firmly believe that because, and only because, of my brother's testimony and the hope that he gives people, more people have beat their cancer, trusting God in all things!

JACOB LAVALLEY: *16, Pageland, SC*
Mount Moriah Baptist Church and South Pointe Christian School, Pageland, SC

TEMPTATION

"No temptation has overtaken you except what is common to humanity. God is faithful, and He will not allow you to be tempted beyond what you are able, but with the temptation He will also provide a way of escape so that you are able to bear it." —1 Corinthians 10:13

Temptation is something that we all deal with. It is a real problem and Satan knows that, so he loves to use temptation on teenagers. It's strong. Be careful! If you let it, it can control your entire life. Temptation can cripple every step you take in your walk with Christ. In fact, temptation will keep you from making any more steps forward with Christ. Temptation will keep you spiritually still. Every day you wake up, you wish you could shake this thing, but temptation is a stronghold, and it grows stronger every day when we do not deal with it. Don't let temptation take control of your life. It's not worth it. Trust me, if you are dealing with a temptation, remember that God will always provide a way of escape. Control your temptation; don't let it control you. "Submit to God . . . resist the Devil, and he will flee from you" (James 4:7).

CHRISTIAN SMITH: *17, New Orleans, LA*
Franklin Avenue Baptist Church and New Orleans Charter Science and Mathematics High School, New Orleans, LA

LIVING WITHOUT FEAR

"For God has not given us a spirit of fearfulness, but one of power, love, and sound judgment." —*2 Timothy 1:7*

I've been a very competitive person all my life. From Little League all the way through high school, I've always wanted to win at everything I've been involved in. I would prepare in practice and work hard to be the best I could be for every practice and for the big game. I would be confident and ready to go all the way up to game day, but there was always a moment of weakness I could never prepare for—pregame fear. For some reason I could never overcome it, and it would leave my body in knots. The pressure of it being the big game would throw me into a panic. One day I was in Sunday school, and the subject was David and how he had responsibility and felt the pressure of millions of lives that were at stake. Everybody was watching him. Talk about a humbling lesson. Reading about David and then coming across the Scripture in 2 Timothy helped me to realize that no fear was too big for God to help me overcome. So whether it's the big game, final exam, or even having the courage to preach the gospel, God has given us everything but a reason to fear anything we face.

PATRICK STANFORD: *18, Albany, GA*
Sherwood Baptist Church and Sherwood Christian Academy, Albany, GA

DON'T GO BACK!

"For we are His creation, created in Christ Jesus for good works, which God prepared ahead of time so that we should walk in them."

—*Ephesians 2:10*

Many of us know what it feels like to be forgiven of a sin that has been in our life for a while. It is that amazing, indescribable feeling that just takes over your whole body. It makes you so happy and proud that you finally overcame it. But, here comes the challenging part—keeping it out of your life. Once Satan realizes that he failed, he will try again and again to succeed, which brings a lot of temptation to give in and do it just one more time. But you have to stay strong! I know, easier said than done, but take a moment and think about it. Whenever you are stuck in a situation like this, just remember how that awesome feeling felt when you confessed and repented of your sin, knowing that God had forgiven you. You don't want Satan to win, do you? Well, that's exactly what you're doing every time you give in just one more time and go back to your old lifestyle. Jesus is our victory!

BRANDON CARROLL: *17, York, SC*
Hillcrest Baptist Church and York Comprehensive High School, York, SC

SHYNESS

"The fear of man is a snare, but the one who trusts
in the Lord is protected." —*Proverbs 29:25*

We pray for the opportunity to do God's work, but when we see it right in front of us and get pumped about it, we freeze. The opportunity passes and we move on, sad that we were too shy to step up and make the opportunity a moment for God. How do we find the courage to take a chance for God without fearing the worst will happen as a result? How will people react if we act in a godly way and do the right thing? The verse above tells us that we can overcome this fear by knowing we will be protected by Him, as long as what we do is truly for God and ordained by Him. This means no harm will come to us as a result of doing His will. We might be hesitant to do the right thing, but knowing God is with us will give us a sense of confidence that is necessary, as we trust God that good results will follow. Who knows, someone may see you do the right thing and come to know the Lord because of your actions. Being willing to obey the commandments of Christ is the first step. He promised to be a lamp unto our feet and a light to our path.

DAVID JOSEPH DALESANDRO: *14, York, SC*
Hillcrest Baptist Church and York Comprehensive High School, York, SC

TURNING A BAD DAY AROUND

"Is anyone among you suffering? He should pray. Is anyone cheerful? He should sing praises." —*James 5:13*

My normal morning schedule includes me taking a shower immediately after I wake up. One morning it wasn't until I was ready to leave home that I realized I was already thirty minutes late for school. When I eventually got to school, I remembered that I had forgotten to do some of my homework. Yuck! When I got to lunch that day, another unusual thing occurred: the cafeteria had run out of food. Then I went to baseball practice, and it turned out I forgot my gear. I'm sure most of us, if not all of us, have had at least one day like the one I just described. They have the potential to ruin your week. Then the next day, I got up on time and got to school early. At lunch, they served my favorite food. Coach decided to give us a day off. This was the exact opposite of the day before. James 5:13 says, "Is anyone among you suffering? He should pray. Is anyone cheerful? He should sing praises." All I had to do was pray. You shouldn't let one bad day ruin the rest of your week. If you continue to have bad days, change the way you are praying. If you have a good day, and even if you have a bad day, give thanks to God. Prayer is a powerful thing. If you are having a bad or a good day, if you are sick or healthy, if you are wealthy or poor, prayer is one of the most important parts of your relationship with God.

BRANDON BOHN: *16, Springdale, AR*
Cross Church Springdale Campus and Shiloh Christian School, Springdale, AR

PUT YOUR TRUST IN THE LORD

"Trust in the LORD with all your heart and do not rely on your own understanding." —*Proverbs 3:5*

Have you ever had a problem, a question, or any kind of situation where you didn't know what to do? Did you do what you thought was right, but the situation didn't turn out the way you wanted it to? Maybe it was because you did not ask God or trust in God. Matthew 7:7 says, "Keep asking, and it will be given to you. Keep searching and you will find. Keep knocking, and the door will be opened to you." Maybe if you had asked and sought, like it says in Matthew 7:7, the outcome could have been different. Maybe if you had set your trust in the Lord, like it says in Proverbs 3:5, and not done what you thought was right, the situation might have gone another way. We all run into problems and questions at some time in our lives, but we need to remember Matthew 7:7 and Proverbs 3:5 so that we can ask for the answer, search it out, and trust that God will do what is right in our life.

CLAYTON TEAL: *17, Pageland, SC*
Smyrna Baptist Church and South Pointe Christian School, Pageland, SC

THE BOLDNESS OF NIGEL

"In Him we have boldness and confident access through faith in Him."
—*Ephesians 3:12*

I've known Nigel since the fifth grade, and God has turned his life completely around. Our church did several mission projects in a broken-down neighborhood in our city, and that is where I met Nigel. You could say Nigel was not the best person in the world. He was certainly not living for the Lord. He cursed all the time, and his lifestyle was very bad. God laid him on many people's hearts, including mine. I became friends with him when he started riding our church bus to church. I watched as God began to work in his life, and he started becoming more open to the Word. Next thing you know, he got saved. Now two years later, he is the strongest Christian I know. Nigel has been called by God to be a pastor and a politician. Now Nigel goes and witnesses to people in the very same place people witnessed to him. He never gets scared of what might happen, and he's not worried when he gets rejected. Nigel's life is a perfect example of Ephesians 3:12. When we go to share the gospel with the world, we should be bold and not be afraid to face persecution. Be bold like Nigel.

ANDREW CLEM: *13, Albany, GA*
Sherwood Baptist Church and Sherwood Christian Academy, Albany, GA

WORRYING

"And why do you worry about clothes? Learn how the wildflowers of the field grow: they don't labor or spin thread." —*Matthew 6:28*

Today's Bible verse, Matthew 6:28, talks about having clothes and learning from the flowers of the field. God promises to take care of our needs. He shows us how faithful He is by the example of the birds and wildflowers. They never worry about where they will live, what they will eat, or what they will wear! And He reminds us that He provides for their needs, so why can't we trust Him to do the same for our needs? Worry causes stress; if we have stress, it could cause us to do something we wouldn't have done if we weren't under so much stress. I personally struggle with worrying about different things. Rather than letting worry turn to stress, we should pray. If we are having a hard time with worrying, we need to pray more, and ask God for help. He promised to feed, clothe, and shelter us, but He also promised to be our helper. I need Him in my life. Do you?

GABRIEL PLYLER: *14, Pageland, SC*
Greater Vision Baptist Church and South Pointe Christian School, Pageland, SC

CHOOSING TO LOVE

"Love is patient, love is kind. Love does not envy, is not boastful,
is not conceited, does not act improperly, is not selfish,
is not provoked, and does not keep a record of wrongs.
Love finds no joy in unrighteousness but rejoices in the truth."

—*1 Corinthians 13:4–6*

Sometimes, choosing to love is a very difficult thing, given our circumstances, but it works out for the best for those who love God. No matter what the situation—perhaps a loved one passes away or maybe a breakup occurs in a loving relationship—choosing to love will make a huge difference in how your heart feels. It's not easy; it's not easy at all. I'd probably say it's one of the hardest things to do. High school and people are just rough sometimes, and we don't even understand why people are who they are, but love is a choice we make. We can either choose to love no matter how we have been treated, or we can choose to say "no" to God and run away from His plan for our lives. If we choose to love no matter what, we will see a huge difference in our personal lives, our relationships with our families and friends, and just our basic attitudes. Hard times happen, and they always will. We can't avoid them, although we try really hard. However, if we choose to love, we will find God, and we will find peace and happiness. Wait on His perfect and pleasing plan for your life and choose to love no matter what hardships come. Choose to love no matter how you feel.

KORD OFFENBACKER: *16, Springdale, AR*
Cross Church Springdale Campus and Shiloh Christian School, Springdale, AR

YIELDING TO GOD IS ALWAYS THE BEST CHOICE

"For man's anger does not accomplish God's righteousness."
—James 1:20

I'm a quiet person, not so much because I don't have anything to say—because I do have an opinion most of the time—but because I'm learning to choose my words more carefully. Proverbs 18:21 says, "Life and death are in the power of the tongue, and those who love it will eat its fruit." My mom invited a friend of my older sibling to church. I had become friends with him and had discovered that we both liked gaming. He had outgrown some of his games and was going to pass them on to me. I really wanted to continue that conversation with him the next time I saw him, plus I had a new app I thought he would appreciate. When I saw him in church, sitting on the pew between my mom and my sibling, it seemed like the perfect opportunity. I excused myself as I went across my mom, but before I could say another word, my sibling's angry voice shattered our serene surroundings to everyone's surprise. "He's *my* friend!" That was a moment of split decision, and in church of all places. I sat down right where I was, glad there was still a seat next to my mom. I was embarrassed, humiliated, and just plain mad. After the emotion passed, I remembered the Word of God: "For man's anger does not accomplish God's righteousness." What was God accomplishing here? It may have been to demonstrate humility to this young man. I was proud to be of service. My sibling later signaled me to come over and we all enjoyed the service together. I did get to have that conversation, too.

PAUL CRAIG GALE: *14, New Orleans, LA*
Franklin Avenue Baptist Church and New Orleans Center for Creative Arts, New Orleans, LA

A HUMBLE SERVANT

"When pride comes, disgrace follows, but with humility comes wisdom."
—Proverbs 11:2

We all know what pride is. Being prideful is probably the number one thing Christians rebuke others for, because it's easy to recognize. However, not many people understand what humility is and how it affects our Christian walk. Humility begins with taking your judging eye off of others and moving it onto yourself. Being humble also means acting humbly. The way you live your life should show others that you aren't living for your own glory, but for God's. If you've ever wondered what humility looks like, just turn to the Bible. There is one character whose humble life and complete sacrifice to God led to Him making the ultimate sacrifice, eventually claiming His rightful seat at the right hand of God. Jesus Christ! Jesus had to humble Himself to the lowest of low in the world and allow Himself to be crucified in order to save all of humanity. I know being Christlike is very difficult sometimes, and it even seems like God asks us as believers to do impossible things, but it is not impossible to do away with pride. Plus, God says in Proverbs 11:2, "When pride comes, disgrace follows, but with humility comes wisdom." This means that if we are humble, it will pay off and God will reward us. I'll leave you with this strange yet appropriate illustration: an acorn must first bury itself beneath the earth, with all of its commotion and destruction, in order to be nurtured into a great tree that will give comfort, peace, and nourishment to the world around it.

BRADY FOWLKES: *16, Tuscaloosa, AL*
Valley View Baptist Church and Hillcrest High School, Tuscaloosa, AL

ENCOURAGEMENT

"Anxiety in a man's heart weighs it down, but a good word cheers it up."
—*Proverbs 12:25*

Encouragement is important to give and to receive. Words are very powerful! When you are down and out and feel like you can't do anything, then someone says a few words of encouragement, it brings instant relief. I'm sure all of us have been encouraged at one time, and that moment felt absolutely incredible. I enjoy giving encouragement to those who have never heard the gospel, and when they receive Christ in their lives, it's the ultimate encouragement. I remember a time when it felt like the whole world was on my shoulders and I didn't know what to do. I started remembering past sins and wept to God saying, "Help me, I cannot do this alone." Isaiah 41:10 says, "Do not fear, for I am with you; do not be afraid, for I am your God. I will strengthen you; I will help you; I will hold on to you with My righteous right hand." That moment of encouragement left me feeling like I was reborn into something new; I was changed for a purpose, so that others could feel the same. Whether at school, at home, or just hanging out, if you see someone down or upset, stop and say something encouraging. It will mean the world to them. My hope for you is that you will find people who encourage you to pursue your dreams. If you are discouraged, I pray that this quote by Henry Ford will encourage you: "When everything seems to be going against you, remember that the airplane takes off against the wind, not with it." Even better, we have a pilot that navigates for us, so stay close to Him and soar in His strength.

COLLIN MICHAEL SEELEN: *18, Itami, Hyogo, Japan*
Emmanuel Baptist Church and Kansai Homeschooled Network, Itami, Hyogo, Japan

WHAT DO PEOPLE THINK OF ME?

"Humble yourselves, therefore, under the mighty hand of God, so that He may exalt you at the proper time." —*1 Peter 5:6*

My family and all my friends could tell you I'm not perfectly humble, but I do my best. I used to really care what people thought of me. I'm still not great, but I'm better than before. When I was thirteen, we went camping with a couple of other families. At that time in my life, I was super worried about what people thought about me. I always felt like they were watching me, and every move had to be just right. An older boy and I went to climb a cliff. It was about 100 feet tall. We climbed from the top to the bottom and then back up. Halfway up, a crowd gathered at the bottom and watched. This is my chance, I thought. I had to show them what a good climber I was. The older boy said we should go back down and find a better way up. I thought that since I was a great climber I could climb it, but I got stuck! Instead of going down I stopped, and I just got weaker and weaker. My legs had pretty much no grip, and I was hanging by my arms. I hung until all my strength was gone— which wasn't long. I slipped, but the Lord gave me strength and I caught myself and hung on just till my wiser friend's dad lowered a rope. It was humiliating, but I learned to not care about impressing people. I have great friends that like me no matter what I do.

JOSHUA COOKSEY: *15, McMinnville, OR*
Valley Baptist Church, McMinnville, OR; Homeschooled

ARMOR OF GOD

"Be strengthened by the Lord and His vast strength. Put on the full armor of God so that you can stand against the tactics of the Devil."

—*Ephesians 6:10–11*

Temptations abound because of the devil's constant battle for our souls. He tries to bring as many people with him into hell as possible. If we accept God into our hearts, it might seem that the battle is over; but it is far from done. Our battle is against the rulers, authorities, and spiritual forces of evil in the heavens. We do this by putting on the armor of God so that we are able to take a stand for Him. God hates lies and doesn't want us to deceive. We need to be prepared to tell others and answer questions about our salvation. We should have faith in His promises of protection. "Take the helmet of salvation, and the sword of the Spirit, which is God's Word. Pray at all times in the Spirit with every prayer and request, and stay alert in this with all perseverance and intercession for all the saints" (Ephesians 6:17–18). Salvation, which was made possible by Christ's death, seals us as Christians. The devil can't take us away from God's loving arms. God's Word is a powerful weapon against the devil and his temptations. Memorizing it and quoting it during temptation is so much easier than trying to do it in our own strength.

MATTHEW COOKSEY: *13, McMinnville, OR*
Valley Baptist Church, McMinnville, OR; Homeschooled

TRIALS

"Consider it a great joy, my brothers, whenever you experience various trials." —*James 1:2*

Why is God letting such bad things happen to me? This is a question I think everyone asks, though maybe not in the exact words. So what's the answer? Why do we face troubling times or see terrible things on the news? Or, rather, why does God allow them to happen? And how do we deal with trials, hard times we face, the loss of a loved one, a certain sin we struggle with, or a severe injury to you or someone close to you? You see, trials are God's way to sanctify us, which means to set us apart, to make us holy. We can either respond to trials by blaming God; or we can turn to Him in prayer and faith, looking to Him for help and strength, which leads to sanctification. Therefore the purpose of a trial is to grow in strength, yet we are not asked or left to do it on our own. This is where the Holy Spirit comes in. He's here to help us respond correctly. Even when we fail, we need to know that God loves us and wants us to learn from that mistake, to repent of it, and to grow in our trust of Him. By doing that, we have really learned what God wanted, and His goal is still ultimately accomplished.

JOSHUA JOHANSEN: *18, Shrewsbury, MA*
Bethlehem Bible Church, West Boylston, MA; Quinsigamond Community College, Worcester, MA

FREEDOM

"And whatever you do, in word or in deed, do everything in the name of the Lord Jesus, giving thanks to God the Father through Him."

—*Colossians 3:17*

Don't you hate the questions, "What do you want to be when you're older?" or "What is the Lord's will for your life?" You usually get those questions from family at reunions, friends in the hallway, guidance counselors, and people at youth conferences. Christians know there are other more important questions to be asking, like "How do I better myself in the way of the Lord?" "What do I need to do now in order to be a godly future husband and father?" and "How do I make disciples who make disciples?" Why? Because God, our Father, will guide us to what He wants us to do as a job. In the Bible, He has already expressed His will for the lives of His children. Matthew 28:19 says, "Go, therefore, and make disciples of all nations," and the verse for today tells us to do everything in His name and to give thanks. Whatever your career choice, do it in the name of Jesus. Many will influence your life, but Jesus is the ultimate influence. Jesus died for you, what more do you need? There will be some people who don't want to see you rise and succeed. Just dust them off your back and call to Jesus. Express excellence in whatever you choose to do with your life. He is the Redeemer and Savior, and He will always be there loving us, freeing us, and restoring us. So remember, "Whatever you do, in word or in deed, do everything in the name of the Lord Jesus, giving thanks to God the Father through Him" (Colossians 3:17).

IFE AKINBOYO: *15, Seymour, TN*
Sevier Heights Baptist Church, Knoxville, TN; The King's Academy, Seymour, TN

GOD'S CALLING ON OUR LIVES (PART 1)

"Therefore, brothers, make every effort to confirm your calling and election, because if you do these things you will never stumble."

—2 Peter 1:10

It is very common for Christians to struggle to know God's calling on their lives, and I think this is a major concern for teen boys. It has been a struggle for me. I would stay awake at night and just pray that God would give me insight into what He wanted me to do with my life. Finally, at age fourteen, God told me what my calling is: pastoral ministry. Knowing what God has called me to do has brought a sense of peace and calm, and it has led me to know what to study in school and how to prepare for the future. However, whether you are called to full-time ministry or not, we are all called to spread the gospel. The Great Commission, which is found in Matthew 28:19–20, is our command to spread the gospel. It says, "Go, therefore, and make disciples of all nations, baptizing them in the name of the Father, and of the Son and of the Holy Spirit, teaching them to observe everything I have commanded you. And remember, I am with you always, to the end of the age." No matter how old we are, what career we enter, God has given all of us the ability and a calling to carry His word, the gospel message, to the entire world. Teens tend to worry about what they are to do, but we need not worry. God will teach us and guide us.

CALEB PAYNE: *18, White House, TN*
Long Hollow Baptist Church, Hendersonville, TN; Volunteer State Community College, Gallatin, TN

GOD'S CALLING ON OUR LIVES (PART 2)

"Therefore, brothers, make every effort to confirm your calling and election, because if you do these things you will never stumble."

—*2 Peter 1:10*

Many times people have said, "What can you do? You are only a kid" or "You can't do that because you are too young." However, in Timothy 4:12, "Let no one despise your youth; instead, you should be an example to the believers in speech, in conduct, in love, in faith, and in purity." We are all called to spread the gospel to the entire world. So, I want to leave you with a challenge. It may be hard, but you will be making an impact for the kingdom of God. I challenge you to go and share the gospel with your friends, go on an overseas short-term mission trip, or go be the friend to that person you know no one else wants to be friends with. Seek God about the place or the person He wants, so you will be spreading the gospel. Pray about it and see what God wants you to do, and He will guide your life like He did for the Israelites in the desert with the pillar of fire. I know you can do it, because He has called you, and as His child you want to obey. Remember that His Word teaches us that we can do all things, even what seems impossible, through Christ.

CALEB PAYNE: *18, White House, TN*
Long Hollow Baptist Church, Hendersonville, TN; Volunteer State Community College, Gallatin, TN

HONESTY

"You must not spread a false report. Do not join the wicked to be a malicious witness." —*Exodus 23:1*

For most children and teens, honesty is one of the hardest things to be consistent with. Growing up, being honest was difficult for me because, first of all, no one wants to be in trouble, and kids often wonder what the consequence would be if they tell the truth. When younger and into my teens my whole family taught me and my sister to tell the truth. Dad's parents taught him to always tell the truth, no matter what! I told a lot of lies trying to get by and hardly ever told the truth, but I am here to tell you to listen to your parents! When they say your lies will find you out, they know it! When we tell one lie, we often have to tell another to cover the first one up, and the situation keeps getting bigger and bigger. Soon we have told so many lies it becomes difficult for others to trust us. John 8:44 says, "You are of your father the Devil, and you want to carry out your father's desires. He was a murderer from the beginning and has not stood in the truth, because there is no truth in him. When he tells a lie, he speaks from his own nature, because he is a liar and the father of liars." The Bible says that all wrongdoers, fornicators, murders, and liars will have their part in the lake of fire forever. It's important to tell the truth. The truth sets us free and our truthful responses in difficult situations could be what cause others to want to know about Jesus.

AUSTIN HARGETT: *15, Marshville, NC*
Bethel Baptist Church, Marshville, NC; South Pointe Christian School, Pageland, SC

FEBRUARY

Wisdom Brings Happiness

Happy is a man who finds wisdom and who acquires understanding, for she is more profitable than silver, and her revenue is better than gold.

She is more precious than jewels; nothing you desire compares with her.

Long life is in her right hand; in her left, riches and honor.

Her ways are pleasant, and all her paths, peaceful.

She is a tree of life to those who embrace her, and those who hold on to her are happy.

The Lord founded the earth by wisdom and established the heavens by understanding.

By His knowledge the watery depths broke open, and the clouds dripped with dew.

Maintain your competence and discretion. My son, don't lose sight of them.

They will be life for you and adornment for your neck.

Then you will go safely on your way; your foot will not stumble. When you lie down, you will not be afraid; you will lie down, and your sleep will be pleasant.

Don't fear sudden danger or the ruin of the wicked when it comes, for the Lord will be your confidence and will keep your foot from a snare.

(Proverbs 3:13–26)

GOD'S WORD

"For the word of God is living and effective and sharper than any double-edged sword, penetrating as far as the separation of soul and spirit, joints and marrow. It is able to judge the ideas and thoughts of the heart." —*Hebrews 4:12*

There are many things we struggle with when reading God's Word. One of the biggest challenges I face in my walk with Christ is the temptation to dismiss the need to study. The Bible is a big book and somewhat intimidating. There are days when I decide that my schedule is too important, that worldly pleasures are more fun, and sometimes I simply don't feel like spending time reading it. We can get bored when we feel as though God's Word is not relevant. God's Word is relevant. The Bible is not some old book that has lost all power or effectiveness. Hebrews 4:12 tells us that it is living and effective. It is sharper than any two-edged sword and penetrates into souls. Psalm 119:105 tells us that the Bible is a lamp to our feet and a light to our path. Ephesians 6:17 tells us that the Bible is a sword that we are to take and use. The Bible is a weapon that exposes sin in our lives, shows us the Savior, and teaches us how to live. We are commanded to use it in our own lives and to share it with others. The Bible does have effectiveness. Without hearing the gospel presented to me using verses such as John 3:16, Romans 3:23 and 6:23, and 1 John 1:8–9, I would not have a relationship with Jesus. God's Word is a gift with power to expose our imperfections, to show us how to live a godlier life, teach us about our Savior, and protect us from our enemy, Satan. So, don't waste the gift of God's Word!

JOSIAH MCGEE: *15, Kansas City, MO*
Summit Woods Baptist Church, Lees Summit, MO; Homeschooled

ABSOLUTE CHAOS

"But grow in the grace and knowledge of our Lord and Savior Jesus Christ. To Him be the glory both now and to the day of eternity. Amen."
—*2 Peter 3:18*

When I was in middle school, my brother, my best friend, and I decided to start a band. We called ourselves Burning Flame. One day we knew we would be the next MercyMe or Casting Crowns. We decided to write our first song. It was appropriately named "Absolute Chaos." Basically, we all played different notes in different keys in different rhythms at the same time very loudly. Our parents graciously recorded this premiere performance, and we were quite proud of it. We watched the video many times (and we still have it today!). The only problem was that we were terrible! However, all of us took lessons and improved greatly over the next few years. We continued to play together and actually became part of the youth praise band at our church. We had a blast playing every Wednesday for the youth service and we were actually pretty good. The key was personal growth in music. Our passage tells us to grow in the grace and knowledge of the Lord. Just as we grow physically and work to grow intellectually or musically, we must grow spiritually too. Our growth in music required consistent practice and there were times we felt like quitting, but practice brought improvement. In Luke 2:52 we see the growth in Jesus' life: "Jesus increased in wisdom and stature, and in favor with God and with people." Growth takes work and time. We must put forth the effort to study God's Word in order to understand His grace and His will for our life. Then, we must consistently apply the truths that we learn to the glory of God.

LUKE PERSTROPE: *17, St. Peters, MO*
First Baptist Church of St. Charles, St. Charles, MO; Fort Zumwalt East High School, St. Peters, MO

OVERCOMING TEMPTATION

"A man who endures trials is blessed, because when he passes the test he will receive the crown of life that God has promised to those who love Him." —*James 1:12*

Temptation is Satan's way of pulling us as far away from our relationship with God as possible. One of the most motivating things I've learned is that God will never allow us to be given more than we can handle. And He will always provide us with a way out of what is tempting us. Our best chance of resisting temptation comes when we take ourselves out of the situation and turn to God. What I like to do when I feel that I'm being tempted is to stop what I'm doing and either pray to God or just open my Bible and start reading. This helps me a lot because I know that either way, I will be hearing what God wants to tell me at that moment. Another thing I've learned is that temptation is a form of spiritual warfare between God and Satan. If we think pure thoughts, we have already won. Colossians 3:2 says, "Set your minds on what is above, not on what is on the earth." God even gives us a list of what to think about in Philippians 4:8: "Finally brothers, whatever is true, whatever is honorable, whatever is just, whatever is pure, whatever is lovely, whatever is commendable—if there is any moral excellence and if there is any praise—dwell on these things." So if you are faced with temptation, don't be overwhelmed. Remember that God is always there for us and that He has already won the war. As long as we keep His Word in our life, temptation will never triumph.

JESSE NIEMAN: *18, Ocala, FL*
Church @ The Springs and Forest High School, Ocala, FL

MOTIVATION

"I am able to do all things through Him who strengthens me."
—*Philippians 4:13*

Golf is one of my favorite sports, and I get a lot of motivation from my dad and coaches. Motivation is a good thing to have if, of course, you use it the way God intended it to be used. Our goal as Christians should be to spread the gospel to all who need to hear, but our motivation should be Jesus Christ, who died for us so that we could be with Him forever. Those who motivate you also encourage you, because you cannot make somebody do something they are not prepared or equipped to do. You can only encourage them to do better and help them to be better at whatever it may be. When Christ was on the earth, He was literally perfect. Can we not be motivated to be like Christ? Even though we are born with a sin nature, we can always encourage and motivate one another to be more like Christ. He should be a Christian's role model, the one we look up to. It is hard to do something without encouragement or motivation. If we are striving to be like Christ, then it should show in our attitude and behavior, and others will be able to see Christ in us. Just as Christ affects us, we should affect those who need to be led to Him. Motivation is a good thing to give to others.

ZACHARY TREMBLAY: *13, Pageland, SC*
South Pointe Fellowship and South Pointe Christian School, Pageland, SC

LIVING FOR GOD TODAY

"This is the day the LORD has made; let us rejoice and be glad in it."
—*Psalm 118:24*

It's easy to look forward to the future and miss out on the great plans God has for you right now. Whether you are a freshman or a senior, the next year always seems more exciting than the one you are in currently. The fact that I will soon move away from my parents and start life on my own is becoming more and more real. It is great to be excited about the plans God has for your future. As Jeremiah 29:11 states, "'For I know the plans I have for you'—this is the LORD's declaration—'plans for your welfare, not for disaster, to give you a future and a hope.'" Plans for the future are beyond exciting, but if you aren't careful you could miss out on having an impact for Christ where you are now. This played out in my senior year in the way I interacted with younger kids and the way I invested in their lives. During the beginning of my senior year, I was more worried about where I was going to go to college or how I was going to pay for it than I was on making a mark for Christ. Then I realized that God was calling me to reach out to underclassmen by simply saying "Hi" in the halls or including them in events. Living in the present and trusting God with the future has been great for my relationship with the Lord. Living with an attitude that is excited about the day God has me in now has also allowed me to experience the joy of reaching out to those in my current environment. Be encouraged to not only be excited about God's future plans for you but to also live for God in the present. What plans does the Lord have for you in your current circumstances?

AUSTIN SOUTHERN: *18, Thailand and Mississippi*
Chiang Mai Christian Fellowship and Grace International School, Chiang Mai, Thailand

REPUTATIONS

"Also, the LORD will provide what is good, and our land will yield its crops." —*Psalm 85:12*

Do you want to have a good reputation? Of course you do! Who wouldn't want to have a good and honorable reputation? We all want to be liked by everyone and have lots of friends. But, what if we didn't worry about ourselves as much and focused solely on God and on His goodness? God will always provide for you: He will never let you go hungry. But what are you putting into your body? Are you putting in healthy things such as God's Word? Are you memorizing Bible verses and keeping pure thoughts? Or are you filling your heart with things that are of this world, not pure and not good? Feed your heart with the things of God, and He will always provide for you and give you the desires of your heart. Keeping our reputation in good standing with God is what we all want. We want His best, right? But how do we do that? Well, feed your heart healthy things and take care of it by keeping the Word of God in it and by practicing what you know is right. Your heart is your most prized possession; it is where Jesus dwells inside of you. So, will you choose to be healthy and allow God to provide a good reputation for you? It is a decision only you can make.

KORD OFFENBACKER: *16, Springdale, AR*
Cross Church Springdale Campus and Shiloh Christian School, Springdale, AR

HABITS

"When you pray, don't babble like the idolaters, since they imagine they'll be heard for their many words." —*Matthew 6:7*

"Old habits die hard" is a statement I'm sure you've heard at least once before, though probably more. It's a very true statement so you should hear it often. It is very difficult to break a bad habit because most people learn by repetition; and a habit, by definition, is an action we perform repeatedly. So when we create a sinful habit, it is very difficult to break. It's like when we tell one lie and it becomes easier to tell another, and then another on top of that, in order for us to cover up the last one. The good news, fortunately, is that we can do the same by creating new habits—things like reading the Bible every day, praying, keeping our word, and telling the truth. The bad news is that it is a lot harder to create a habit out of these things. It takes discipline, hard work, and strength that can only be found in God. Now don't take the word *habit* the wrong way. I don't mean for us to get so used to doing these things that we get into mindless repetition. In other words, I want us to keep our hearts in it instead of doing it just to say we did it. We need to have the proper motives and, like everything in life, our goal should be to bring glory to God. May He give us the strength to create good habits, and may those habits never die.

JOSHUA JOHANSEN: *18, Shrewsbury, MA*
Bethlehem Bible Church, West Boylston, MA; Quinsigamond Community College, Worchester, MA

LOVE
(PART 1)

"Dear friends, let us love one another, because love is from God, and everyone who loves has been born of God and knows God."

—*1 John 4:7*

We should be aware of and focus on love in our lives and in the lives of others. Love is an essential of all life. No matter what the circumstances are, you should always know that you are deeply loved and wanted by God. Psalm 36:5 says, "Lord, Your faithful love reaches to heaven, Your faithfulness to the clouds." God's love is much stronger than you can ever realize. He sent His only Son to die for you, so that you might have eternal life in heaven with Him. We should also love the Lord. First John 4:19 says, "We love Him because He first loved us." In 1 Corinthians 8:3 we are told, "But if anyone loves God, he is known by Him." God wants us to love Him and our love for Him provides a personal relationship with Him. God also wants us to love others. When others see our love, they will want to know where that amazing love comes from. Your influence may lead others to eternity with the Lord. In John 15:17 God commands us to "Love one another." In Matthew 22:39 and in many other places in the Bible, we are told to "Love your neighbor as yourself." To do this, you must first know God's unconditional love. As amazing as that is, He has also provided us with the capacity to love others with His love. Are you loving others the way Christ loves you?

LUKE HUMANIK: *15, Jefferson, SC*
Mt. Olive Baptist Church, Marshville, NC; South Pointe Christian School, Pageland, SC

LOVE
(PART 2)

"Dear friends, let us love one another, because love is from God, and everyone who loves has been born of God and knows God."

—*1 John 4:7*

God wants us to love others with the same love that He offers us. It is unconditional and it lasts for all eternity. We see in Psalm 136:23 that "He remembered us in our humiliation; His love is eternal." *Eternal* means never-ending. In order to love others we also need to learn to love ourselves, which can be difficult at times. But if we don't love ourselves, it is impossible to love our neighbors. There are so many teenagers walking around today who never really feel loved, so they look to the world to provide a few moments of satisfaction in the place of the love they don't know. They need to know the love of Jesus. When someone knows they are loved, they may be changed forever. You may be the only one who can ever plant the seed of the Word in their hearts or even lead them to salvation. Love can solve anything. In Proverbs 10:12 we see that "Hatred stirs up conflicts, but love covers all offenses." Please realize God's incredible love for you. When everyone else's love fails, the love of God prevails! Love yourself and honor yourself. God made you perfectly. Spread your love. Show others that they are worth something and they are wanted. Keep love as a priority in your life. Remember that in 1 Corinthians 8:3 we are told, "But if anyone loves God, he is known by Him." We cannot ask for anything more, right?

LUKE HUMANIK: *15, Jefferson, SC*
Mt. Olive Baptist Church, Marshville, NC; South Pointe Christian School, Pageland, SC

SERVING THE NEEDY

"Then He will answer them, 'I assure you: Whatever you did not do for one of the least of these, you did not do for Me either.'" —*Matthew 25:45*

I see them! I know some of them! Who am I talking about? That man who lives under the bridge with his grocery cart of belongings, or the single mother who works hard but can barely provide for her children. When I see them, I usually feel sorry for them and might possibly say a quick prayer. But is that enough? What does Jesus say about those struggling to make it through the day? In today's verse, Matthew 25:45, it basically says that if we don't do anything to help those in need, it's like doing the same to Jesus. What if the man under the bridge was Jesus? Would you drive on by without doing anything? This thought troubles me, because I almost never do anything for those who need help. Jesus came to serve, and that included the lowest and neediest of people. Imagine if we as Christians strived to have a servant's heart like Jesus. How radically the world would change! What's holding us back from serving? Pride? Fear? Greed? We have so much compared to the poor and the downtrodden. I've realized that God has blessed me with much and I often take it for granted. The Lord may prompt us to help others out financially, and He wants us to tell them about the love of Christ. That's the most important gift we could give them! Let's constantly be in prayer and ask God to open our eyes to the ways we can help others. When we help the needy, we're doing what Jesus did. That's one of the most rewarding things we can do. Why not try doing something for someone less fortunate than you?

AUSTIN CANFIELD: *18, Tulsa, OK*
Evergreen Baptist Church, Bixby, OK; Homeschooled

ARE SISTERS COOL?

"Whatever you do, do it enthusiastically, as something done for the Lord and not for men." —*Colossians 3:23*

The Bible commands us to love our sisters. I'm not writing about loving our sisters, but showing them love. It's easy to be embarrassed about our sisters; we want to be tough. We don't want a tender heart—we're men! We may think that the rest of the world will think badly of us if we show love to them. God gave us our sisters as part of His plan to raise us into manhood. You're probably not mean to your sisters, but you don't want to open the door for them or even sit next to them. You probably would do all these things at home, but in public it's different. Being there for your sisters is just preparing for your future. Opening the door for your sister is great! You don't have to run across the room to open the door for her or lift everything she reaches for. All you have to do is be willing to help her and make her feel as valued as all the rest of your friends. The main thing is just to treat her special and put her above yourself. Don't make it obvious, which would be pleasing men: you just have to give her priority. Your sisters do a lot more for you than you may think. Even if they don't, it doesn't change anything. You need to treat your mom the same way, except that your mom gets even more respect. When you treat your mom and your sisters right, the world will see you as a respectable young man. But more than that, God will.

JOSHUA COOKSEY: *15, McMinnville, OR*
Valley Baptist Church, McMinnville, OR; Homeschooled

UNDERSTANDING AND EXHIBITING FORGIVENESS

"And be kind and compassionate to one another, forgiving one another, just as God also forgave you in Christ." —*Ephesians 4:32*

Forgiveness is what the people of this world desperately need, whether from God or from our peers. Forgiveness, remember, is something for you, but it is also for the one who offers to forgive. The person that has done you wrong will go on living unaffected whether you forgive them or not; but if you hold a grudge, you will never truly be happy with yourself. You must let the grudge go. Believe me, you'll feel much better than the person you forgave. My friends and I film movies, and we use real weapons. On one of the days we were filming, one of my friends misjudged the distance between yours truly and his sword, and my hand was sliced. My dad rushed me to the hospital to get stitches that remained in my hand for two weeks. I bring this up because I had never even thought about holding a grudge over my friend's head. I knew it was an accident and, if anything, I felt sorry for him, wondering how I would feel if I had sent a friend to the hospital. Some people might have stayed upset about an injury like that, but the reason I think I didn't is because I put myself in his place and felt his pain. We have a harder time forgiving someone close to us, like friends or family, than we do complete strangers. If someone close to you does something upsetting or snaps at you, instead of snapping back, ask how their day went. Maybe then you can understand what they're dealing with and respond the way Christ wants with love and forgiveness.

JASON MCKEE: *15, Anchorage, AK*
First Baptist Church of Anchorage and Service High School, Anchorage, AK

STRENGTH COMES FROM GOD

"Youths may faint and grow weary, and young men stumble and fall, but those who trust in the Lᴏʀᴅ will renew their strength; they will soar on wings like eagles; they will run and not grow weary; they will walk and not faint." —*Isaiah 40:30–31*

Strength comes from God. I am not saying that God gives us superpowers. I am saying that He will give strength to stand up for those who need it, including ourselves. God's strength will help us overcome any obstacle, enabling us to stand up for ourselves and our faith without growing tired and faint. It is a mental and physical strength, not a strength gained through lifting weights or running for miles on end. We get this strength from believing and trusting in the one true God. Our God! Other religions believe that their gods will help them, that a piece of gold can heal. The truth is, none of that comes from their gods; it happens the way that God wants it to. That may seem off topic, but it truly isn't. If those lost souls were to believe in God, they would receive strength from Him. When bullied, I may want to punch the guys in the face, but then God gives me strength to resist that urge. Then they are confused as to why I did not fight back. That turns into a perfect opportunity to witness to them. I don't tell them I think retaliation is bad, I tell them I know it's bad. I can then share God with them. It starts with you and me.

TERRELL STRAIN: *13, Spokane, WA*
Airway Heights Baptist Church, Airway Heights, WA; Medical Lake Middle School, Medical Lake, WA

HOW MANY TIMES, LORD?

"Then Peter came to Him and said Lord how many times could my brother sin against me and I forgive him? As many as seven times?"

—*Matthew 18:21*

Forgiveness is a blessing from God. In the verse above, Jesus answered that we are to forgive seventy times seven. In other words, He was saying that we should always forgive those that have wronged us. After Jesus said this, He told the parable of the unforgiving servant. The parable is about a servant who owed a king ten thousand talents. The servant pleaded and begged for the king to give him more time, promising that he would pay the king back. The king felt compassionate and forgave the servant his entire debt. Later, that same servant was asked by a fellow servant who owed him only one hundred talents if he could have more time. The servant who had his debt forgiven by the king was not willing to do the same for another. The king found out and summoned the servant whose debt he had forgiven and said to him, "You should have had compassion on the servant as I had compassion on you." The king became angry and sent the servant to the tormentors until he could pay his debt. Like the king, we are to forgive everyone. The Golden Rule applies here: Do unto others as you would have them do unto you. Be forgiving, as God has forgiven us.

RHETT CHAPMAN: *15, Pageland, SC*
South Pointe Fellowship and South Pointe Christian School, Pageland, SC

TEEN MISSIONS

"Let no one despise your youth; instead, you should be an example to the believers in speech, in conduct, in love, in faith, in purity." —1 Timothy 4:12

One of my greatest experiences as a teenager was a week-long mission trip to Northeast India. Approximately twenty teens traveled to the Himalayan foothills of West Bengal and lived in a mountainous village. We shared our faith that week, taught in the local school, and touched the lives of elementary-aged children. It was an eye-opening experience for me, because it showed me that God can use a teenager like me for ground-shattering ministry work. After returning from the India trip, God opened up other doors for me to get involved in local ministries in my city. God has greatly blessed me through those opportunities. It is extremely exciting to see how creative He is in bringing the lost to Himself. The cool thing is that He can use normal teenagers like you and me in the work as well. If you aren't currently involved in missions work, whether local or international, it is definitely something worth being a part of. Not only is God able to use teenagers in kingdom work, He wants to use you. Being young is not a limiting factor for growth in your Christian walk and involvement in sharing God's love. Often, we teens say things like "I'll live like that when I'm older" or "I'm too young," but I encourage you to go against the norm and make an impact for God even in your youth. Missions work is an incredibly rewarding way to live this out.

AUSTIN SOUTHERN: 18, Thailand and Mississippi
Chiang Mai Christian Fellowship and Grace International School, Chiang Mai, Thailand

WHAT DOES AWESOME MEAN?

"Let the whole earth tremble before the Lord, let all the inhabitants of the world stand in awe of Him." —*Psalm 33:8*

Teenagers use adjectives to describe how we feel about something. Some words are used so often that they become flippant. Too easily we exaggerate what we are talking about to our peers, or we describe something far greater than what we are actually discussing. Before you know it, the meaning of the word has been lost. One word that is misunderstood is *awesome*. I use it often and sometimes forget why I am using it. It has become almost second nature. Every once in a while I have to remember what *awesome* really means. Psalm 33 gives an explanation of the word *awesome* and when it is to be used. *Awesome*, quite simply, is a form of the word *awe*. Awe is a form of fear, but it is the good kind of fear. It comes from natural respect for someone because of their immense power and authority. Imagine that you received an invitation one day to see God face-to-face. When you arrive at the meeting place, you immediately fall to your face. You are overcome with emotion and respect at the sight of God and the sound of His voice. This is awe. Psalm 33 details God's character and commands all people to stand in awe of Him. God is described as "just, all powerful, merciful, righteous, faithful, holy, and trustworthy." Awe is meant to be reserved for the only one who deserves that title. When we use the word *awesome*, we are using the same word that describes our feelings for the Creator, the Lord of lords, and the King of kings. Nothing we experience matches the awesome qualities of God.

JOSIAH MCGEE: *15, Kansas City, MO*
Summit Woods Baptist Church, Lees Summit, MO; Homeschooled

49

RESPECT

> "Honor your father and your mother so that you may have a long life in the land that the LORD your God is giving you."
>
> —*Exodus 20:12*

Respect isn't exactly common in our society. Kids are disrespectful to their parents, people shoot police officers, and women are beaten by their husbands. Obviously, the first one mentioned would apply most often to teenagers. I have a huge problem with respecting my parents. I often want them to understand what I think is right. I get easily irritated with them, and I speak to them in ways that are far from what they deserve. Now, I could blame part of this on them. I could say, "Well, if they just weren't so hard to get along with, I would act better." Wrong answer! My dad often reminds me of a truth. He says that my responsibility as a teenager is to respect and honor my parents. Academics, sports, music, whatever, those are all fine and good; but I need to respect my parents. From the time we are toddlers, we learn how to honor God as we learn to obey our parents. In the verse above, we see that God wants us to honor our parents. Ephesians also reminds us to obey our parents as we would the Lord, because this is right. So, if we believe in the Lord and truly wish to do His will, we must learn to consider everyone, but especially our parents, better than ourselves and obey them as we would the Lord. We can do this only with an attitude of humility.

LUKE MERRICK: *15, Springdale, AR*
Immanuel Baptist Church and Shiloh Christian School, Springdale, AR

ACCOUNTABILITY

"Woe to the world because of offenses. For offenses must come, but woe to that man by whom the offense comes." —*Matthew 18:7*

As a high school senior, it gets harder and harder to stay on your walk with Christ. Sin is thrown at you constantly, and you find yourself having nobody to share your struggles with. Thankfully, there are those good friends that hold me accountable for what I do. I can go to my two best friends about any temptation or problem I have. As their friend, I also have to try to give them the best advice I can. When I give them advice, I go to Scripture first to make sure it's God's advice. As a brother in Christ, you want to lead your friends in the best direction possible. There is a group of guys that would do whatever they can to lead me and other peers astray, but they call themselves Christians. Jesus says in Mark 9:42, "But whoever causes the downfall of one of these little ones who believe in Me—it would be better for him if a heavy millstone were hung around his neck and he were thrown into the sea." I don't know about you, but that doesn't sound too exciting. I don't want to be a stumbling block to anyone. We need each other, so always remember to keep your brothers in Christ accountable. They will be thankful for your concern and care for them in the future.

CHRISTOPHER COLEMAN BAILEY: *17, Albany, GA*
Greater Second Mt. Olive Baptist Church and Sherwood Christian Academy, Albany, GA

LISTENING TO GOD

"'For I know the plans I have for you'-this is the Lord's declaration-'plans for your welfare, not for disaster, to give you a future and a hope.'" —Jeremiah 29:11

The verse above is a promise from God to all Christians, saying that if we are saved He has a perfect plan for our lives. But many teens find it hard to understand and submit to the will of the Lord. A really important lesson for all of us to learn is that if we do submit to His plans for our lives, He will show us. Isaiah 55:8 says, "For My thoughts are not your thoughts, and your ways are not My ways." As guys, we have the natural tendency to do two different things that are very harmful to our walks with Christ. First, we pray for things and expect them to be answered immediately. If God doesn't answer the request quickly, we become impatient and try to fix things ourselves. Second, we try to figure everything out and make our own big plans. But God knows this, and in His providence He has a much better plan for our lives than we ever could! Listen, we can't even imagine the good that God has planned for us. This is a really hard concept for us to grasp sometimes, but our job is to keep our eyes on Him for everything. Pastor and author Charles Swindoll said, "Fix your eyes upon the Lord! Do it once. Do it daily. Do it ten thousand times ten thousand times. Do it constantly. . . . Look at the Lord and keep on looking at Him" (*Bedside Blessings: 365 Days of Inspirational Thoughts by Charles Swindoll*, Nashville: Thomas Nelson, 2011). God has huge plans for your life. He wants you to get out of the way so He can lead you through this journey we call life. Will you look to God for guidance in your life today?

WILLIAM DAVID ORR: *17, Albany, GA*
Sherwood Baptist Church and Sherwood Christian Academy, Albany, GA

RUNNING THE RACE

"Don't you know the runners in a stadium all race, but only one receives the prize? Run in such a way to win the prize. Now everyone who competes exercises self-control in everything. However, they do it to receive a crown that will fade away, but we a crown that will never fade away. Therefore I do not run like one who runs aimlessly or box like one beating the air. Instead, I discipline my body and bring it under strict control, so that after preaching to others, I myself will not be disqualified."

—1 Corinthians 9:24–27

The runner who wins the prize is the one who trains the hardest, pushes through the pain and hardships with determination, and stays on a strict training schedule. Serious athletes have a regular training routine, which they stick to in order to be prepared to do well when they compete. In the same way, the Christian life requires effort. By Christ's awesome power, peace, and joy, we can push through hardships and devote ourselves to spending time with God and being filled with His Holy Spirit, so that we are fully prepared for each day. Like a runner with a training strategy, we must purposely and faithfully commit ourselves to spiritual training and prayer, constantly growing in our faith. The Christian is like the boxer; but instead of senselessly swinging at punching bags or each other, we fight against our own flesh. By doing this, we can remove anything in us that keeps us from living for Him. Why do we do all this? So we won't be disqualified from the prize cup. We run in a way as to win the prize—a prize that, unlike the temporary prizes of this world that become corrupted and faded, will last eternally. The God-given prize is worthy to be sought after with determination.

CONNOR HOWINGTON: *17, West Monroe, LA*
First Baptist West Monroe and Northeast Baptist School, West Monroe, LA

PURITY

"For this is God's will, your sanctification: that you abstain from sexual immorality." —*1 Thessalonians 4:3*

If a vote was taken, I think it would be safe to say most teenagers hope to get married someday. At the very least, they hope to date someone. Fact is, the two situations shouldn't be separated like that. The point of dating should be to find someone who could be your husband or wife. We should want to have only one boyfriend or girlfriend, not as many as possible. I know there are always a lot of questions regarding dating: when you should be allowed to date, what you should be allowed to do while dating, etc. The best way I can answer both of those questions is: Listen to your parents. They do, in fact, know what's best for you. If you are allowed to date, I think it would be wise to do your part in keeping them involved. And a little heads-up—the Bible says very little about dating. It does have a lot to say about purity and its importance. Several times we are called to stay pure, to refrain from sexual immorality. We know that if we repent and turn to God, He is ready and willing to forgive us of our sins. Depending on what your parents say about the topic, I think these are some good reminders for the guys: get a job, have a plan to support a family, be a godly leader, and build your relationship on the Word. It's good to set personal boundaries that will protect you from sinful desires. If that means no kissing or holding hands then don't. Be the example, honor God by honoring your parents, and stay away from sexual immorality.

JOSHUA JOHANSEN: *18, Shrewsbury, MA*
Bethlehem Bible Church, West Boylston, MA; Quinsigamond Community College, Worcester, MA

BEING A HUSBAND AND FATHER

"For I have chosen him so that he will command his children and his house after him to keep the way of the LORD by doing what is right and just. This is how the LORD will fulfill to Abraham what He promised him."

—*Genesis 18:19*

One day I hope to be married to a beautiful woman of Christ and be a father of wonderful children. It seems like the perfect life, but I know there will be challenges in living this life as I show loving leadership to my wife and children. I wish the Christian role models in my life would show me how to overcome the challenges that I don't see on the surface. How do I handle the pressure of raising kids along with having a healthy relationship with my spouse? This is the biggest question I wish to see answered when I look to my mentors, and it is a hard question to answer. Many of them have different ways of handling it, but one thing comes to the center of all their answers. Make sure God is first in everything. Make sure God is the center of the family. With the firm core of Christ, you know whatever happens is for a good reason and it will all play out in the end. Things will be tough, but with Christ all things can be overcome.

ZACH WATKINS: *16, Henderson, NV*
Highland Hills Baptist Church and Green Valley High School, Henderson, NV

BEING A LIGHT IN A DARK WORLD

"You are the light of the world. A city situated on a hill cannot be hidden. No one lights a lamp and puts it under a basket, but rather on a lampstand, and it gives light for all who are in the house. In the same way, let your light shine before men, so that they may see your good works and give glory to your Father in heaven." —*Matthew 5:14–16*

We live in a dark world. Our friends, our schools, and our communities are in desperate need of Christ. It's obvious that it is time to rise up as a body of believers and proclaim the truths of the gospel. We tend to forget the great responsibility that we have. Our mission is to be a light in a dark world, a city on a hill. However, believers often do not accept this challenge. We settle for something less, a dim light in a dark world. To some, a flicker of light in a dark world is adequate. Many teens even resort to the comforts found under the basket. However, this way of living exercised by many fellow brothers and sisters deeply concerns me and should concern you. As a body and as ambassadors of Christ, we should strive to shine brighter and brighter. John 3:19 tells us, "people love darkness rather than light." The natural tendency of humanity is to reject the light. It is our duty to shine the light so that men may "see your good works and give glory to your Father in heaven." By living as a light, we glorify God. Today, I would like you to examine your life and determine if you are being a light in a dark world. Pray that God would eliminate the fears of taking a stand. Pray that, through your light, many would come to know God personally.

LUKE PERSTROPE: *17, St. Peters, MO*
First Baptist Church of St. Charles, St. Charles, MO; Fort Zumwalt East High School, St. Peters, MO

WIN THE PRIZE

"Brothers, I do not consider myself to have taken hold of it.
But one thing I do: Forgetting what is behind and reaching forward
to what is ahead, I pursue as my goal the prize promised
by God's heavenly call in Christ Jesus." —*Philippians 3:13–14*

This is a prime example of the forgiveness of Christ: No matter what you have done, it can be completely cleared from your record, as if it never happened in the first place. This doesn't mean you can keep living in sin and say, "Oh, I can do this because God will forgive me." If you say that every time you want to do something wrong, you will never truly have faith in the Lord. To experience true forgiveness, you must completely turn away from your sin. Now, I'm not saying you won't ever sin again, because you are human and every human has a sin nature. Philippians 3:13–14 shows us it can be a very difficult task to live out your faith. It specifically says it will be a strain, and you will have to push on to the ultimate prize of eternity with our Lord Jesus Christ. To do this, we must be firmly grounded in Scripture and be in a continuous state of prayer. This will keep you in contact with the Lord at all times, so when you sin you can immediately repent from it. Another way this helps us, since we are constantly in contact with the Lord, is that if He wants you to reach out to someone, you know right then and there what to do to live out your faith. God wants to use you right where you are, but you must know Him and His Word to be able to hear what He is calling you to do for Him.

REED REYNOLDS: *15, Albany, GA*
Sherwood Baptist Church and Sherwood Christian Academy, Albany, GA

TEASING HURTS!

"Instead, it should consist of what is inside the heart with the imperishable quality of a gentle and quiet spirit, which is very valuable in God's eyes." —*1 Peter 3:4*

Have you been teased before? I have and it hurts! It all started in third grade. Since then, I've often been a target for being teased. I've been talked about because of my weight, the fact that I wear glasses, the fact that I suffer with allergies, and because I was considered to be "weird." When I graduated middle school, I thought it was all over, but in high school the teasing got even worse. Once, I even got my lunch taken from me! Really? In high school! It was just bad. But, as I got older and learned more about Jesus, how much He loves me and that He loves me for who I am, I realized I shouldn't try to be someone I'm not. So having confidence in God helped me deal with the abuse. Always remember that God made you who you are, and God doesn't make mistakes. You are God's perfect creation. In the Song of Songs 4:7 we are told that, "You are absolutely beautiful, my darling, with no imperfection in you." Don't worry when people call you weird; you're a different kind of normal, a kind of normal that God loves. Psalm 139:14 says, "I will praise You because I have been remarkably and wonderfully made. Your works are wonderful, and I know this very well."

CHRISTIAN SMITH: *17, New Orleans, LA*
Franklin Avenue Baptist Church and New Orleans Charter Science and Mathematics High School, New Orleans, LA

SELF-HARM

"You are not to make gashes on your bodies for the dead or put tattoo marks on yourselves; I am Yahweh." —*Leviticus 19:28*

Self-harm is a very sensitive subject for many teens, because so many struggle with it or know someone who does. Everyone who suffers from this horrible choice to try to ease the pain inside them needs a friend, one who shows them what God has to say about the body. We should also trust our parents and God for help. They love us more than anyone else and they always want what's best for us. Finding Bible verses that guide us and help us to see truth is helpful. I found a favorite book of the Bible, Leviticus. In Leviticus 19:28 it states, "You are not to make gashes on your bodies for the dead or put tattoo marks on yourselves; I am Yahweh." To me, this means that we are never to cut ourselves in any way or for any purpose. This can be hard for those who feel neglected and feel internal pain. When they hurt inside, some of these people turn to cutting or other forms of self-harming. After they harm themselves, the relief leaves, and they realize they have only added pain on top of the pain they already felt. If you are thinking about self-harming, talk to a trusted adult as soon as possible. Turn to God and ask Him to help you through it. It hurts God when you hurt yourself.

DAVID JOSEPH DALESANDRO: *14, York, SC*
Hillcrest Baptist Church and York Comprehensive High School, York, SC

PSSSST!

"Keep your tongue from evil and your lips from deceitful speech."
—*Psalm 34:13*

When I think of gossip, I think of those four or five girls in the corner mumbling to each other while looking at everyone else like they have issues. What I found out later in my high school career is that guys do it too, and we are equally as bad. We have a tendency to spread rumors without even thinking about it, and it's usually about a girl. Our female friends are delicate and should be treated like sisters in Christ, no matter what their reputation. The most common gossip that guys in high school hear is, "Did you hear what she did?" And, sadly, we hear most of that from guys we know and that we call friends. It is important that we protect the innocence of whomever we know about. It is their job to repent, and they will if they know they are wrong. It is not our place to judge. I will admit I have spread rumors before, and I felt guilty for it. I went back to those people and apologized and asked for forgiveness. It's not easy to hold something you were told, but it doesn't benefit anyone when there are rumors in the air. We are to hold our tongue always unless it is edifying to the Lord.

CHRISTOPHER COLEMAN BAILEY: *17, Albany, GA*
Greater Second Mt. Olive Baptist Church and Sherwood Christian Academy, Albany, GA

MARCH

The Straight Path

My son, pay attention to my words; listen closely to my sayings.

Don't lose sight of them; keep them within your heart.

For they are life to those who find them, and health to one's whole body.

Guard your heart above all else, for it is the source of life.

Don't let your mouth speak dishonestly, and don't let your lips talk deviously.

Let your eyes look forward; fix your gaze straight ahead. Carefully consider the path for your feet, and all your ways will be established.

Don't turn to the right or to the left; keep your feet away from evil.

(Proverbs 4:20–27)

ARE YOU SOARING FOR JESUS?

"But those who trust in the LORD will renew their strength; they will soar on wings like eagles; they will run and not grow weary; they will walk and not faint." —*Isaiah 40:31*

Hard to believe, I know, but we Christians don't always put our trust in the Lord. We may say we trust in Him; but do we live it out naturally or do we possess some pretend attitude, living a lie before others? Do we worry about an upcoming test, game, or homework assignment? Or, even more important for the long-term, do we trust Him with our futures—college, marriage, purchasing a home, and all the other major things we young men will face not too many years after we graduate from high school? Trusting the Lord is giving your worries to God and knowing He has a plan even when we may not understand it at the time. When I think of an eagle, I think of greatness. It has the ability to spread its wings and soar unlike anything else God has created. I think God intentionally used an eagle in today's verse for that reason. As Christians, we are not called to just fly but to soar. We need to trust God with our lives so that we can soar. Don't be a spiritual chicken, which can barely get off the ground. Be an eagle. Soar! Soar for Christ!

CHANDLER SMITH: *16, Springdale, AR*
Cross Church Springdale Campus and Shiloh Christian School, Springdale, AR

PASSIONS AND PLATFORMS

"Whatever you do, do it enthusiastically, as something done for the Lord and not for men." —*Colossians 3:23*

What do you like to do? What are you passionate about? Is it sports, music, marching band, or maybe academics? Aren't we all passionate about something? But I want you to just think for a second: What are you most passionate about apart from God? I know a man who is completely on fire for the Lord. He's a baseball player and he taught me everything I know about God and how to live a Christ-centered life! He uses the sport of baseball as a platform for Christ. He doesn't play baseball just for the fun of it or for the cheers and praises. He plays for the one who gave him the ability to play! No matter what he does in baseball or in life, it is a platform for Jesus Christ. What are you passionate about? Is it sports, marching band, music, or maybe academics? Well, once you know your passion, use it as a platform for your Savior! I encourage you to make your passion a platform for Jesus Christ.

KORD OFFENBACKER: *15, Springdale, AR*
Cross Church Springdale Campus and Shiloh Christian School, Springdale, AR

PRAISE THE LORD!

"Sing to Yahweh, for He has done glorious things. Let this be known throughout the earth." —*Isaiah 12:5*

The meaning of the first phrase, "Sing to Yahweh," is to tell God how great He is. In this case, it is through singing. This can be done in church as well as in the car, the shower, and in your bedroom. My friend and I were sitting on the bus when I pulled out my iPod. He asked to look at my songs. He found an album with a song that he liked. So, we enjoyed that one and then we played some other songs that he also liked. The one we really liked is called "Break It Down" by Lecrae. In it is a modern-day version of 1 Corinthians; it speaks about someone who moves away from the truth and says that anyone can come back to God's truth. The excellent thing that God does is to bring people to know His truth and love, and He teaches them how to love one another. My friend, who is a Christian, liked the words and the rhythm, and he shared what it was about with some of our friends. We can all think about the excellent things God has done. The greatest thing He has done was to send His Son to die on the cross so that we could spend eternity with Him. Music can be a tool to spread the gospel to all nations, starting on the bus!

AARON THOMPSON: *13, Tiger, GA*
Clayton Baptist Church and Rabun County Middle School, Clayton, GA

DON'T LUST

"Don't lust in your heart for her beauty or let her captivate you with her eyelashes." —*Proverbs 6:25*

Have you ever caught yourself staring at a young woman or simply wishing that you could be like some other guys, always surrounded by beautiful ladies? Sometimes it is hard to admit that you have fallen into the temptation of lust, but realize that it is in every male's nature to be attracted to the opposite gender. Lust is not just a problem for men; it is something women deal with too. Everyone is tempted by lust throughout their lives. We were called by God to be fruitful and multiply in Genesis 1:22. However, it is easy to cross the line and desire something for yourself, outside of God's intentions. As men, we want to be seen as someone who is loved, which is not wrong, but it's easy to become so focused on ourselves that we ignore the need for God in our lives. If we will simply pray for our future relationships, God will fulfill His purpose for us to find a partner in His own time. We must first continue in our relationships with Christ, day-by-day, and blessings will flow abundantly for our devotion to the one who loved us so much that He sent His Son to die for our sins. Be strong in your daily life and realize that attraction is human but lust is sinful.

JONATHAN DISMUKES: *17, Mobile, AL*
Redeemer Fellowship Church and Cottage Hill Christian Academy, Mobile, AL

LOVE

"If I speak human or angelic languages but don't have love
I am a sounding gong or a clanging cymbal. If I have the gift
of prophecy and understand all mysteries and all knowledge and if
I have all faith that I can move mountains but do not have love,
I am nothing. And if I donate all my goods to feed the poor and I give
my body in order to boast but do not have love I gain nothing."

—1 Corinthians 13:1–3

In the verses above it says you could be the most holy person, but if you don't have love you are basically nothing. We are called to love everyone, and that includes our enemies. Jesus said if our enemy is hungry, we are to feed him; and if he needs clothes, then we are to clothe him. Jesus even said to love your neighbor as yourself, which can be really hard for some of us. But, don't you suppose that some of our neighbors have problems loving us too? Loving our neighbors enough to meet their needs is what God wants us to do. We need to do what God tells us to do, and we need to read the Bible so that we will know what that is!

RHETT CHAPMAN: *15, Pageland, SC*
South Pointe Fellowship and South Pointe Christian School, Pageland, SC

JUDGING OTHERS (PART 1)

"He will not judge by what He sees with His eyes, He will not execute justice by what He hears with His ears, but He will judge the poor righteously and execute justice for the oppressed of the land." —*Isaiah 11:3–4*

How often do we judge another? And by what standards do we hold them accountable? I find that I, all too often, judge by what I see on the outside of a person. It is a very bad habit, because I have no way of seeing what is in a person's heart. As cliché as it may sound, it is not often thought of or taken seriously. It is not my duty to judge others; it is the Lord's job. Why? Because God is a righteous judge and He will judge by His standards and not mine. My standards are twisted, and not like God's, regardless of what I may think of the person I am judging. As Isaiah 64:6 says, "All of us have become like something unclean, and all our righteous acts are like a polluted garment: all of us wither like a leaf, and our iniquities carry us away like the wind." This means that our righteousness, in the unfathomable comparison with God's, is like a polluted garment, filthy and unfit for service, all because of our sin. With that way of thinking, no man can judge another with righteousness. Yet the Lord came to the earth, perfect and sinless, and He chooses to hang out with us? Amazing!

JESSE D. SANDO: *13, Pleasant Hill, OH*
First Baptist Church, Vandalia, OH; Homeschooled

OTHERS (PART 2)

"He will not judge by what He sees with His eyes, He will not execute justice by what He hears with His ears, but He will judge the poor righteously and execute justice for the oppressed of the land." —*Isaiah 11:3–4*

Jesus didn't converse or socialize with the Pharisees or religious leaders, yet He spoke against them and their false teachings. The Lord was constantly found with the poor, the tax collectors, and the sinners. Can you guess why? He looked inside their hearts, seeing the Pharisee's hypocrisy and the sinner's brokenness. Yet to both parties, the mourning and the prejudiced, He spoke with love and compassion. He did not judge by what He saw on the outside, and He did not execute justice through what He heard. Instead, He looked within and saw the contrite heart of the sinner. He forgives the repentant offender, you and me. One day, we will all pass from this earthly home into eternity, and on that day we will stand before God, a righteous judge, and be given either what we do deserve (death, which leads to hell), or what we do not deserve (grace, which leads to heaven). So, the next time you are quick to judge a person by act or appearance, just ask yourself something: "By whose standards am I judging this person, and do I know the true intention of his or her heart?" Only God knows that, so He is to be the only judge. He can be trusted to do the perfectly righteous thing.

JESSE D. SANDO: *13, Pleasant Hill, OH*
First Baptist Church, Vandalia, OH; Homeschooled

STRENGTH

"God is our refuge and strength, a helper who is always found in times of trouble." —*Psalm 46:1*

Strength may be that one thing we all need or desire, but not all of us have it. There are many types of strength. For instance, some of us might have brute or physical strength, while others have brain or mental strength. Not that there's anything wrong with either of those, but the Bible tells us that God should be our strength, not our mental or physical abilities. For example, let's look at two verses that speak of strength in the Lord. "Finally, be strengthened by the Lord and by His vast strength" (Ephesians 6:10). "The LORD is my strength and my song; He has become my salvation" (Psalm 118:14). Now, if you didn't catch on, both of those verses clearly state that God is the writer's strength. I have an older brother who is in the Marine Corps, and he is quite strong and muscular. When he was in boot camp, he knew it was going to be grueling. He also knew that he was in shape and that he had a great chance of making it through. But, he soon found out that boot camp didn't require as much physical strength as it did mental strength. It was so challenging mentally that he knew that he couldn't do it on his own. So he placed his trust in the Lord, knowing that God was right by his side and that He was the only one who could give him the strength to pull through. We can't do it on our own, we can't be God, but we can let Him be our strength. "I am able to do all things through Him who strengthens me" (Philippians 4:13).

JOSH DANIEL: *14, Troy, OH*
Two Rivers Community Church, Vandalia, OH; Homeschooled

LOVING NO MATTER WHAT!

"Whosoever humbles himself like this child—this one is the greatest in the kingdom of heaven. And whoever welcomes one child like this in My name welcomes Me." —Matthew 18:5

I have a younger brother and sister who are sometimes annoying. I'm trying to do something, why do they keep doing that? Now why would they say that? I get angry—sometimes too angry. Jesus says in Matthew 18:3–5, "'I assure you,' He said, 'unless you are converted and become like children, you will never enter the kingdom of heaven. Therefore, whoever humbles himself like this child—this one is the greatest in the kingdom of heaven. And whosoever welcomes one child like this in My name welcomes Me.'" So, we can remember these verses when our siblings get on our nerves to the point of being annoying. We can also try to remember that we used to be just as bad as they are, if not worse, when we were their age. And most importantly, never give in to anger. Matthew 18:6 says, "But whosoever causes the downfall of one of these little ones who believe in Me—it were better for him if a heavy millstone were hung around his neck and that he were drowned in the depths of the sea!" Have you ever seen a millstone? It's huge! Swimming would be impossible if one was tied around your neck. We should try to remember how God feels about children when dealing with our younger siblings.

MATTHEW COOKSEY: *13, McMinnville, OR*
Valley Baptist Church, McMinnville, OR; Homeschooled

GOD WILL PROVIDE AND TAKE CARE OF YOU

"Protect me as the pupil of Your eye, hide me in the shadow of Your wings." —Psalm 17:8

God will provide for all of your needs. He will take care of you and provide for you, as He promised in His Word. God is the source of everything you need. He is the God of all comfort, and He gives us peace. You see, nothing can separate us from God's love. He gives us what we need to live for Him. He is the Author and Finisher of our faith. God will provide! Romans 8:28 says that "We know that all things work together for the good of those who love God: those who are called according to His purpose." The Bible also gives us encouragement, like in Deuteronomy 31:6 where we are told to "Be strong and courageous; don't be terrified or afraid of them. For it is the Lord your God who goes with you; He will not leave you or forsake you." Let's remember not to be afraid and not to forget that God will provide. God will provide for all your needs and, as His Word also promises, He will never leave you or forsake you, no matter what. That is something to cling to, don't you agree?

HANK F. GRIFFIN: *14, Pageland, SC*
White Plains Baptist Church, Jefferson, SC; South Pointe Christian School, Pageland, SC

JEALOUSY

"A tranquil heart is life to the body, but jealousy is rottenness to the bones." —*Proverbs 14:30*

Jealousy is a destroyer, causing people to go absolutely savage. Yet it can be a good thing when God says "I am jealous for you." The reason He says He is jealous for you is that He loves you. Think about it: If you had something or made something and someone took it, you would be jealous to get it back. God is the same way. He wants you and is jealous for you. You might think, *Well, why doesn't He just save us from the evils of life?* Good point, but what if your parents did the same thing? What if every time they thought something might bring harm to you, they didn't let you do it? For example, what if your parents didn't let you drive or even play sports because they thought it was too dangerous? The world would be full of weak people who are unable to do anything, because we would be so fearful of everything out there in the real world. Like your parents, God loves us and lets us do things that might knock us down, but He will be there to pick us right back up and nudge us on.

HUNTER TREMBLAY: *14, Pageland, SC*
South Pointe Fellowship and South Pointe Christian School, Pageland, SC

THE ARMOR OF GOD

"I have treasured Your word in my heart so that I may not sin against You." —*Psalm 119:11*

Bible study is one of the most important parts in maintaining a relationship with God. Studying God's Word every day will help us grow and mature in our walk with Christ. If we hide God's Word in our hearts, like He has commanded us to do, then we will have the strength to resist the devil. Ephesians 6:10–19 reminds us, "Finally, be strengthened by the Lord and by His vast strength. Put on the full armor of God so that you can stand against the tactics of the Devil. For our battle is not against flesh and blood, but against the rulers, against the authorities, against the world powers of this darkness, against the spiritual forces of evil in the heavens. This is why you must take up the full armor of God, so that you may be able to resist in the evil day, and having prepared everything, to take your stand. Stand, therefore, with truth like a belt around your waist, righteousness like armor on your chest, and your feet sandaled with readiness for the gospel of peace. In every situation take the shield of faith, and with it you will be able to extinguish all the flaming arrows of the evil one. Take the helmet of salvation, and the sword of the Spirit, which is God's word." And James 4:7 tells us to "submit to God. But resist the Devil, and he will flee from you." So, if we put on the spiritual armor of God every day and resist the snares of the devil, he will flee from us with God's help!

ZACH M. BYRD: *15, Jefferson, SC*
Bethlehem Baptist Church, Buford, SC; South Point Christian School, Pageland, SC

THINKING ABOUT RELATIONSHIPS

"All a man's ways seem right to him, but the LORD evaluates the motives. Commit your activities to the LORD, and your plans will be achieved."
—Proverbs 16:2–3

You may have read this title and verse and thought, *What does that verse have to do with relationships?* Well, let me explain. As teenagers, it seems like everyone is getting a new boyfriend or girlfriend every month. All the drama that goes along with that can get ridiculous. I think most guys would agree that we would all like to have a girlfriend at one point or another. I mean, not too many of us want to be single forever. But how do we know which girl to be in a relationship with? It can be tough and confusing. But before doing anything, you need to think about some things. If you get into that relationship, will it last? I've asked myself this many times. I've had opportunities to be in relationships, but since I could tell it wouldn't last, I kept it on a just-friends level. If you get into relationships that don't last and keep breaking up, those are kind of like mini divorces. It's not healthy practice for marriage. Also, you have to almost be picky and set standards for both you and a girl. You want a girl who truly loves God more than you, and you need to get to the point where you love God more than her. If you're not at that point, you shouldn't be in a relationship. God has to be at the center of every relationship! Finally, be patient and pray. God has a plan. He has someone for you and will bring that person into your life. Pray for your future wife and for yourself. Turn your focus to God, commit your activities to Him, and He will provide!

AUSTIN CANFIELD: *18, Tulsa, OK*
Evergreen Baptist Church, Bixby, OK; Homeschooled

ANXIETY

"Don't worry about anything, but in everything, through prayer and petition with thanksgiving, let your requests be made known to God."

—*Philippians 4:6*

Anxiety is the feeling of fear or an uneasiness about something that has not even happened. People can become anxious about anything, including their families, work, future, health, death, or even their salvation. Sometimes people have trouble finding the exact cause of their anxiety. God's Word tells us that we do not need to be anxious about anything. He offers His peace, which is far beyond anything humans can comprehend, to guard our minds and hearts. God offers much encouragement for Christians to consider when we are anxious. God is with us all of the time and in every situation. Psalm 139:7 says, "Where can I go to escape Your Spirit? Where can I flee from Your presence?" God promises to never leave us or forsake us (Hebrews 13:5), that we can do anything through Christ (Philippians 4:13), and that He will supply all of our needs according to His riches (Philippians 4:19). God's character also provides encouragement: His holiness, which refers to His perfect purity; His power, grace, goodness, mercy, wisdom, and justice. God loves and cares for you. God cannot lie (Hebrews 6:18). First Peter 5:7 says, "Casting all your care upon Him, for He cares about you." When you focus your attention on God and trust that His Word is true, you can find peace in place of anxiety. There have been many times when I've been anxious, but I found His peace in prayer. If you are anxious, seek God's help and confess your anxiety, asking His forgiveness for not trusting Him. He forgives and encourages us into a deeper relationship with Him. He stands ready to meet us, even now!

DAVID MARTIN: *15, Pageland, SC*
Mount Moriah Baptist Church, Marshville, NC; South Pointe Christian School, Pageland, SC

HE KNOWS JUST WHAT YOU NEED

"For the word of God is living and effective and sharper than any double-edged sword, penetrating as far as the separation of soul and spirit, joints and marrow. It is able to judge the ideas and thoughts of the heart." —*Hebrews 4:12*

Have you ever just opened your Bible and started reading, and right where you opened the page was exactly the verse or motivation you needed at that very moment? Hebrews 4:12 states, "For the word of God is living and effective and sharper than any double-edged sword, penetrating as far as the separation of soul and spirit, joints and marrow. It is able to judge the ideas and thoughts of the heart." Since the Word of God is living and active and judges the thoughts and intents of the heart, it knows exactly what you need. As soon as you open your Bible and open the pages, whether it is words of encouragement, help with a problem you are having, or motivation, God knows what you need to hear. It says in John 1:1 that "In the beginning was the Word, and the Word was with God, and the Word was God." The Word has always been around since the beginning of time, and so has God. If the Word is God, that is just another reason to show you He knows what you need and He will lead you to it. So I encourage you to open and read your Bible, because He knows what you need to hear.

KYLE SUTTON: *16, Pageland, SC*
First Baptist Church and South Pointe Christian School, Pageland, SC

INTEGRITY

"The integrity of the upright guides them, but the perversity of the treacherous destroys them." —*Proverbs 11:3*

It is a great honor to be known as a man of integrity. Why? I'm afraid I'll have to answer that with this question: What is integrity? Integrity is living up to one's moral standards. It is honesty, it's keeping our word. To be a man of integrity requires that we uphold God's rules. His Word sets the standard! Without integrity we will destroy ourselves. In today's world, it is often seen as OK to take something small, like a pen or pencil, from school or church for your own personal use. And it's seen as normal to tell a white lie to cover something you did wrong, or to excuse yourself for doing that wrong instead of taking responsibility. Christians need to be different from the norm. By being men of integrity, we can open up many opportunities to share the gospel. Now, to be clear, being a person of integrity also means that when we tell the truth, we don't do it partly, we do it all the way. For example, let's say you were asked to do the dishes before your parents got home and you got your sibling to do them for you. When asked later if you did the dishes, the wrong answer would be, "Yeah, the dishes got done." That would be deceitful. The point is, even though you might technically be telling the truth, your answer does not show integrity. We must ask God for the strength to be men and women of integrity as He prepares us for adulthood, parenthood, and for being leaders in our churches and communities. It's only by His power that we can.

JOSHUA JOHANSEN: *18, Shrewsbury, MA*
Bethlehem Bible Church, West Boylston, MA; Quinsigamond Community College, Worchester, MA

FAITH

"Now faith is the reality of what is hoped for, the proof of what is not seen. For our ancestors won God's approval by it. By faith we understand that the universe was created by God's command, so that what is seen has been made from things that are not visible." —*Hebrews 11:1–3*

Faith is one of the most important things in the world. This can be seen in just about everything we do. Without faith, we wouldn't have things like the Bible. Without faith, the history of the world would be drastically different. Faith is the basis of every religion. If the world lacked faith, none of us would be here because it was faith that saved Noah. It was faith that gave Abraham the chance to be the father of nations. It was faith that saved Isaac when God told Abraham to sacrifice him. Without faith, we would have nothing but suffering and pain. With faith comes the gift of knowing that we will get to go to heaven by the grace of God. With the knowledge that our path leads to heaven, we can relax and do what God has put us here to do—spread His Word, the gospel message!

DYLAN KNOLES: *13, Jefferson, SC*
South Pointe Fellowship and South Pointe Christian School, Pageland, SC

HEARING GOD

"And the peace of God, which surpasses every thought, will guard your hearts and minds in Christ Jesus." —Philippians 4:7

Hearing what God wants you to do is somewhat difficult. More than likely, you haven't literally heard God tell you to do something. When we refer to hearing God we are talking about knowing in our hearts what God wants us to do. Why can't we always understand Him? Why must we pray to be shown what He wants us to do? Today's verse tells us that God's knowledge is far superior to our own knowledge; and when He tells us to do something He will confirm it through His Word, through godly counsel, through circumstances, and as we talk to Him and He talks to us in prayer. God will show us what He means, but we must pray for the wisdom to understand what He wants us to do. We have to take Him at His word. Sometimes we have to do crazy things, but we should always do what God asks us to do no matter how crazy or risky it may seem. God has more for us behind the next door. He has more for us over the next hill. All we have to do to receive these blessings is to listen to Him, and He will teach us and guide us to the next step. He will always be there with us. He can be trusted.

DAVID JOSEPH DALESANDRO: *14, York, SC*
Hillcrest Baptist Church and York Comprehensive High School, York, SC

OUR REFUGE AND STRENGTH IN TIMES OF TROUBLE

"God is our refuge and strength,
a helper who is always found in times of trouble." —*Psalm 46:1*

Did you know that God is our refuge and our strength, and He has promised to be a helper who is always available to us in times of trouble, no matter what? He is available to us even when the burdens we carry are so painful that we fear that if anyone found out we could suffer for the rest of our lives. Even in the worst of situations and the most fearful times in our lives, God is with us to provide a safe shelter. He is our refuge! So, if you are going through troubles, and it matters not what those troubles are, please trust in God, for He can be trusted! Proverbs 3:5–6 encourages us with these words: "Trust in the LORD with all your heart, and do not rely on your own understanding; think about Him in all your ways, and He will guide you on the right paths." How amazing is that? The Bible, God's Word, also says in Psalm 91:11, "For He will give His angels orders concerning you, to protect you in all your ways." There is no place or person on the earth that will provide a safe refuge for us, and no other can give us strength in times of trouble but God. Think about it!

HANK F. GRIFFIN: *14, Pageland, SC*
White Plains Baptist Church, Jefferson, SC; South Pointe Christian School, Pageland, SC

PLAYING FOR HIS GLORY

"Whatever you do, do it enthusiastically, as something done for the Lord and not for men." —*Colossians 3:23*

Let's put ourselves in the world of sports for a few minutes. Most guys have probably either played or are currently playing a sport. Sports can be really fun because as an athlete you can use your speed to make the goal or your strength to make the tackle. But none of us could do what we do on our own. All our talents and abilities come from God. He made each of us with certain talents that we can use to build skills for what He has in store for us in the future. But this verse can also be applied to our athletics right now. When you play your sport, you should play and work as hard as you can. Do not do it for yourself: do it only to glorify God. Your hard work and good attitude are reflections of Christ. When you are on the field or in the gym practicing and playing to the best of your abilities, your motivation should be "for the Lord and not for men." Whether you're playing football, basketball, soccer, or any other sport, do it all to glorify God! Let Him be the victor in your life all the time.

ANDREW CLEM: *13, Albany, GA*
Sherwood Baptist Church and Sherwood Christian Academy, Albany, GA

DEATH AND ETERNITY

"We will certainly die and be like water poured out on the ground, which can't be recovered. But God would not take away a life; He would devise plans so that the one banished from Him does not remain banished."

—2 Samuel 14:14

There is no debate; we all will die one day. But there is a question that needs to be answered in our hearts. The question is, where will we spend eternity, heaven or hell? It is my understanding that eternity is a long, long time! Eternity has no end. So if a person goes to hell, the pain will never ease off. So, be ready, the Bible tells us in Matthew 3:2 to "Repent, because the kingdom of heaven has come near!" Obviously, we need to be ready and not put off until tomorrow the most important decision we will ever make, because none of us knows when our time will come. The Bible also says in Psalm 89:48, "What man can live and never see death? Who can save himself from the power of Sheol?" Since we know that we will all die, it seems very important to think about the question I asked you earlier about where you will spend eternity. The question is the most important one you will ever answer. It is time to seek God and know His perfect will for your life, and that includes heaven. But you must make the decision to confess, repent, and accept Him as your Lord and Savior. There is no other way to get into heaven except by knowing Jesus. Now, that is something to think about—and something to think about now!

HANK F. GRIFFIN: 14, Pageland, SC
White Plains Baptist Church, Jefferson, SC; South Pointe Christian School, Pageland, SC

WORKING

"Whatever you do, do it enthusiastically, as something done for the Lord and not for men." —*Colossians 3:23*

Getting your dream job when you're twenty-five isn't an instantaneous thing. It sometimes starts taking shape when you're twelve! A huge part of being employable is learning how to be a good worker when you're young, when simple tasks are building blocks to greater responsibilities. You can begin by helping your parents by doing chores, mowing the lawn, weeding the flower beds, etc. A good work ethic is important to employers, and someone who has a good work ethic will excel in almost any work environment. There is no room for lazy or unprepared people in the workplace. Do you want to be an engineer? Work hard on your math now so that you can learn advanced calculus later on. Want to own your own business? Maybe you can start a home business like a lawn-mowing service or baking cookies, etc. There is always something you can do that will prepare you for the future, so think ahead and be creative now. Just be sure that you aren't structuring your whole life around getting the perfect job. The only thing that can ultimately make you happy is to follow God's will and glorify Him with your life.

MICAH COOKSEY: *19, McMinnville, OR*
Valley Baptist Church, McMinnville, OR

OBEY, REALLY?

"'For I know the plans I have for you'—this is the LORD's declaration—'plans for your welfare, not for disaster, to give you a future and a hope.'" —*Jeremiah 29:11*

What comes to mind when you hear the word *obedience*? *Obedience* has been defined as submission to one's authority. The Bible talks extensively about obedience. One of the Ten Commandments says to obey your father and mother. God commanded Moses to free His people and Moses obeyed, and Abraham was told to travel to distant lands and he obeyed. There are many stories like these where God commanded something and the followers obeyed, but can you see the other thing involved in these men's lives? It is called adjustment, becoming suitable to the circumstances. God has given me a plan for my life, and I want to chase after it with all my heart, but I know when I pursue it there will be adjustments on my part. I must prepare for those moments. I have gone through many adjustments in my life; even now I am adjusting to moving to a new city during my senior year. Maybe you are experiencing God's call to obedience and struggling with adjusting your life to it. Remember, God loves us and He has a grand plan for each of us. Although I have a dream, God might change that, and I will have to obey His command and adjust to this new idea. My favorite verse is Jeremiah 29:11 because it has an awesome promise and reminds us that He hasn't forgotten us. We must obey His commands, following His plans for us. Life is incredible, and it will be rewarding if you know what God's purpose for your life is, and you chase after that with all your heart.

COLLIN MICHAEL SEELEN: *18, Itami, Hyogo, Japan*
Emmanuel Baptist Church and Kansai Homeschooled Network, Itami, Hyogo, Japan

TIME MANAGEMENT (PART 1)

"Teach us to number our days carefully so that we may develop wisdom in our hearts." —Psalm 90:12

Like many people, especially guys in their teens, I struggle with time management. Simply put, it is a problem! Between all the schoolwork, tests, sports, and the desire to have at least some sort of social life, I sometimes put God on the back burner. Why are the church and God the first things to go when we don't have a lot of free time? The fact of the matter is, God should be at the top of our list because He's the most important, and then we should try to fill in all the other stuff behind Him. The problem is that we, as Christians, have bought into the mentality of this world. Achieving in school so we can grow up and get a successful job are good things, and we do need to do those things to the best of our ability to glorify God. But what is the point if we end up missing God? None of us wants to be on our death bed and think, *Wow I did all this stuff, but where did I see God in my life?* We have to start spending our time better now, because if we don't we'll just continue to spiral and drift away. If we choose to put God on the back burner now, it could be months or years before we ever start to spend the time we should've been spending with Him all along.

CLAY NORMAN: *18, Albany, GA*
Sherwood Baptist Church and Sherwood Christian Academy, Albany, GA

TIME MANAGEMENT (PART 2)

"Teach us to number our days carefully so that we may develop wisdom in our hearts." —*Psalm 90:12*

For a lot of men in mid-life, time management sort of comes under the heading of, "Don't let this happen to you!" Men need to learn early on the importance of making time for what is necessary and for what is important. Giving time to God every day to worship and praise Him and to learn from His Word has to fit under both categories: making time for what is important and for what is necessary! Trust me, even as a teenager, I've had to learn this lesson the hard way! There is nothing so important in our lives now or in the future that we should put it above God. God left us His Word, which teaches us that He has a purpose and a direction for our lives. We are here to honor and glorify God and to spread the gospel. If we are too busy to fulfill God's purpose, we have to realign our priorities and remember to keep God first. Our days are numbered here, but we will spend eternity with Him. It will be a major blessing when God looks at us and says, "Well done, good and faithful servant!"

CLAY NORMAN: *18, Albany, GA*
Sherwood Baptist Church and Sherwood Christian Academy, Albany, GA

EXAMPLES OF THE CHRISTIAN WALK

"Listen, my sons, to a father's discipline, and pay attention so that you may gain understanding." —*Proverbs 4:1*

We often can overlook our own parents as a source for guidance and as worthy examples of how we should live our lives. But aren't they the strongest influence on our lives? We are given to our parents so that they may raise us in the knowledge of the Lord and impart wisdom from their own experiences. By law, we are under their authority for eighteen years but remain as students throughout our lives, constantly seeking their help in tough circumstances. No one on the earth loves you more than your parents, even if it often seems otherwise. Just realize how much they do for you. They pay the way for your education, feed you when you are hungry, provide clothing, etc. We often take these blessings for granted, but let me challenge you to stop and be thankful for the care you have and the love your parents have for you. Even more important is that we learn from their teachings and use their example to follow the Lord in His Word. It is foolish to forsake the availability of great knowledge and fail to gain wisdom from the time you spend with your parents. Ask questions and take more time to be more involved in your family. Most important, pray that you will recognize the love your parents have for you and seek to learn from their example.

JONATHAN DISMUKES: *17, Mobile, AL*
Redeemer Fellowship Church and Cottage Hill Christian Academy, Mobile, AL

CHRIST'S RETURN (PART 1)

"Your heart must not be troubled. Believe in God believe also in Me. In My Father's house are many dwelling places; if not, I would have told you. I am going away to prepare a place for you. If I go away and prepare a place for you, I will come back and receive you to Myself, so that where I am you may be also." —*John 14:1–3*

Christ's return is sooner than we can imagine. So, as the Bible says, "The time is at hand." It is time to turn from your unbelief and turn to God. Salvation, becoming a born-again Christian, is the only way! Salvation is as easy as A, B, C. You must first *admit* that you are a sinner, then *believe* that Christ died for you and that He rose again. Finally, *confess* that God is the Savior of all who believe on His name, repent of your sins, and ask Jesus Christ to save you. If you are not saved, I invite you to take that next step in your life before it is too late. Mark 1:15 says that, "The time is fulfilled, and the kingdom of God has come near. Repent and believe in the good news!" The scariest part of it all is not what the Bible tells us about the fire and gnashing teeth. It is that you will be separated from God forever. In Revelation, it says that Jesus will come like a thief in the night, which means that we won't even know when He's coming; we have no clue. Being ready to meet Christ on that day is the most important thing we can do on this earth. Are you ready to go?

ZACHARY TREMBLAY: *13, Pageland, SC*
South Pointe Fellowship and South Pointe Christian School, Pageland, SC

CHRIST'S RETURN (PART 2)

"'Your heart must not be troubled. Believe in God; believe also in Me. In My Father's house are many dwelling places; if not, I would have told you. I am going away to prepare a place for you. If I go away and prepare a place for you, I will come back and receive you to Myself, so that where I am you may be also.'" —John 14:1–3

Even though your house now may be nice, this is just a temporary home. Do you want to be with Christ in paradise or with Satan in the worst place you have ever been? John 14:2–4 says, "In My Father's house are many dwelling places; if not, I would have told you. I am going away to prepare a place for you. If I go away and prepare a place for you, I will come back and receive you to Myself, so that where I am you may be also. You know the way to where I am going." I've heard it said that if you are unsaved, life here on the earth is the best you will ever have; but if you are saved, the earth is the worst you will ever have. This is very true, for if you are going to heaven there is no fussing, fighting, or sadness; there is no sin, no death, no pain or suffering. In heaven we will be with God and know Him by sight. We will be with God forever. If you are unsaved, you will spend eternity in hell where there is only sharp, stinging fire that never dulls in its intensity. The day of the Lord is coming and He will take all of the ones who are saved with Him. There is no time to waste. Be ready to meet Christ!

ZACHARY TREMBLAY: *13, Pageland, SC*
South Pointe Fellowship and South Pointe Christian School, Pageland, SC

THE TRINITY

"For His invisible attributes, that is, His eternal power and divine nature, have been clearly seen since the creation of the world, being understood through what He has made. As a result, people are without excuse."
—Romans 1:20

Want a brain teaser? How can someone be three people and three people be someone, and the three parts are completely inseparable yet completely distinct? The Trinity—Father, Son, and Holy Spirit—is an entirely confusing subject. We know God is one God, a single omnipotent, omnipresent God, who created the world and saves us. Yet we also know God the Father, Jesus the Son, and the Holy Spirit that lives in us all also exist. So how is it that we recognize three different entities as being God but still claim to worship just one God? It is very hard to understand the Trinity because there is nothing like it in this world. We can imagine a fruit, which has seeds, meat, and skin and say that's what it must be like. But we can cut open an apple and slice the skin off and remove the seeds and make everything separate, but God cannot be separated. God has always and always will exist. If we can't explain the Trinity, are we wrong? Does God not exist this way? God does exist as three in one! Let the Trinity be evidence of God's glory and might. "Ascribe power to God. His majesty is over Israel, His power among the clouds" (Psalm 68:34).

CODY BRANDON: *17, Old Hickory, TN*
The Fellowship at Two Rivers, Nashville, TN; Mt. Juliet High School, Mt. Juliet, TN

HELPING THE NEEDY

"And the King will answer them, 'I assure you: Whatever you did for one of the least of these brothers of Mine, you did for Me.'" —*Matthew 25:40*

On a mission project in Atlanta, Georgia, our team went around the city and brought sandwiches to homeless people living under bridges. We spent time talking and praying with them as they ate. This was a unique experience for everyone in our youth group. The reality and my expectations were very different. The people weren't all drug addicts who made poor decisions to mess up their lives. One guy looked not much different than I do. Some were victims of unfortunate events, loss of jobs in a bad economy, lack of a good family, and sometimes sinful choices. They were grateful for the lunches we passed out. Many prayed with us. Jesus spent a lot of His time with the poor. If Jesus was doing His ministry today, He would spend some time under the bridges. We should help those less fortunate than we are. We have to look at the people all around the world who are living in poverty that is incomprehensible to many. Thousands of children will take their final breath today due to a preventable disease; starvation is prominent; and clean water is hard to come by in many places in the world. Christ reminds us that "whatever you did for one of the least of these brothers of Mine, you did for Me." We serve Christ when we serve the poor. Ignoring the poor, leaving them to perish, ignores God's call. When desperate for a Savior, Christ met our need. We must help meet the needs of others.

LUKE PERSTROPE: *17, St. Peters, MO*
First Baptist Church of St. Charles, St. Charles, MO; Fort Zumwalt East High School, St. Peters, MO

APRIL

A Father's Example

Listen, my sons, to a father's discipline, and pay attention so that you may gain understanding, for I am giving you good instruction.

Don't abandon my teaching.

When I was a son with my father, tender and precious to my mother, he taught me and said:

"Your heart must hold on to my words.

Keep my commands and live. Get wisdom, get understanding, don't forget or turn away from the words of my mouth.

Don't abandon wisdom, and she will watch over you;

love her, and she will guard you.

Wisdom is supreme—so get wisdom.

And whatever else you get, get understanding.

Cherish her, and she will exalt you, if you embrace her, she will honor you.

She will place a garland of grace on your head;, she will give you a crown of beauty." (Proverbs 4:1–9)

FORGIVENESS IS ESSENTIAL FOR CHRISTIANS

"For if you forgive people their wrongdoing, your heavenly Father will forgive you as well. But if you don't forgive people, your Father will not forgive your wrongdoing." —*Matthew 6:14–15*

Forgiveness is an essential part of a Christian's life. Without forgiveness there would be no Christians, because a Christian is a person whose sins have been forgiven by God through the acceptance of Jesus Christ. And, according to Matthew 6:14–15, we are only forgiven of our sins if we forgive others. Also Christians should forgive others not only to be forgiven, but because we were forgiven we should want to forgive others. It is like gifts at Christmas—not only do you receive gifts, you also give gifts to others. So, Christians should treat forgiveness like presents, not only receiving but also giving forgiveness. Forgiving others is the right thing to do, and when you do forgive there will be a great peace with you. Just like watching friends or family open the presents you gave them and seeing the joy on their faces, you will have joy in their reactions. But this verse also tells us that if we do not forgive others of their wrongdoings, then God will not forgive us of our wrongdoing. In other words, if we do not give any gifts, then we will not receive any gifts. Forgiving others is a difficult but necessary part of a Christian's life. Without forgiveness, a Christian cannot live his life the way God meant him to.

MICHAEL LOWE: *15, Pageland, SC*
Wolf Pond Baptist Church and South Pointe Christian School, Pageland, SC

KEEP IT BURNING!
(PART 1)

"Grace be with all who have undying love for our Lord Jesus Christ."
—*Ephesians 6:24*

Many times I've found that I have no motivation to do much of anything. Sometimes I will wake up in the morning and I just don't want to go to school or do anything else. Don't get me wrong. I like school, and I know that we all learn and grow there and get to spend time with friends. But, when days like this come, I will just lie in my bed and not get up because I feel like there is no point. I'm certain that I am not the only teen boy to ever feel this way. I went on a school retreat about three years ago and while sitting around a bonfire one night, one of my friends started talking. He was going on about the fire and I found myself totally confused. I had no idea where he was going with this conversation. But I listened to what he said, and I started to understand. He said that sometimes we feel like we are in this place where there is no point to anything in our lives. We think to ourselves, What is the point? That can lead to some pretty dangerous thoughts. We find that not only have we lost touch with what we need to do, but in times like that we can lose touch with Jesus too. We lose touch with Him, our Savior. We know that idle time is the devil's workshop, so it is important that we, particularly teens, keep our hearts and minds focused on what God wants us to do with every day.

DANIEL BAEHR: *17, Manassas, VA*
Emmanuel Baptist Church Youth Group and Emmanuel Christian School, Manassas, VA

KEEP IT BURNING!
(PART 2)

"Grace be with all who have undying love for our Lord Jesus Christ."
—*Ephesians 6:24*

I'm sure a lot of people have experienced going on a retreat or something similar and being on a big spiritual high: "Oh, my gosh, I love Jesus!" and all that stuff. Then we get back home and have a retreat letdown, because we're back to our normal environment and the same boring routine. What we need to do is find a way to stay on that spiritual high. We cannot ride on another's high: we need to allow the Lord to show us how to live out His grace and victory without getting bored! Now the connection to the fire is this: What is it that keeps a fire burning? Wood! Wood is the fuel that keeps the fire burning. We need to find the fuel in our Christian lives to keep the fire going, so that we can keep burning for God. I'm not going to lie; I have not always found my fuel in every situation, and many I know struggle with finding theirs for everything that comes up in their lives. But we need to be the generation that finds the fuel that God has for us so that we can be balanced in our Christian life. To do that we need to be on guard, and we need to be willing to get into the Bible, and to also be willing to get up and get going! Are you lying around just waiting for something to fuel your life? Remember that God's Word, the Bible, offers us what we need to get us fueled for God.

DANIEL BAEHR: *17, Manassas, VA*
Emmanuel Baptist Church Youth Group and Emmanuel Christian School, Manassas, VA

COURAGE

"In God whose word I praise, in the LORD, whose word I praise, in God I trust; I will not fear. What can man do to me?" —*Psalm 56:10–11*

As the Christian men we aspire to be, we are expected to live a life of courage. After all, faith in Christ is not easy. It is by far the easier road to be afraid and to hide behind those things that we think will protect us. Pride in Christ is no longer considered a good attribute in our culture today. These two verses in today's devotional can be considered a battle cry of fearless, proud Christian men. It is an encouragement to praise God in all circumstances. It describes a man who takes pride in God with bold confidence, even in the face of negative consequences. It can also be a challenge to us in our daily walks as Christians. Are you prepared to trust God in all situations? Will you take pride in God no matter who is around you or who is trying to get you to move away from what you know to be right? Are you willing to be fearless for the cause of Christ?

JACKSON REESE: *18, Pageland, SC*
South Pointe Fellowship and South Pointe Christian School, Pageland, SC

GIVING IT ALL TO GOD

"We know that all things work together for the good of those who love God; those who are called according to His purpose."

—*Romans 8:28*

Stuff happens in life that doesn't go according to our plan, like not getting into the college you were hoping for or not making the basketball team. Whatever the situation, we all come to the same conclusion in the end. Life isn't fair! But let me ask you this question: Whose plan was it to begin with? Your plan, or God's (see Jeremiah 29:11–14)? God plants a seed that encourages us to work toward goals and attain skills that will help us to achieve them. We may not see things the same way God does. God has a time and place for everything, and each has a significant purpose that will affect not only us but everyone we come in contact with. One summer day riding home from the store on our scooters, my friends and I were holding ice cold Slushies in our hands. We decided to take a different route home than usual. I pointed out a shaded area and suggested we stay there and relax. About twenty minutes later, we continued our trip home. The chapel across the street was having an Ultimate Frisbee game, and we were invited to join. When we turned them down, one of the youth leaders, again, ran to ask us to join them. This time we did. They reached out to us and made us welcome. I still attend the youth group functions and have made several new friends there. When I look back on this, I realize God was in control. There was a purpose for us taking a different route home that day. After that I began to give everything to God. I let Him control every aspect of my life. Are you willing to do the same?

NICHOLAS BERGER: *15, Fairchild Air Force Base, Airway Heights, WA; Airway Heights Baptist Church, Airway Heights, WA; Homeschooled*

VOLUNTEERING

"Then I heard the voice of the Lord saying: Who should I send? Who will go for Us? I said: Here I am. Send me." —*Isaiah 6:8*

Imagine this, you're sitting in class and you are tuned in to what your teacher is talking about. She pulls out a prize you really want, like a new iPhone or iPad, and she asks, "Does anyone want to volunteer?" I can almost guarantee that you will volunteer! But wait, how many of us will do that same thing when God calls a volunteer for His service? The rewards for doing God's will are things that will last for all eternity, not just until the next new electronic item arrives on the market. When God calls us to do something for His kingdom on the earth, would you speak up and say, "I'll do it, Father, choose me!" It does not matter when, or where, or what you're doing at the time! You just need to do it for His glory. Just like Isaiah, "Here I am. Send me." God loves it when His own children volunteer for Him. He loves using us for His plan! So, when God needs a volunteer, how about we just go ahead and do it to bring Him glory?

KORD OFFENBACKER: *16, Springdale, AR*
Cross Church Springdale Campus and Shiloh Christian School, Springdale, AR

ADVERSITY

"For He will conceal me in His shelter in the day of adversity; He will hide me under the cover of His tent; He will set me high on a rock." —*Psalm 27:5*

There will always be adversity in life, no matter where you go there will be trouble. But when there is trouble, you should look to God. He will get you on the right path. Job 42:11 tells us, "All his brothers, sisters, and former acquaintances came to his house and dined with him in his house. They sympathized with him and comforted him concerning all the adversity the Lord had brought on him." The story of Job is a good example of adversity, because Job was tested by God and was in trouble, but he stayed faithful to God and got back more than he had before. Ecclesiastes 7:14 says, "In the day of prosperity be joyful, but in the day of adversity, consider: God has made the one as well as the other, so that man cannot discover anything that will come after him." When trouble comes, keep trusting in the Lord. He will help you through and you will be better than when you were when the trouble came. "A friend loves at all times, and a brother is born for a difficult time" (Proverbs 17:17). You will be closer to God as well as people after trouble. Your bonds with friends will be stronger, and you will be a better friend because of it.

NOLAN MARTIN: *16, Marshville, NC*
Mount Moriah Baptist Church, Marshville, NC; South Pointe Christian School, Pageland, SC

FIRST DAY OF SCHOOL

"Your word is a lamp for my feet and a light on my path."
—Psalm 119:105

Moving can be scary! One summer my family moved from south of Atlanta, Georgia, to Missouri. One of the hardest things about moving is starting at a new school. On the first day of school, I got up early, put on my new clothes and Nikes, ate a good breakfast, and my mom took my picture before leaving for school like she always does on the first day of school, regardless of the weather. That was the easy part of the day. Then, I entered the school and went to my first hour class, or what I thought was my first hour class. After not hearing my name called on the classroom role, my teacher looked at my schedule and told me to go to the A gym. She asked me if I knew where the gyms were located. I had absolutely no clue! She then gave directions that didn't make any sense (don't you hate it when that happens?). So when I walked out of the classroom, I was on my own. I wandered around the school and finally found the gyms. I was so relieved. But, of course, I walked into the wrong gym. Someone finally told me I needed to go to the gym next door. After arriving in the correct gym, I sat down not knowing anyone and feeling pretty embarrassed. This story can sometimes be compared to life. People who don't know God and don't read the Bible can wander through life, not knowing where to go or what to do. As Christians, the Bible should be the guide to light our paths. We should apply the truths of God's Word. He tells us how to live in this life, and we should be trying our best to live like Christ.

MICAH PERSTROPE: *13, St. Peters, MO*
First Baptist Church of St. Charles, St. Charles, MO; Dubray Middle School, St. Peters, MO

GOD'S LOVE

"For I am persuaded that not even death or life, angels or rulers, things present or things to come, hostile powers, height or depth, or any other created thing will have the power to separate us from the love of God that is in Christ Jesus our Lord!" —*Romans 8:38–39*

Now before you start thinking, Oh, yeah, I've heard this so many times, and I know that God loves me, let me ask you to just hear my story. Hopefully it will encourage you or give you a new perspective on God's love. A few years ago I was struggling with depression. It felt to me like I was loved by no one. While this was totally not true, I believed the lies I was fed. One night after some events, God brought me to my knees crying. I couldn't understand how He could love me. Although none of us can ever fully realize the amount of love God has for us, I caught just a glimpse of it that night. It was enough to break down the walls I had built up. Just sit and think, the Creator of the galaxies, mountain ranges, humans, and DNA coding loves me so much that He sent His only Son to die for me—a person who continually violates His rules and dishonors Him. That's crazy! I find it hard to love the people that even slightly annoy me, let alone someone who would disobey, dishonor, and not listen to me countless times. One of my favorite worship songs says, "Your love never fails, it never gives up, it never runs out on me." We can't comprehend this kind of love! It's a love no human could possibly ever express apart from knowing God. Realizing a little of how much God loves you can totally change your life! How awesome it is to serve a God whose love will never fail and who never gives up on us, no matter what we have done or will do! Awesome!

AUSTIN CANFIELD: *18, Tulsa, OK*
Evergreen Baptist Church, Bixby, OK; Homeschooled

DEATH

"Jesus said to her, 'I am the resurrection and the life. The one who believes in Me, even if he dies, will live.'" —*John 11:25*

Death is always a sad thing to experience, but it is something that we must deal with during our lives. We will have friends, relatives, and acquaintances all pass away from old age, sickness, and accidents. Yet, in these trying times, we must remain focused on the Lord to provide comfort and realize that everything has a purpose to bring glory to God. Oftentimes, it helps to seek out those that have successfully overcome this trial and look to them for guidance. It is much easier to deal with something with the help of another and to lean on an understanding shoulder. However, death also allows for an opportunity to share the message of Christ and how we do not have to fear death on this earth due to His sacrifice. In troubling situations, most people seek answers and are open to any relief. As Christians, we must take advantage of the chance to bring security to their lives with the comforting power of our Lord. No earthly pleasure can match God's ability to put man's mind at ease and heart to rest. Search for those who have recently dealt with death in their lives and share the all-loving character of the Lord, so that they might find peace during the storm.

JONATHAN DISMUKES: *17, Mobile, AL*
Redeemer Fellowship Church and Cottage Hill Christian Academy, Mobile, AL

TRUST IN GOD

"Trust in the LORD with all your heart, and do not rely on your own understanding; think about Him in all your ways, and He will guide you on the right paths." —Proverbs 3:5–6

Do you trust God? It's not always easy, but you need to do it so God can lead you. Proverbs 3:5–6 says to trust in God, and He will lead you in the right path. God's ways are the best ways, and He won't lead you to where you don't need to be. Psalm 56:4 says "In God, whose word I praise, in God I trust; I will not fear. What can man do to me?" This means if you trust in God, you shouldn't fear what man could do to you. If you trust in God, it doesn't matter what people say, think, or do to you. God will take care of you if you trust in Him. Second Kings 18:5 says "Hezekiah trusted in the LORD God of Israel; not one of the kings of Judah was like him, either before him or after him." Hezekiah trusted in God and he was the greatest ruler of his time. God made Hezekiah a great king because he trusted in Him. If you trust in God, you can do great things. Psalm 31:6 says, "I hate those who are devoted to worthless idols, but I trust in the LORD." You shouldn't put your trust into false idols like money and possessions. You should put all your trust in God. Don't worry about anything else, just trust in God and you will be fine. As Psalm 19:7 says, "The instruction of the LORD is perfect, renewing one's life; the testimony of the LORD is trustworthy, making the inexperienced wise."

NOLAN MARTIN: *16, Marshville, NC*
Mount Moriah Baptist Church, Marshville, NC; South Pointe Christian School, Pageland, SC

EVERYBODY MAKES MISTAKES

"But God proves His own love for us in that while we were still sinners, Christ died for us!" —*Romans 5:8*

The Bible tells us that everyone sins and falls short of God's standard. Although we all do sin, God's grace and love is great enough that He forgives us when we confess and repent. But, this does not mean that we can just go around all day and every day sinning as much as we want saying, "It's OK because God will forgive me anyway." It doesn't work that way. We need to know the truth and practice it. There are some vital steps that we must take when asking for forgiveness. The first one is admitting it (confession). Yes, actually admitting that you sinned. I know it's hard to do, but this is the first and most important step. Next, we have to be sincere and really want to be forgiven (repenting). Don't just go through the motions. Once God forgives you, you will not believe the feeling you will get! You feel so clean, like a new person! But take caution and be aware so that you do not fall back into the same sin you just were forgiven for. There is an old saying that applies here: "God hates sin and loves the sinner!"

BRANDON CARROLL: *17, York, SC*
Hillcrest Baptist Church and York Comprehensive High School, York, SC

GOD'S STRENGTH

"The LORD is my strength and my song; He has become my salvation. This is my God, and I will praise Him, my father's God, and I will exalt Him."

—*Exodus 15:2*

We often limit ourselves to what we believe is the peak of our capability to take in—what our stress limit is and things that we just can't take. In tough situations, when we feel as if our strength is not enough, and we feel overwhelmed and overstressed, we can always find renewed strength in God. Because we are only human, it is hard for our physical brains to comprehend God's power. I often find myself trying to think of great things that God can do, but I know that no matter what my brain can comprehend, it is still not even close to what our Creator can actually do. When we simply sit outside and look up to the sky, we can only see so much. But beyond what we can see lies massive amounts more of God's creation, in vastness above us that we cannot even imagine. So, in a situation when you might feel discouraged and out of energy, look to God, because He is available all the time and will aid you in ways seen and even unseen. How awesome is that?

JACOB LAVALLEY: *16, Pageland, SC*
Mount Moriah Baptist Church and South Pointe Christian School, Pageland, SC

LISTEN AND ACCEPT ALL THAT GOD HAS FOR YOU

"Listen to advice and accept instruction,
that you may gain wisdom in the future." —*Proverbs 19:20*

It is hard to listen to counsel and to receive instruction. Today's verse brings our parents to mind: most of us hear them, but most of us don't actually listen. If you have godly parents, you need to understand that they are doing their best to instruct you according to God's will. Our parents are human too, and they make mistakes. Be quick to forgive, because they are doing their best for you. What about other people in your life that impart wisdom to you? If you don't think you have someone like that in your life, do one of two things. Look a little closer, because you could be overlooking that person God already has in your life, or start looking for someone that God may put in your life. Having a mentor is awesome. I have had many different mentors and have learned from each one. It is important to realize that no mentor, even if you think he is the godliest person alive, is perfect. They will mess up, and they might even offend you sometimes. Though mentors are awesome to have, it is Jesus who is the example you need to strive to be like. Don't try to mimic any man, because every man is imperfect. Jesus is the #1 mentor for life, so look to Him before you look to anyone else. Take time and pray that God would put someone in your life who will model wisdom based on His truths and biblical lessons. Also, pray that God would always guide you as you look to Him as your true mentor.

TREY SUEY: *16, Mt. Juliet, TN*
The Fellowship at Two Rivers, Nashville, TN; New Life Academy, Mt. Juliet, TN

REJOICE, PRAY, GIVE THANKS!

"Rejoice always! Pray constantly. Give thanks in everything, for this is God's will for you in Christ Jesus."

—*1 Thessalonians 5:16–18*

To rejoice, to pray, and to give thanks to God now, that is His will for us. Well, it sounds like we need to make those three things the most important in our life. Why shouldn't we rejoice? God has given us another day, He has safely guided us wherever we are going, and He is always protecting us! Rejoice always! Be happy! I can't think of anything to be unhappy about in Christ Jesus! Can you? A very wise man once reminded me that the Bible says, "You do not have because you do not ask" (James 4:2). I am learning to ask God to meet my needs. So, you can ask God for what you need in prayer as you spend time with Him! Seek God in your prayer life, and I can guarantee you that God will give you the desires of your heart, according to His perfect will. It is also important to be thankful, even when things just aren't the way you think they are supposed to be. It's hard when things aren't the way we would like; when something is wrong in life it often freaks us out. But wait, didn't God wake us up this morning? Don't we have a family or some friends to be around? Don't we have the Savior of the world in our hearts if we are saved? Well, those three things are definitely things to be thankful for. Even when things aren't right, we can still trust and thank God. Rejoice always, pray no matter what, and give thanks to the One who gave us eternal life and gives us all things to be thankful for!

KORD OFFENBACKER: *16, Springdale, AR*
Cross Church Springdale Campus and Shiloh Christian School, Springdale, AR

LAZY BONES

"And whatever you do . . . do it all in the name of the Lord Jesus."
—*Colossians 3:17*

Laziness is a sin and all too common. Many have defeated this sin and become hard workers. Laziness can be overcome by working for God rather than man. Paul said, "And whatever you do, whether in word or deed, do it all in the name of the Lord Jesus, giving thanks to God the Father through Him." If we work in our daily lives like we would for a sovereign God, then our laziness will subside. Christians need to study the ant, which, "without leader, administrator, or ruler, it prepares its provisions in summer; it gathers its food during harvest" (Proverbs 6:7–8). The ant hardly ever stops for a break, but works night and day with minimal sleep. Ants usually live for about 45–60 days, and almost that whole time is spent working. The queen ant lays all the eggs and the worker ants forage and defend her and her eggs. Even at night, these tiny creatures move the eggs and larvae deep inside the ant nest to protect them. Once daylight comes, they move the eggs to the top so that the larvae can absorb the sun's heat. You can see why we are instructed to watch these amazing creatures! Humans cannot go without sleep, so God has given us time for both work and sleep. Man struggles with hard work because of sin, which is the root of laziness. If laziness is a problem, ask God to help you to work hard so that He will get all the glory.

LUKE ABENDROTH: *16, Lancaster, MA*
Bethlehem Bible Church and Bethlehem Bible Church Homeschool Co-op, West Boylston, MA

WHEN IT'S COOL TO BE UNCOOL!

"So if anyone purifies himself from anything dishonorable, he will be a special instrument, set apart, useful to the Master, prepared for every good work." —2 Timothy 2:21

I've always wanted to be used by God. A lot of Christian teens talk about being used to serve, and preachers use it as a point of emphasis during sermons. The idea of the God of the universe using me to do His work is amazing. One thing, though, that many people forget to tell us is how hard it is to be set apart for God's calling on our lives. In high school I'm always surrounded with the temptations to live like the world. No one wants to be out-of-the-loop or made fun of. Many times I've gotten the "Jesus freak" name-calling, and sometimes I'll be the one not invited to the big party because people know my views on drinking alcohol and things like that. The only thing I can do is to pray and ask God to be with me. I know if I ask for His comfort He'll be there for me no matter what the situation. It's definitely a struggle to constantly stay pure in a corrupt society. I just hold true to the promises God gives us, that when we discipline ourselves and live for His glory, He will use us to fulfill His will. So my advice for anyone who feels like an outsider is to let God comfort your hurt. Take heart in the truth that God won't leave us nor forsake us, and His Spirit dwells in us always.

PATRICK STANFORD: *18, Albany, GA*
Sherwood Baptist Church and Sherwood Christian Academy, Albany, GA

WORSHIP THE LORD

"Come, let us shout joyfully to the LORD, shout triumphantly to the rock of our salvation! Let us enter His presence with thanksgiving; let us shout triumphantly to Him in song."

—Psalm 95:1–2

I've been privileged to visit several churches and, in a lot of ways, they were very different. Some had one service, some had multiple services; some were very small, and some had thousands of members. I've attended church services in school gyms, warehouses, the YMCA, and traditional church buildings. Some of the churches had choirs and orchestras, some had praise bands, some did hymns, and some used very contemporary praise songs. Though the styles and the buildings were all different, all the churches seemed to desire to worship the Lord. The psalm above says that worship should be exciting. The writer talks about shouting and being triumphant and says that we should be thankful. We have a great God who has done so many great things for us, and we should remember how blessed we are. Psalm 95:6 says "Come, let us worship and bow down; let us kneel before the LORD our Maker." Worship should also humble us. We should recognize how awesome and mighty our God is. Worship is a personal as well as a corporate experience. Psalm 95:7 says, "For He is our God, and we are the people of His pasture, the sheep under His care." God is our shepherd and we are sheep under His care, so we should rejoice and be grateful in worship. Whether we meet in a school building or a church with a steeple, the goal is to exalt our great God. We should also remember that worship doesn't happen just on Sunday, but we should worship Him daily.

MICAH PERSTROPE: *13, St. Peters, MO*
First Baptist Church of St. Charles, St. Charles, MO; Dubray Middle School, St. Peters, MO

DESIRES

"Take delight in the LORD, and He will give you your heart's desires."
—Psalm 37:4

Psalm 37:4 is well-known, but the meaning is often mistaken. The first part of the verse pretty much explains itself. It tells us to delight in the Lord by not being afraid to show the love we have for Him. Showing our love for God becomes natural with our parents, friends, fellow students, team members, coworkers, etc. To delight in the Lord, we must find our joy in Him and in His Word. Limited joy can be found in such things as sports, X-box, or dating. There is nothing wrong with these activities, but our real joy should come from getting to show Christ. A good friend of mine gave a perfect example of showing God through sports. A soccer team we played once was being really rough and used vulgar language. During the game, my friend was knocked down by one of their players and, as he fell, the player insulted him with foul language. Instead of doing what most of us would, firing back with the same type of insult, he simply got up and looked at the offender and said, "Jesus loves you." This is a perfect example of how to show God in our daily activities. This verse also tells us that God will give us the desires of our hearts. Most people think that if there is someone you want to date and you delight in the Lord, then God will give you the opportunity to date that person. However, once you begin to delight in the Lord, you begin to think more like God, and then your desires become what God wants for you. Those are the desires God will grant you.

DUSTIN BRECHT: *17, Lancaster, SC*
Spring Hill Baptist Church, Lancaster, SC; South Pointe Christian School, Pageland, SC

PURSUE

"But you, man of God, run from these things, and pursue righteousness, godliness, faith, love, endurance, and gentleness."

—*1 Timothy 6:11*

My favorite teacher was also the hardest teacher I have ever had. He was determined to push us to our limits. He assigned a lot of homework every day and every weekend. We typically read a novel every week. Every day he assigned thirty minutes of a math program. He was a tough teacher. When we were off school for a week with bad weather, he called us and gave us homework, because he was so passionate about learning. Not only was he a passionate teacher, but he was a great Christian man. He truly pursued godliness and exemplified love to his students at my public school. I also went to church with him and his focus on Jesus was evident. He lived the example of 1 Timothy 6:11. All of us can be distracted from following God's will. The devil throws many temptations in our lives. This verse tells us that there are things we need to run from, like false doctrine, evil actions, and the love of money (see 1 Timothy 6:3–10). The world often tells us that money and materialism are the things that matter in life: where you live, what you drive, what you wear, and where you vacation are the priorities the world concentrates on. As believers, we should run from the world's priorities and focus on God's priorities. Whether we attend public school, private school, or are homeschooled, we must pursue God's teaching in His Word and seek to live it. Just as my teacher was passionate about teaching his students, we need to be passionate about learning God's truth and living it. My teacher was a great example to me, and God wants us to be a great example to others.

MICAH PERSTROPE: *13, St. Peters, MO*
First Baptist Church of St. Charles, St. Charles, MO; Dubray Middle School, St. Peters, MO

TEMPTATIONS

"Finally brothers, whatever is true, whatever is honorable, whatever is just, whatever is pure, whatever is lovely, whatever is commendable—if there is any moral excellence and if there is any praise—dwell on these things." —*Philippians 4:8*

Temptation can be a hard thing to overcome, and everyone on the earth is tempted at many times in their lives. Even Jesus Himself was tempted in the Garden of Gethsemane. One good way to fight against temptation is to think about Philippians 4:8. This verse gives us six categories of things to think about: things true, honorable, just, pure, lovely, and commendable. If anything does not fall under one of these six categories, it may be something that is evil. But if anything that is part of one of these categories is right, it cannot be an evil thing. Let's use cheating as an example. Cheating cannot be considered as any one of these six things, so you know it is bad and you should not think about it. If you only think about the things listed in this verse, you can escape the clutches of temptation. Next this verse says that if there is anything that is considered morally excellent, or anything that is worthy of praise, then do these things. Next time you are tempted, think about Philippians 4:8 and the six categories it tells us to think about.

DUSTIN BRECHT: *17, Lancaster, SC*
Spring Hill Baptist Church, Lancaster, SC; South Pointe Christian School, Pageland, SC

TRIALS

"Consider it a great joy, my brothers, whenever you experience various trials, knowing that the testing of your faith produces endurance. But endurance must do its complete work, so that you may be mature and complete, lacking nothing." —*James 1:2–4*

Recently I started working out in preparation for the upcoming baseball season. We had long- and short-distance running, bench pressing, regular press, squats, pull-ups, etc. Many nights I would go home worn out and wake up sore the next morning. However, my cardiovascular endurance increased, as well as my muscular strength and endurance. Though painful, it was ultimately beneficial. James tells us that we should rejoice when we face trials, because our trials produce spiritual endurance. Our spiritual muscles grow as we face trials. In the gym and in life, we can try to avoid trials that cause pain and discomfort, but we won't grow in endurance. James says, "Endurance must do its complete work." Giving up before your reps are finished short-changes you, so remain faithful to finish all of your exercises to achieve the goal of strength and endurance. Spiritual trials can cause you to give up on God or get angry with God. Trials of different types make you feel alone and overwhelmed, but God wants to use the trials you are facing to make you spiritually strong and to shape you to look more like Jesus. If you need God's wisdom as you go through the trials, James says to call on God (James 1:5). This verse tells us that God will give us the wisdom we need, and He will not criticize us for asking for His help. We will grow spiritually wiser and stronger as we call on Him.

JOEL PERSTROPE: *15, St. Peters, MO*
First Baptist Church of St. Charles, St. Charles, MO; Fort Zumwalt East High School, St. Peters, MO

HONOR

"Honor your father and your mother so that you may have a long life in the land that the LORD is giving you." —*Exodus 20:12*

Kids these days don't want to obey their parents like the last generations did. Children don't listen, so they keep making the same mistakes, and some parents don't discipline them as they should. The Bible clearly states that children who do not obey their parents will not have a long life and may not prosper. In biblical times, children obeyed their parents. For some in history and even in some locations of the world today, children are killed for acts of disobedience! The Lord commands that all children honor their fathers and mothers. Quoting Moses Mark 7:10 says, "Honor your father and mother and whosoever speaks evil of father or mother must be put to death." We're pretty blessed to be living in these times where we don't have to worry about being killed for not obeying our parents. Let's honor our parents, which is the first commandment with a promise. Always tell the truth and never lie. Listen to your parents. We are known by our behavior. So respecting our parents is a great way to let others know that we love our parents and God. Remember that what others see is the impression they get about who we are on the inside. Behaving well influences how they think about our earthly parents and our heavenly Father!

AUSTIN HARGETT: *15, Marshville, NC*
Bethel Baptist Church, Marshville, NC; South Pointe Christian School, Pageland, SC

ASKING FOR FORGIVENESS

"John came baptizing in the wilderness and preaching a baptism of repentance for the forgiveness of sins." —Mark 1:4

When we hurt people we love with our poor choices or bad behavior, we need to humble ourselves and go to them with repentant hearts. You ask to be friends again or for the chance to regain their trust; hopefully that will reflect the mercy God has shown us. Forgiveness is a big deal. Sometimes people just won't forgive, instead holding things against people who have done something wrong to them. No matter what the circumstance, you should always forgive someone when they wrong you, no matter how bad it hurts. To be able to forgive someone, we need to always remember how Jesus forgave our sins. When the Holy Spirit convicted your heart, you came to realize that He loved you and forgave you, and He continues to forgive you when you ask Him to. Forgiveness is most important. When we forgive it clears the air of past sins and helps us to begin to rebuild wounded relationships. Try forgiving, and be willing to ask for forgiveness. It is what God wants us to do. It blesses Him.

AUSTIN HARGETT: *15, Marshville, NC*
Bethel Baptist Church, Marshville, NC; South Pointe Christian School, Pageland, SC

IMPORTANCE OF OUR WORDS

"No foul language is to come from your mouth, but only what is good for building up someone in need, so that it gives grace to those who hear."

—*Ephesians 4:29*

An innocent little girl who was made fun of at school and alienated became so sad and lonely that she saw no other option than to take her life. There are many stories of bullying like this one that take place daily. One bully was recently shot in school because of the intense hatred he evoked in another student. Yes, bullying can manifest itself in wrong and deadly actions. Words can be devastatingly painful. We know in our hearts that we would rather be attacked with "sticks and stones" than internally decimated by what others say to us. Sadly, I hear Christians in conversation with each other, and with nonbelievers, that I'm sure makes the Lord Jesus cringe. Jesus came to bind up the brokenhearted and set the captives free, and He is obviously the opponent of negative communication. Ephesians says that our words are to build others up. Wow! That messes me up, because I see a culture where sarcasm is prevalent and may be used jokingly, not meant to be taken seriously. The Bible says that if it isn't lifting up the Lord Jesus, or lifting up others, I need to reevaluate my speech. Christians are to love our brothers and sisters in Christ, and be good representatives of Christ for those who are on the outside. I see attitudes, words, and actions in Christians that would utterly repel me if I was looking in from the outside. Not to be legalistic or to criticize because I, too, struggle, but we need to demonstrate Jesus' love in our words, laying aside our standard conversation to build up others in Christ.

LUKE MERRICK: *15, Springdale, AR*
Immanuel Baptist Church and Shiloh Christian School, Springdale, AR

HIGH SCHOOL WITNESSING (PART 1)

"Go, therefore, and make disciples of all nations, baptizing them in the name of the Father and of the Son and of the Holy Spirit, teaching them to observe everything I have commanded you. And remember, I am with you always, to the end of the age." —*Matthew 28:19–20*

Religion can be hard to bring up in a conversation at school, especially when you are continually surrounded by different people throughout the day who continually put down God and anything related to Him. The sad thing is that we sometimes consider these people our best friends. I used to be friends with a person who told me God was angry at him, and that God wouldn't have anything to do with him even if he prayed and asked Him for His help. I found myself just being quiet during times like these. I was scared that my friend would become angry with me if I pushed the subject any further. God told me to have the courage to tell my friend about His love and that He was always there with me, even if I felt like I was the only person there to spread the message. I later went up to my friend and explained how God loved him and that God is a forgiving God, no matter what sin had been committed. I had a strong feeling come over me, as if I had just gotten rid of a weight that had been pushing me down. I felt like God was telling me, "Well done, My good and faithful servant." Telling others about Christ is not just something foreign missionaries are supposed to do. We are called to be messengers for God every day, everywhere; and that means in our own home, in our school, and even in the church. Are you telling the good news?

BILLY RAMSEY: *17, Sharon, SC*
Faith Baptist Church, Clover, SC; York Comprehensive High School, York, SC

HIGH SCHOOL WITNESSING (PART 2)

"Go, therefore, and make disciples of all nations, baptizing them in the name of the Father and of the Son and of the Holy Spirit, teaching them to observe everything I have commanded you. And remember, I am with you always, to the end of the age." —*Matthew 28:19–20*

Once I was willing to tell someone else about what God can do for them as a witness from my own experience, I knew that I had just conquered one of my biggest fears and that Jesus was with me every step of the way. God will always be with you in anything that uplifts His kingdom. Many lost people will try to counter a Christian witness by saying that God is a loving God who would never send somebody to hell. It was never intended by God to send anyone to hell, but He can't let sin enter into heaven, so the lost are cast into hell (see Romans 6:23). God gave each of us a chance to have a second chance, so that we might escape hell. He loved us so much that He allowed His only Son to die for a corrupt people. The born-again children of God know how much God loves each of us, and we are to show that love to others. Our nerves may flare when we witness to a lost person in our school, but we must always remember that Jesus Christ is our strength and that He will never forsake us or leave us on our own (see Philippians 4:13). Being a witness is something we are all called to do, as Matthew 28:19–20 reminds us. We can go without going and still do the will of God right here at home!

BILLY RAMSEY: *17, Sharon, SC*
Faith Baptist Church, Clover, SC; York Comprehensive High School, York, SC

MORE THAN JUST A BOOK

"Take the underwear that you bought and are wearing,
and go at once to the Euphrates River and hide it in a rocky crevice."

—*Jeremiah 13:4*

One problem with trying to get friends to go to church is that the only thing they know of church is sitting and listening to a preacher talk. One thing I have learned through my walk with God is that being a Christian goes way beyond Sunday school. Two years ago, I challenged myself to read the Bible from Genesis to Revelation, and I came upon today's passage in Jeremiah 13:1–11. As I read it, I could not keep myself from laughing out loud because of the decision God made to use underwear in telling the story. These verses helped me realize that the Bible is more than a book of rules. The Bible has rules in it that are extremely important, but it also tells a story. When God created the Bible, His goal was not to force us to endure through these passages and hate every minute of it. He wanted to give us a resource that could excite us and tell us His plan for our lives through the events and people of the past. This book has the death of great warriors, outrageously funny stories, and extraordinary adventures that all lead to the exciting life of Jesus Christ. We have this resource and can learn from all of these stories. We live in an age where we can simply get online and search for the passages that might interest us, or we can simply pick the Bible up and start from the beginning. My prayer is that you will be inspired and not only want to read the Bible, but also to share all you are learning with those who never thought of the Bible as a source of entertainment and inspiration.

CHRIS NATION: *15, Gallatin, TN*
The Fellowship at Two Rivers, Nashville, TN; Station Camp High School, Gallatin, TN

IT'S NOT ABOUT ME

"Therefore, whether you eat or drink, or whatever you do, do everything for God's glory." —*1 Corinthians 10:31*

Have you ever stopped to think about why you are doing something or whether it is right to have all the credit for your successes? I have struggled with a major pride issue for a long time. I am often tempted to think that when I do something, it is for me and I deserve the credit for the things that I do. As a teen that is moving toward a point of independence in decision-making, it is important that I understand why I do what I do. First Corinthians 10:31 has really helped me to understand this. This verse tells me that whatever I do, it should be for God's glory, not mine. Knowing this, I should be making decisions that will lead to God being glorified. In order for this to happen, God must be recognized. If we allow people to think that our success or blessings have come from our work only, then God is left out. Instead, when someone compliments us, we should say, "Thank you, God has been good." Glorifying God requires a conscious decision that His glory is worth more than the stoking of personal pride. We must decide whose glory is worth more to us. Once we establish whose honor and glory we value more, then we will begin to make better decisions. We must decide what the end goal is in order to make wise decisions for the journey God has mapped out for us. Once we understand that the goal in life should be to glorify God with our actions, and that God deserves the glory, then we will be well on our way to making wise decisions.

JOSIAH MCGEE: *15, Kansas City, MO*
Summit Woods Baptist Church, Lees Summit, MO; Homeschooled

MAY

My son, don't forget my teaching, but let your heart keep my commands;

for they will bring you many days, a full life, and well-being.

Never let loyalty and faithfulness leave you.

Tie them around your neck; write them on the tablet of your heart.

Then you will find favor and high regard in the sight of God and man.

Trust in the Lord with all your heart, and do not rely on your own understanding;

think about Him in all your ways, and He will guide you on the right paths.

Don't consider yourself to be wise;

fear the Lord and turn away from evil.

This will be healing for your body and strengthening for your bones.

Honor the Lord with your possessions

and with the first produce of your entire harvest; then your barns will be completely filled, and your vats will overflow with new wine.

Do not despise the Lord's instruction, my son,

and do not loathe His discipline; for the Lord disciplines the one He loves, just as a father, the son he delights in.

(Proverbs 3:1–12)

TEMPTATION

"Stay awake and pray, so that you won't enter into temptation. The spirit is willing, but the flesh is weak." —*Matthew 26:41*

Drugs, sex, and alcohol are just a few of the things that Satan uses to tempt us, especially teens. It doesn't matter what it is because the devil knows what appeals to each of us. He will find your weakness and attack you with the thing you're the most vulnerable to. It's easy to give in. Almost every teenager in the school system knows this. The world is full of battle zones. One of those battle zones is inside you, and a battle is raging all the time. My advice is to find a spiritual friend you can lean on and be completely honest with, so that when you're bombarded with temptation you can turn to that friend. Also, never forget that your parents understand and that there is no one who loves you more than your dad and mom. Pray, love God, and dig into the Word of God. God wants you to be as pure as possible, and it hurts when we fail. He said to be holy as He is holy. I'm sure that He is in heaven smiling when we beat temptation, because it brings us one step closer to holiness. So, love life; build strong, healthy relationships; and be there for your brothers and sisters. Proverbs 27:17 says, "Iron sharpens iron, and one man sharpens another." Use this verse and build your brothers and sisters up in Christ so that together we can resist temptation.

DAVID WOODY: *16, Greencastle, PA*
Greencastle Baptist Church and Greencastle-Antrim High School, Greencastle, PA

HAVING FAITH IN PRAYER (PART 1)

"Jesus answered them, "I assure you: If you have faith and do not doubt, you will not only do what was done to the fig tree, but even if you tell this mountain, "Be lifted up and thrown into the sea," it will be done. And if you believe, you will receive whatever you ask for in prayer.""

—Matthew 21:21–22

The verse for today gives the account of the fig tree. After having left Jerusalem and spending a night in Bethany, Jesus is coming back to the city, and He's hungry. Seeing a fig tree off to the side of the road, He goes up to it, but as He gets closer He finds it to be fruitless. He spoke to the tree and told it to never bear fruit again. Matthew records that the fig tree immediately withered and died. Jesus' disciples, who were watching the whole event, are dumbstruck! Jaws drop and they ask Him how He did that. Verses 21–22 record Jesus' powerful answer, which is summed up in two words: by faith! Simple? Maybe not! It seems a lot of teens have trouble believing in the power of prayer. I remember feeling as if my prayers were hitting the ceiling, that God was nowhere to be found, and that He did not ever hear me. I was discouraged that God apparently did not hear my prayers and was not answering. I found that I didn't have the faith to keep praying regularly and, of course, because I didn't pray, nothing I had been praying for ever happened in my life! Please don't get caught in that cycle. God does hear the prayers of His children, but His answers do not always come on our timetable. He never gives up on us, so we need to continue to pray and trust Him to answer us in His time and with what He thinks is best for us. After all, He is all-knowing!

CONNOR HOWINGTON: *17, West Monroe, LA*
First Baptist West Monroe and Northeast Baptist School, West Monroe, LA

HAVING FAITH IN PRAYER (PART 2)

"Jesus answered them, "I assure you: If you have faith and do not doubt, you will not only do what was done to the fig tree, but even if you tell this mountain, "Be lifted up and thrown into the sea," it will be done. And if you believe, you will receive whatever you ask for in prayer.""

—*Matthew 21:21–22*

The story of the fig tree is one that teens need to consider. We are still growing in our faith, and sometimes we allow other things like our busy schedules to interfere with the time we need to spend with God in prayer. We want to pray and get a quick answer, and when it does not come we tend to move on. Sometimes we just make things happen, even if it is not the answer God would have given us. I remember learning Jeremiah 33:3, which says, "Call to Me and I will answer you and tell you great and incomprehensible things you do not know." During a very lonely time I had to ask myself if I really believed that God would really answer my prayers. It became a matter of faith and trust. Did I have the faith to believe that God would answer and was my trust in Him strong enough to thank Him for whatever His answer would be? I thank God that at that moment He gave me the faith to believe that He does answer my prayers, with the best answer for me as His child. This was a tremendous step in my Christian life. So it's time to decide: Do you really believe that God will answer your prayers?

CONNOR HOWINGTON: *17, West Monroe, LA*
First Baptist West Monroe and Northeast Baptist School, West Monroe, LA

GRACE

"But God, who is rich in mercy, because of His great love that He had for us, made us alive with the Messiah even though we were dead in trespasses. You are saved by grace!" —*Ephesians 2:4–5*

Grace is what you give someone out of the goodness of your heart. It is not expected that they pay it back, but to show kindness in return. God showed how much grace He had when He sent His Son to die on the cross for our sins. He knew that we could not save ourselves, and He certainly knew we could never repay Him for what He gave us. We should show how much we appreciate that gift by telling others about God's awesome grace. We can also show God how grateful we are for what He did for us by having joy and thanksgiving in our hearts as we live our lives for Him. He shows us grace through forgiveness, even though we don't deserve it. He forgives us by grace for the sins we commit each day. It is important that teens show that grace to our peers, as we live in front of them the way God tells us to in the Bible. Can you do that today? Tomorrow? For the rest of your life?

DREW G. JENKINS: *13, Pageland, SC*
Grace Baptist Church and South Pointe Christian School, Pageland, SC

TRUSTING IN THE LORD

"Trust in the Lord with all your heart, and do not rely on your own understanding; think about Him in all your ways, and He will guide you on the right paths." —*Proverbs 3:5–6*

Oftentimes, we feel that life's burden is too heavy for us to carry all alone. We might attempt to walk a few steps by ourselves, only to crash face-first into the ground. Multiple trials such as this only lead to depression—the thought that we are too insignificant to perform successfully. Ultimately, this is true. We cannot live up to the call God has placed on our lives. So why does He give us a task impossible to complete, you ask? And, of course, the answer is so that we have to look to Him for help and guidance. He wishes for His children to trust solely in His power and love, so that we might grow to know Him better. If we do not spend time reading the Word for wisdom and praying to God for direction, we cannot advance in our relationships with our Creator. However, if we do seek Him for understanding, then He will be faithful to guide us in the right path. Jeremiah 29:11 says, "For I know the plans I have for you . . . plans for your welfare, not for disaster, to give you a future and a hope." We can trust the Lord to protect and lead us correctly. So, next time you are faced with a difficult situation, first call upon Christ for wisdom on how to continue.

JONATHAN DISMUKES: *17, Mobile, AL*
Redeemer Fellowship Church and Cottage Hill Christian Academy, Mobile, AL

LIFT OTHERS UP

"Whoever conceals an offense promotes love,
but whoever gossips about it separates friends." —*Proverbs 17:9*

Do you know someone who is a blabbermouth? Someone who is like a dog that spreads everybody's trash? Well, now that you have someone in mind, stop! Look at yourself. You do the same thing and, to be honest, at some point in our lives we all gossip and talk bad about others. So, why is it so intriguing to talk about everybody else's problems? Does it make us feel better about ourselves? Does it help that person change? No! The Bible says to lift one another up and to not tear down. We strip each other of confidence until we have none left ourselves. Gossip not only destroys relationships, it also destroys lives. It is easy to buy into Satan's lies that people aren't worthy or that they will always be this way. The truth is that God loves everyone equally, no matter what they have done. The rapist or murderer has the same chance to get into heaven as you do. All they have to do is confess and repent of their sins and trust Christ as their personal Savior. We all need to realize that it is not our place to talk about the sins that people have committed, because the fact is that we all sin on a regular basis. We just need to work on our own problems and not everyone else's. Take some time today to pray that God would fill your heart with love and compassion for people, instead of feeling the need to talk about their issues. Pray that He would bring you to pray for the people who are the topics of the gossip chains.

TREY SUEY: *16, Mt. Juliet, TN*
The Fellowship at Two Rivers, Nashville, TN; New Life Academy, Mt. Juliet, TN

WHY WE SHOULD OBEY GOD

"As for the eye that ridicules a father and despises obedience to a mother, may ravens of the valley pluck it out and young vultures eat it."

—Proverbs 30:17

Obedience is a very important part of life. Any good leader was once a follower and had to obey their authority. We should always obey authority, even in the menial tasks. Cleaning our rooms, cutting the grass, and taking out the trash may not be anyone's idea of a fun Saturday, but our parents give us these chores for a reason. We should be thankful for our parents because they only want the best for us, even though it may not always seem like it. We must also remember that our parents are human and they make mistakes every day, like we do. Obeying school teachers, parents, and preachers also teaches us about a good submissive relationship with God. God has a plan for all Christians, and many miss out on the wonderful blessings God has in store for them because they choose to disobey Him. A poem by Martha Snell Nicholson entitled "His Plan for Me" is a good example of disobeying God and regretting it when we miss out on God's many rewards in heaven. When we say no over and over to God, we miss out on all His blessings making life harder on ourselves. Ephesians 6:1–3 says, "Children, obey your parents as you would the Lord, because this is right. Honor your father and mother, which is the first commandment with a promise, so that it may go well with you and that you may have a long life in the land."

ZACH M. BYRD: *15, Jefferson, SC*
Bethlehem Baptist Church, Buford, SC; South Point Christian School, Pageland, SC

RESISTING TEMPTATION

"Stay awake and pray, so that you won't enter into temptation. The spirit is willing, but the flesh is weak." —*Matthew 26:41*

Temptation is Satan's way of getting someone to disobey God's commandments and laws. He memorizes our habits and actions, and from them he tempts us to do what God does not want us to do. In the Bible it states, "Stay awake and pray, so that you won't enter into temptation. The spirit is willing, but the flesh is weak." When we are tempted, we have to always ask ourselves what God would do in that particular situation. We have to meditate and pray on the problem first so that the advantage will be ours. God will always do His part in taking care of His children, so we have to trust Him. He always has and always will lead the way for us. It will always help to pray about the situation, even if it is something small.

RAJ PATEL: *15, Jefferson, SC*
South Pointe Fellowship and South Pointe Christian School, Pageland, SC

MEANINGLESS!

**"'Absolute futility,' says the Teacher. 'Absolute futility.
Everything is futile.'"** —*Ecclesiastes 1:2*

If you read the book of Ecclesiastes, you will find the word *futile* multiple times. However, the teacher does not stop there. If he was to, he certainly would leave the odd impression that we exist for absolutely no reason. But I believe that he wanted us to see that everything we know and do is actually futile—apart from God that is. Later he clarifies this and states that this is the reason that all is futile. There is an amazing truth to this. You see, the average life of a human is eighty or so years. Yet eternity is unfathomably longer! What do we live for then? Well, since everything we put away on the earth will perish or decay with the world, everything truly is pointless. Matthew 6:19–21 says, "Don't collect for yourselves treasures on earth, where moth and rust destroy and where thieves break in and steal. But collect for yourselves treasures in heaven, where neither moth nor rust destroys, and where thieves do not break in and steal. For where your treasure is, there your heart will be also." We need to do more for the kingdom of God, and less for ourselves. The more we do for ourselves, the more we will lose. But the more we do for the kingdom of God, the more we will gain. So next time you are posed with the question, "Is it beneficial," simply ask yourself, "Will it be accomplishing anything for the kingdom of God?" If the answer is no, then you need to rethink how you are investing your time here on the earth. Is there eternal value in what you are doing?

JESSE D. SANDO: *13, Pleasant Hill, OH*
First Baptist Church, Vandalia, OH; Homeschooled

TRUST GOD FOR ENDURANCE TO DO THE JOB

"But those who trust in the LORD will renew their strength; they will soar on wings like eagles; they will run and not grow weary; they will walk and not faint." —*Isaiah 40:31*

While in St. Vincent on a mission trip, my family helped to renovate a church that was in disrepair. The stage was rotten, and the paint on the whole outside of the building was chipping and looked terrible. There were also some doors that needed to be replaced. We thought the repairs would take a couple of months or up to a year. We diligently started working in the morning from around 8:00 until the sun went down. At the end of every day, we were very tired and it only took about thirty seconds for us to fall asleep. The first couple of days we chipped what paint we could from the sides of the building. My dad and my brother were working on the stage and the doors inside. We primed the surfaces and then we painted. After about a week of hard work and much sweating in the sun, which was incredibly hot, we finished painting the three sides of the church that were visible from the street, repaired and carpeted the stage, put up curtains to block the sun, and replaced the doors. The church looked magnificent! By God's grace we finished jobs we thought might take a year. The pastor e-mailed us and told us that people had noticed the church because it was painted and looked terrific. The Lord can do great things through us if we are willing to go and do what we can. He gives strength and grace to do things our bodies couldn't do without Him. We need to trust God with our plans, and He will bring about His will in our lives.

ELI JONES: *15, Tulsa, OK*
Evergreen Baptist Church, Bixby, OK; Mingo Valley Christian School, Tulsa, OK

AVENGING

"Don't say, 'I will avenge this evil!' Wait on the Lord, and He will rescue you." —*Proverbs 20:22*

It is very easy because of our human nature to try and get back at those who are unkind or cruel to us, but the verse for today tells us that revenge isn't biblical. Now that we're Christians, God will protect us and punish those who persecute us. Persecution for our faith honors God and we, though it's very hard, should rejoice like Paul the apostle at persecution. Here's Romans 12:17: "Do not repay anyone evil for evil. Try to do what is honorable in everyone's eyes." When we remain calm and are not angry when we have been wronged, the accuser will wonder how we come by this great peace, and we will be a wonderful witness and light for God. So we know now that we shouldn't avenge offenses, but listen to this: "Don't resist an evildoer. On the contrary, if anyone slaps you on your right cheek, turn the other to him also. As for the one who wants to . . . take away your shirt, let him have your coat as well. And if anyone forces you to go one mile, go with him two" (Matthew 5:39–41). Wow, that's hard. Not only does God not want us to take abuse, but we should also not protest at all and allow him to be rude or unkind to us. Why would God want us to do that? Well, I think He wants us to forgive people. Remember that God forgave us for everything we've done wrong. Instead of hating people who aren't Christians and who do wrong things, we should love them, pray for them, and witness to them, all in hope of their salvation. We too, once, didn't know the Lord.

MATTHEW COOKSEY: *13, McMinnville, OR*
Valley Baptist Church, McMinnville, OR; Homeschooled

PORNOGRAPHY (PART 1)

"But each person is tempted when he is drawn away and enticed by his own evil desires. Then after desire has conceived, it gives birth to sin, and when sin is fully grown, it gives birth to death." —James 1:14–15

Far more often than not, Christians flip the metaphorical page once the topic of pornography is presented. They either think it's a dangerous topic or they're affected by it directly. Either way, they must deal with it. Pornography is a dangerous topic, but sometimes people don't give it enough attention, especially in times when they need to reach out and help that one who has been caught in the downward spiral of pornography. Pornography doesn't always have to be online or in provocative videos; pornography is anything that causes lust in a person's heart. This can be a picture, a song, or a book. Pornography in today's world glorifies vulgar sexual acts, marginalizes women, and taints the God-given gift and beauty of sex. Pornography is tearing apart families and changing our standard of purity. God's Word has much to say about what we look at and about lust. Looking at porn causes all of us to lust. God wants us to have pure hearts and intentions. Porn instilled in our minds and hearts is an abomination to God. We need to turn away and seek the Lord, by knowing God and His Word, by praying, by being open with our parents, and by surrounding ourselves with Christian friends for accountability.

PAUL RICHARDSON: *17, Huntsville, AL*
Whitesburg Baptist Church and Whitesburg Christian Academy, Huntsville, AL

PORNOGRAPHY (PART 2)

"But each person is tempted when he is drawn away and enticed by his own evil desires. Then after desire has conceived, it gives birth to sin, and when sin is fully grown, it gives birth to death." —*James 1:14–15*

The ultimate key to defeating pornography is the Word of God. Yes, we have to physically remove ourselves from the temptation, but ultimately human power will fail. Psalm 119:9 says, "How can a young man keep his way pure? By keeping Your word." We have to make Jesus an intimate part of our lives, and we must do that daily. Romans 8:5 says, "For those who live according to the flesh think about the things of the flesh, but those who live according to the Spirit, about the things of the Spirit." If you are subject to the trap of pornography, you have to realize you are not alone. Though it is important to find accountability, whether it's your dad, youth pastor, close friend, or whomever; just someone who can check on you and encourage you. There are also many books on living with a godly sexuality, like *Every Man's Battle* by Stephen Arterburn and Fred Stoeker. But most importantly, rely on God. And we need to remind ourselves to get our eyes off computer screens and television and, as it says in Romans 12, "Look to God."

PAUL RICHARDSON: *17, Huntsville, AL*
Whitesburg Baptist Church and Whitesburg Christian Academy, Huntsville, AL

PORNOGRAPHY (PART 3)

"But each person is tempted when he is drawn away and enticed by his own evil desires. Then after desire has conceived, it gives birth to sin, and when sin is fully grown, it gives birth to death." —James 1:14–15

"Let no one despise your youth; instead you should be an example to the believers in speech, in conduct, in love, in faith, in purity" (1 Timothy 4:12). Living a life of purity is the essential key to defeating the desire for pornography. When dealing with sin, we cannot rationalize. We have to completely defeat the desire for it, and we do this by removing the situations from our lives that cause temptation. If you're tempted by something on Twitter or Facebook, you may need to unfollow or unfriend someone, or even delete your accounts completely if they are causing you to be tempted. When tempted, flee the situation no matter what it is.

A few facts on pornography show its prevalence in today's world:

- The photograph was invented in 1839, and by 1850 the word *pornographer* appeared in the dictionary.
- Every second in the United States, 28,258 people view pornography online. Of the 28,000 people, 72 percent are men and 28 percent are women.
- Every 39 minutes, a new porn video is created in the United States.
- According to a 2009 survey by Pastors.com, 54 percent of pastors surveyed watched porn the week before.
- People from the ages of 35 to 49 years old view the most amount of pornography.

God has given us His Son and the resource we need is His Word to combat the evils of pornography, so let's get busy and use them for His glory and our good!

PAUL RICHARDSON: *17, Huntsville, AL*
Whitesburg Baptist Church and Whitesburg Christian Academy, Huntsville, AL

DON'T LOOK BACK

"He comforts us in all our affliction, so that we may be able
to comfort those who are in any kind of affliction, through
the comfort we ourselves receive from God." —2 Corinthians 1:4

Excuses about how sinful we are and how unworthy or incapable we are can keep us from the life that God wants us to live. With both of my parents involved in the student ministry at the church we attend, I hear these kinds of stories all the time. I've even heard them from other adults. They say things like, "Why would God want to use me?" or "How am I supposed to serve and represent Jesus with the past that I have?" Students sometimes feel guilty about the things they have done and feel as if they are too bad to be a servant of God. The truth about these situations is that they are just bad excuses. Do you think that Jesus' disciples were perfect or even came close? No, they weren't, but they were willing to get past that and let God use their lives to be examples to others. The fact of the matter is, God wants to use us right where we are. No matter how messed up we are, or were in the past, God wants to take our whole being and minister to others through us. Our past, and the good and bad we've been through, matters to God. As the verse says, He wants us to use our afflictions to comfort others. I encourage you to join a small group at your local church where you can give and receive comfort for the struggles you are facing, which will help you get through them and be used by God to bless others.

JESSE NIEMAN: 18, Ocala, FL
Church @ The Springs and Forest High School, Ocala, FL

GOD'S LOVE, OUR LOVE

"For God loved the world in this way: He gave His One and Only Son, so that everyone who believes in Him will not perish but have eternal life."
—John 3:16

"Dear friends, let us love one another, because love is from God, and everyone who loves has been born of God and knows God. The one who does not love does not know God, because God is love" (1 John 4:7–8). Love is when you show how much you care for or about someone. It is not just showing emotion—you know that touchy-feely stuff—and it is not something you just show on Valentine's Day. God sent His only Son, Jesus, into the world just to save the sinful race of humans on the earth. He showed us how much He cared for us and how much love He had for us by giving His most precious gift to stand in the place of our sins. God's love isn't based on how you act, how you think, or what your outward appearance is. In 1 John 4:8, it says the person that does not have love in his heart doesn't have God in his heart either, because God is love. Today would be a great time to get to know the love of God. Read 1 John and ask God to show you His love. He will do that for you!

DREW G. JENKINS: *13, Pageland, SC*
Grace Baptist Church and South Pointe Christian School, Pageland, SC

A PROUD HEART

"Everyone with a proud heart is detestable to the Lord; be assured, he will not go unpunished." —*Proverbs 16:5*

Pride is the feeling we experience when we think we are better than others or that we have accomplished more than others. Pride also tends to cause an elevated sense of respect for oneself. Pride causes all of us to become arrogant, but pride is not acceptable to God. A prideful person will want to think more of himself than of others, and it will cause him to become haughty and unattractive. Today's verse is saying that a proud (prideful) spirit will always be punished. Christians are to be humble, and when we do fall short and become proud, then we have to ask God for His help. He always has, always is, and always will be there for us no matter the circumstances. We have choices to make in every situation, but we have to be sure that God is the one leading us through those choices, and that has to be the case every time. This will always make a prideful person become humble. As Proverbs 29:23 states, "A person's pride will humble him, but a humble spirit will gain honor."

RAJ PATEL: *15, Jefferson, SC*
South Pointe Fellowship and South Pointe Christian School, Pageland, SC

139

BROTHERLY LOVE

"Show family affection to one another with brotherly love."

—*Romans 12:10*

When we started attending a new church, I was invited to go with my brothers to Monday Night Guys, which is a small group Bible study that meets at different homes of guys in the church. At first, I was pretty nervous because I was the only middle school student who came on a regular basis. I was in a Bible study where everyone was bigger than I was, older than I was, and most knew more about God's Word. But once I met the high school students, I found my fears were unfounded. Though I was younger than these guys, they were some of the most loving people I had ever met. I was encouraged, cared about, and loved in this small group of guys and most are now role models to me in my Christian walk. I have really grown in this group, and they continue to challenge me to learn more about God's Word. I want to go to church more often because I feel like I am important to this group of guys. It was cool how they took me in and treated me like I was their brother. They have even let me teach a couple of times. I would say this to the high school guys in your church and especially in youth group: There are middle school students who need you to make friends with them. Work hard to be a good example to them, and show them some brotherly love just like Romans 12:10 teaches. Also, to those who have younger siblings, work hard to be a godly example and to show them the love of Christ. I am thankful for my older brothers who bring me to Monday Night Guys and to all the high school guys at my church who are making a difference in my life.

MICAH PERSTROPE: *13, St. Peters, MO*
First Baptist Church of St. Charles, St. Charles, MO; Dubray Middle School, St. Peters, MO

BLESSED BLIND BEGGARS

"As they were leaving Jericho, a large crowd followed Him. They were two blind men sitting by the road. When they heard that Jesus was passing by, they cried out, 'Lord, have mercy on us, Son of David!' The crowd told them to keep quiet, but they cried out all the more, 'Lord, have mercy on us, Son of David!' Jesus stopped, called them, and said, 'What do you want Me to do for you?' 'Lord,' they said to Him, 'open our eyes!' Moved with compassion, Jesus touched their eyes. Immediately they could see and followed Him." —Matthew 20:29–34

In today's verse, God is speaking to two groups of people, giving them different messages. The group represented by the "crowd" following Jesus and His disciples includes all those who follow Christ in their life. The other, illustrated by two blind beggars, is unsaved, unchurched, or simply in desperate need. God's message to the first group is: Although your enthusiasm and desire to know Christ and be blessed by Him is amazing and in no way immoral, perhaps you should look behind you at those in desperate need; help them up, call out to the Lord for their sake, and be blessed through their uplifting. Do not be quick to silence and rebuke those whom you find irrelevant, for Christ values them as much as He does you. In fact, He values them enough to call to them by name. As for the second group, God's message is to the lonely, broken, forgotten, or even blind to love: God is calling out to you. When He calls, will you answer? Do you know exactly what it is you want from God? Then tell Him. He longs to hear from His children.

BRADY FOWLKES: *16, Tuscaloosa, AL*
Valley View Baptist Church and Hillcrest High School, Tuscaloosa, AL

TRANSFORMING FROM A WORLD OF CONFORMING

"Do not be conformed to this age, but be transformed by the renewing of your mind, so that you may discern what is the good, pleasing, and perfect will of God." —*Romans 12:2*

Peer pressure. We don't like to talk about it because we like to think we're above it, but the grip of influence from others causes us to give in to peer pressure and go with the status quo. It's easier to swim downstream than upstream. Christians are called to be transformed from this age. Some real issues of this age are drugs, alcohol, pornography, cheating, stealing, lying, etc. These are easy traps to fall into; sin seems fun at first. After a while, though, one discovers the fragility of these pleasures of the world. Ultimately, sin creates separation and a lack of closeness in your walk with God. If we want to be close to God, sinful barriers must be broken down. Christ triumphed over sin, so we know we can win the war against sin! Though we may lose some battles along the way, we know that through Christ we can be transformed from sinners into believers who passionately seek to follow Christ. Transformation is not an easy process and it will require some discipline, but we know that it is what God has called us to do. We should be different from the rest of the world. Today, I would like to challenge you to transform yourself by doing something different. If it is standing up for someone, talking to a loner, asking forgiveness, or simply doing something nice for someone, I pray that you will make a difference for the kingdom!

LUKE PERSTROPE: *17, St. Peters, MO*
First Baptist Church of St. Charles, St. Charles, MO; Fort Zumwalt East High School, St. Peters, MO

LIFE WITH A PURPOSE

"And the world with its lust is passing away,
but the one who does God's will remains forever." —*1 John 2:17*

Everyone wants to be remembered for something good after death has overtaken them. I know that I want to have a life remembered for giving everything to Christ and not being afraid to show in public that He lives in me. Life is too precious to waste on things that will amount to nothing when we get to heaven. Being a friend to someone that the world puts down always turns heads in school, and everyone will notice a person that isn't afraid to be talked about and who is willing to go the extra mile to show Christ's love. We need to make it our purpose to show Christ to the world, so we are remembered for that instead of the sins we committed. Christians don't need to worry if people gossip about the way we express Christ in our lives. It is better for us to build a good, heavenly reputation, instead of one from the world. Riches earned on the earth today will only disappear after death or robbers steal it away. "But collect for yourselves treasures in heaven, where neither moth nor rust destroys, and where thieves don't break in and steal" (Matthew 6:20). Going out on a limb for Jesus will reward us in the end, and that is worth more than the words a person has to say about us.

BILLY RAMSEY: *17, Sharon, SC*
Faith Baptist Church, Clover, SC; York Comprehensive High School, York, SC

THE GOOD SAMARITAN (PART 1)

"But a Samaritan on his journey came up to him, and when he saw the man, he had compassion. . . . Then he put him on his own animal, brought him to an inn, and took care of him." —Luke 10:33–34

We all go through tough time and struggles. Christians are going to face challenges. The Bible actually promises us that we will. The man in our passage for today was stripped of his clothing and left to die. This man was in great need; he was in a state of desperation. Perhaps not for the same reasons as the man in the message today, but have you ever experienced desperation? Most of us have at some time in our life. Imagine the glee that must have sprung forth from his mind and heart when he saw a priest walking down the road toward him! Unfortunately for the half-dead man, the priest walked to the other side of the street. The Levite that came later followed the example of the priest and also walked on the other side of the road. These religious leaders saw the need, made a decision, and kept on walking. However, the Samaritan came along and he bent down and helped the man. This shows the hearts and mind-sets of the three men. As Dr. Martin Luther King Jr. said, "The first question which the priest and the Levite asked was: 'If I stop to help this man, what will happen to me?' But . . . the Good Samaritan reversed the question: 'If I do not stop to help this man, what will happen to him?'" We must also ask, what would our response be?

LUKE PERSTROPE: *17, St. Peters, MO*
First Baptist Church of St. Charles, St. Charles, MO; Fort Zumwalt East High School, St. Peters, MO

THE GOOD SAMARITAN (PART 2)

"But a Samaritan on his journey came up to him, and when he saw the man, he had compassion. . . . Then he put him on his own animal, brought him to an inn, and took care of him." —*Luke 10:33–34*

As we continue to consider the plight of the man left to die on the side of the road and the decisions made by three passersby, we must recognize that the focus of these men was completely different. The religious leaders were more concerned about themselves and what others might think of them, so they removed themselves from the situation. They were not willing to bend down to help the helpless. The Samaritan, however, was concerned about the injured man and was willing to get down where the man was, on his level, to be able to assist him in his hour of great need. My family moved to Missouri the summer before my junior year, not an ideal time in one's life. Though I had my family with me, I needed some church and school friends. Some guys were like the Good Samaritan to me, they saw my need and filled it by coming alongside to be my friends when I was lonely. I am so grateful for the people God has placed in my life. Things would be much harder without them. We must get the mind-set of the Good Samaritan and be willing to get involved in order to help others in their time of need. The world around us is in need of Christ's love. We must learn to put others above ourselves and put that love into action.

LUKE PERSTROPE: *17, St. Peters, MO*
First Baptist Church of St. Charles, St. Charles, MO; Fort Zumwalt East High School, St. Peters, MO

DECEITFUL CHARM OR ONE WHO FEARS THE LORD?

"Charm is deceitful, and beauty is fleeting, but a woman who fears the LORD will be praised." —*Proverbs 31:30*

About the time I turned thirteen, I started noticing girls my age. Thoughts started going through my head like, I wonder what they think about me? and What can I do to impress them? While it was normal to think that way, my parents helped me to realize that it wasn't time yet. It's so tempting to think that if you have a girlfriend you'll be happy. She's so fun and cute and pretty and nice! you may think. My parents just don't understand! The fact of the matter is, however, that God has the perfect person in mind for you to marry. Since it's pretty much impossible for you to know who that person is when you're thirteen, it's very likely that if you let yourself become attached to someone, they're not the person God has set aside for you. In this era where the norm is for all teenage guys to have a girlfriend, how amazing would it be for you to wait for God's plan? What if, rather than spending your teenage years flirting with, exchanging looks, and giving pieces of your heart to people who at the time seem so perfect, you saved yourself wholly and completely for your future spouse? Pray that God will help you to not be focused on impressing girls. Pray, instead, that He will help you prepare yourself for that one He has in mind for you and even to wait to start dating until you and your parents feel that you're ready. If you do this, you will have a much happier marriage.

MICAH COOKSEY: *19, McMinnville, OR*
Valley Baptist Church, McMinnville, OR

FORSAKING RIGHTS, CHOOSING LOVE

"However, we have not made use of this right. . . . But I have used none of these rights . . . For it would be better for me to die than for anyone to deprive me of my boast! No one should seek his own good, but the good of the other person." —*1 Corinthians 9:12, 15; 10:24*

Paul makes a long and complex argument dealing with personal rights. Paul's preference over rights is love! We teenagers sometimes think that we know all about love. It's that warm, fuzzy feeling, right? It's that desire to cuddle up in someone's arms. But what happens when the feeling goes away? Is the love gone? Is love based on our silly, fickle emotions? In Scripture, husbands are called to love their wives "just as Christ loved the church and gave Himself for her." So what is love? Love is a commitment to forsake your own rights for the benefit of your partner; to choose not to fulfill your own desires, but to enrich the life of the other person. Love is sacrifice. God calls us to love our neighbor. Is it not the same love? What does this love look like in our everyday interactions? We can get into arguments with others, trying to justify our actions, trying to show we have a right to do the things we do or say the things we say. Or we accuse someone for not respecting our rights. Bad feelings arise, and we find that we've become enemies with the ones we argue with. How different things would be if we would forsake our individual rights from the start, letting go of our desire to argue and defend ourselves over things that truly don't matter in eternity. Let's choose to come together in unity, realizing "how good and pleasant it is when brothers live together in harmony!" (Psalm 133:1).

CONNOR HOWINGTON: *17, West Monroe, LA*
First Baptist West Monroe and Northeast Baptist School, West Monroe, LA

A TIME FOR EVERYTHING

*"There is an occasion for everything,
and a time for every activity under heaven."* —*Ecclesiastes 3:1*

We often hear our parents say, "It's not the time for that." We quickly write off this advice without realizing that the truth of what they're saying is actually in the Bible. One of the best characteristics to have is self-control, and this passage says that there are, in fact, occasions to be reserved. Each of the actions in Ephesians 3, such as weeping or laughing, are not wrong by themselves, but may be inappropriate due to the circumstances. We must be aware of the situation we are in and act accordingly. Also, one's actions often represent those who have raised that person. Think about how your deeds reflect on your parents. Be careful to acknowledge the responsibility you have in both your reputation and that of your parents. A few simple seconds before reacting to think about what you might do will greatly influence your actual response. Pray daily that you will be quick to think and slow to answer.

JONATHAN DISMUKES: *17, Mobile, AL*
Redeemer Fellowship Church and Cottage Hill Christian Academy, Mobile, AL

BEING GODLY AND STEADFAST IN A GODLESS AND EVERYTHING GOES WORLD (PART 1)

"Because lawlessness will multiply, the love of many will grow cold. But the one who endures to the end will be delivered." —*Matthew 24:12–13*

Abortion is the blatant murder of an unborn baby; and what we have heard about killing a fetus, which is viable at the point of conception, being permissible is an outright lie. What does a God who affectionately asked for the little children to come to Him think of babies being massacred by the millions since 1973? It is important for teens who will be parents, church, and political leaders one day to consider some facts: Close to 55 million babies murders committed: the painful methods used to kill babies range from suction of the brain through a tube to total dismemberment until death is achieved by hemorrhaging. Consider these ratios as we put the numbers into perspective: using a constant of roughly 54.6 million abortions: deaths in the Holocaust=13% of abortions since *Roe vs. Wade*; Joplin tornado=.00000002% (2 billionths of a percent); Hurricane Katrina=.00003% (3 millionths of a percent); September 11, 2001=.000055% (5.5 ten millionths). All combined composes a fraction of the cumulative abortions committed. As Christians, even teen Christians, God wants us to pay attention to what is happening in our world. He wants us to be aware and prepared to be used when He calls up for the battle against these sinful human atrocities. Are you ready?

LUKE MERRICK: *15, Springdale, AR*
Immanuel Baptist Church and Shiloh Christian School, Springdale, AR

BEING GODLY AND STEADFAST IN A GODLESS AND EVERYTHING GOES WORLD (PART 2)

"Therefore, I remind you to keep ablaze the gift of God that is in you. . . . For God has not given us a spirit of fearfulness, but one of power, love, and sound judgment." —*2 Timothy 1:6–7*

Not even two years ago, there was little to make us think that our nation's leaders and even some in the church would become so accepting of what God refers to as detestable. When you turn on the television, you will find commercials and shows that promote homosexuality. We can see, though, that God clearly condemns this version of sexuality in Romans 1:25–26. We will be the politicians, the doctors, the pastors, and workforce of tomorrow. We will be the next generation of believers in a world that increasingly looks down on Christians. In this world where people, many Christians included, condone all manner of evil and wrongdoing (in theory and/or practice), we must continually remember what our convictions are and be willing to stand firm on them. Until Christ returns, the world will become increasingly evil, with sin and lawlessness escalating. As believers in Christ, let us never become involved in the sexual sin that causes this destruction of families, souls, and human lives. We should seek to point the world toward God, remain blameless ourselves, and keep our faith warm and fervent. Let's strive to live God's way!

LUKE MERRICK: *15, Springdale, AR*
Immanuel Baptist Church and Shiloh Christian School, Springdale, AR

150

JOY
(PART 1)

"I have spoken these things to you so that My joy may be in you and your joy may be complete. This is My command: Love one another as I have loved you." —John 15:11–12

Joy is a complex but important word with many lessons that are often tossed around in church, but why is it so important? And how is joy any different from happiness? In 1647 a group of highly intelligent, spiritually wise men came together to answer one of the biggest questions ever to face humankind. In the dialect of the day it read, "What is the chief end of Man?" What is our purpose, what are we doing here? The answer may seem surprising: "Man's chief end is to glorify God, and enjoy Him forever." There are two reasons why this answer is so important. First, it says man's purpose in life is to enjoy God. We were created to find joy and live a life in which God gives an abundance of joy. We were not created to be miserable or angry or defiant. God did not create us to test us and have us suffer; rather, we are here to enjoy Him and His Son. Second, it answers the question on how to find joy. The stated purpose of man almost seems like two things, glorifying and finding joy, but the writers of the Westminster Shorter Catechism intended it to be one unified purpose. We Christians find our joy in glorifying God. When we act according to His will and bring glory to Him, we bring joy into our lives as well as into the lives of others.

CODY BRANDON: *17, Mt. Juliet, TN*
The Fellowship at Two Rivers, Nashville, TN; Mt. Juliet High School, Mt. Juliet, TN

JOY
(PART 2)

"I have spoken these things to you so that My joy may be in you and your joy may be complete. This is My command: Love one another as I have loved you." —*John 15:11–12*

When we find joy in God and His creation we glorify Him, because we are doing what He created us to do. It becomes a never-ending circle of spiritual growth and enjoyment. Our lives will overflow with joy as we glorify God and take delight in Him. The best part is, as we grow more and more joyous in our faith and stronger in Christ, other people will notice and wonder what's going on. Then we have even more opportunities to glorify God and, in turn, spread joy to more and more people. If glorifying God is our chief end then it would behoove us—yes, even teens—to consider all the ways that our meditation, prayer life, Bible study, and every other thing that we do in our daily lives can bring glory to God the Father. It is especially important for teen males to be in a place in our Christian walks to learn all we can about giving glory to God. We will set the example of glorifying God as future leaders, as husbands, and as fathers. It will be up to us to teach by practicing the presence of God. "In the same way, let your light shine before men, so that they may see your good works and give glory to your Father in heaven" (Matthew 5:16).

CODY BRANDON: *17, Mt. Juliet, TN*
The Fellowship at Two Rivers, Nashville, TN; Mt. Juliet High School, Mt. Juliet, TN

JUNE

Listen, my son, to your father's instruction, and don't reject your mother's teaching,

for they will be a garland of grace on your head and a gold chain around your neck.

My son, if sinners entice you, don't be persuaded.

If they say—"Come with us! Let's set an ambush and kill someone.

Let's attack some innocent person just for fun!

Let's swallow them alive, like Sheol, still healthy as they go down to the Pit.

We'll find all kinds of valuable property and fill our houses with plunder.

Throw in your lot with us, and we'll all share our money"—

my son, don't travel that road with them or set foot on their path,

because their feet run toward trouble and they hurry to commit murder.

It is foolish to spread a net where any bird can see it,

but they set an ambush to kill themselves, they attack their own lives.

Such are the paths of all who make profit dishonestly, it takes the lives of those who receive it.

(Proverbs 1:8–19)

MISSIONS

"As He was getting into the boat, the man who had been demon-possessed kept begging Him to be with Him. But He would not let him instead, He told him, 'Go back home to your own people, and report to them how much the Lord has done for you and how He has had mercy on you.' So he went out and began to proclaim in the Decapolis how much Jesus had done for him, and they were all amazed." —Mark 5:18–20

When most people think of missions, they think of people who devote their lives to travel to distant parts of the world, away from home, to share the gospel to people who won't get it otherwise. They devote themselves to the cause of spreading the gospel message. They leave family and friends, leave their jobs, learn a new language, and go to places where they could lose their own lives for believing in Christ and trying to save others. As teenagers, it is difficult to do this, but it doesn't mean we can't participate in missions. God has placed you in a specific area to do great works. When you are at school, look around. There are hurting people who need to hear the message of Jesus Christ. You are in your own mission field right now, surrounded by people who need to feel God's love. Go and proclaim what Jesus has done for you. Tell your friends how great God's love is and that He has died for them. Just because you aren't in a different part of the world doesn't mean you can't help others into the kingdom of God.

ZACH WATKINS: *16, Henderson, NV*
Highland Hills Baptist Church and Green Valley High School, Henderson, NV

PRAYER

"Pray constantly." —*1 Thessalonians 5:17*

Have you ever had a time when you've been so busy with things that you felt like you were suffocating, as if you were running out of time to even breathe? Believe it or not, our spiritual lives are much the same in concept. You see, our prayer lives can be compared to breathing. All the time we spend running around saying we don't have time to pray, we actually don't have time to pray. However, we seem to remember to breathe a lot more often than we remember to pray, at least in my experience. Maybe it's different with you: maybe you do forget to breathe as often as you forget to pray. I would sure hope not, otherwise you could get yourself seriously injured. Charles Spurgeon said, "They [men of God] can no more live without prayer than I can live without breathing" ("Pray without Ceasing," Message delivered at Metropolitan Tabernacle, Newington UK, March 10, 1872). Just like we breathe without ceasing, we should also pray without ceasing by having an open communion with God throughout the day! No doubt we need to make time to pray in secret, yet throughout the day we should talk with God as often as we breathe. If we don't pray, if we don't talk to God, we suffocate ourselves. No prayer means no breath; no breath means no life, and a man without life is a dead man! Prayer, then, would have to be a necessary function of a spiritually living person, as well as studying God's Word. For who can live without breath, and who can have strength without food?

JOSHUA JOHANSEN: *18, Shrewsbury, MA*
Bethlehem Bible Church, West Boylston, MA; Quinsigamond Community College, Worchester, MA

OVERFLOW

"A good man produces good out of the good storeroom in his heart. An evil man produces the evil out of the evil storeroom, for his mouth speaks from the overflow of the heart." —*Luke 6:45*

Today's verse is great and read with many different interpretations. Most focus on the fact that the type of man you are, good or evil, is decided by what's in your heart. This focus usually concludes with the old saying, "It's what's on the inside that counts." I agree with this interpretation, but I want to show you a little more depth to the passage. When looking at the verse, there are several words the author, Luke, intends you to notice; *good, evil,* and *heart* are used repeatedly to highlight their importance. There is one meaningful and descriptive word that stands out, though it's only used once: *overflow.* It's easy to overlook but is possibly the most influential word in the passage. Imagine a cup. You cannot see inside this cup from any angle, therefore you cannot tell what is inside. In fact, the only way for you to know what is inside this cup would be for it to pour over, overflow. Without the overflow, you would not be able to tell whether the cup had purified spring water inside of it or hot, sticky tar. No matter how "glass-half-full" your attitude is, quite frankly, that's not all God calls us to be. He did not call us to be cheerleaders but, rather, examples of Christ; not only through what's inside our cups—what is inside our hearts—but what is filling us to the point of overflowing: God's love.

BRADY FOWLKES: *16, Tuscaloosa, AL*
Valley View Baptist Church and Hillcrest High School, Tuscaloosa, AL

I NEED TO CONFESS

"The one who conceals his sin will not prosper, but whoever confesses and renounces them will find mercy." —Proverbs 28:13

As a teen, I find it is incredibly difficult to say that I am wrong. When someone confronts me about my sins I am quick to deny, to justify my actions, or to attempt to minimize the effect of my actions. The Holy Spirit has given strength and self-control in times when I am tempted to lie about my actions, and I thank God for that. Concealing sin is very serious. When we lie to others, we tell ourselves that we have done nothing wrong, and we conveniently forget to tell someone when we know we have done wrong. A person who does this is denying the fact that there is a problem, and he or she is denying that wrong has been done. When you sin, there is a problem. You have broken God's law and have damaged the relationship there. If you refuse to recognize there's a problem or that you have done wrong, what do you think will happen? If your best friend did something very cruel to you and refused to acknowledge any wrong done, would your relationship be unaffected? God knows all things and we can never truly hide our sin from Him. However, if we pretend that we do not feel guilt or do not understand we have done wrong, then our relationship with God will be affected. God desires strong and loving relationships with us. We are told in the psalms that His mercies are new every morning. We need to have the courage to admit that we have done wrong and accept the consequences. God tells us He will forgive us and we will find mercy.

JOSIAH MCGEE: *15, Kansas City, MO*
Summit Woods Baptist Church, Lees Summit, MO; Homeschooled

MISSING THE MARK (PART 1)

"For all have sinned and fall short of the glory of God."
—Romans 3:23

I had never played a high school sport before. My retirement from baseball occurred back in my middle school days. However, I decided it was time for a comeback. My favorite teacher was the tennis coach, so I decided to join the tennis team. Though the running and conditioning were less than desirable, I have really enjoyed my time with the tennis team. In my first tennis match, I wasn't perfect. With the combination of the Siberian wind chill and my nerves, I had a few serves that didn't make it in the box. I lost several points for my doubles team because I could not hit the ball in the service box. In life, many times we miss the mark. Romans 3:23 tells us that all of humanity falls short of the glory of God. We fall into the traps of sin and fail to live up to the standards that God has for us. Our sin separates us from God. There was a canyon between God and humanity. There was only one way to bridge the gap and liberate us from our condemnation. God sent His Son to make a way for us to enter into heaven. If you are struggling to keep your life inside the very place where God will be your all, you might want to spend time with Him, reading His Word and praying. You will then be on the winning team for all eternity!

LUKE PERSTROPE: *17, St. Peters, MO*
First Baptist Church of St. Charles, St. Charles, MO; Fort Zumwalt East High School, St. Peters, MO

MISSING THE MARK (PART 2)

"For all have sinned and fall short of the glory of God."
—*Romans 3:23*

Once we accept Jesus as our Lord and Savior, through confession of our sins and repentance, acknowledging the sin debt that He paid on the cross at Calvary, we will know that eternity will be spent with Him in heaven. We will not be perfect here on the earth and will fall down many times in our lives. The Bible is full of imperfect people who served a perfect God. David had an affair. Paul (Saul) persecuted the church and killed many Christians. Others doubted. Some even laughed at God. Peter denied Christ. We should feel tremendous joy in knowing that even when we mess up God still loves us. He still cares for us and watches over us. In life, we mess up, yet God loves us with an unconditional love. You may be like me in my first tennis match and lose points, but you can still win. I did end up winning my game. Despite my flaws, I still had victory. Despite our flaws, we can still have victory through Christ Jesus our Lord.

LUKE PERSTROPE: *17, St. Peters, MO*
First Baptist Church of St. Charles, St. Charles, MO; Fort Zumwalt East High School, St. Peters, MO

THE GREATEST GIFT

"For God loved the world in this way. He gave His One and Only Son, so that everyone who believes in Him will not perish but have eternal life."
—John 3:16

I have a friend who enjoys coming to church with me when we have youth activities. We've been friends since fourth grade. Seventh grade was tough for most of our class. Our teachers said it was a transitional grade and we needed to learn to be more responsible before moving to high school. At crunch time before a major test I'd ask my friend to pray with me. One day he asked me to explain this God stuff. Our youth pastor had taught on being prepared to win souls for Christ. Here it was, John 3:16: "For God loved the world in this way. He gave His One and Only Son, so that everyone who believes in Him will not perish but have eternal life." I led my friend in prayer with Romans 10:9: "If you confess with your mouth, 'Jesus is Lord,' and believe in your heart that God raised Him from the dead, you will be saved," and he accepted Christ right there in school. We had no way of knowing at that time that my friend's uncle would be found dead or that he would save his mother's life when he found her having a stroke in the middle of the night. But we both knew that God was there for him. We've both gone on to different high schools, though we still talk from time to time and have remained friends. I'm so glad he has a relationship with Christ and he knows how to pray in the good times and bad.

PAUL CRAIG GALE: *14, New Orleans, LA*
Franklin Avenue Baptist Church and New Orleans Center for Creative Arts, New Orleans, LA

WITNESS

"If I say to the wicked, 'Wicked one, you will surely die,' but you do not speak out to warn him about his way, that wicked person will die for his iniquity, yet I will hold you responsible for his blood. But if you warn a wicked person to turn from his way and he doesn't turn from it, he will die for his iniquity, but you will have saved your life." —*Ezekiel 33:8–9*

If someone asked your friends to characterize you in one word, what word would they use? Would they say, "He's nice," "She's fun," or something like that? What if they said, "She's a Christian"? Wouldn't that be neat? We have opportunities to witness to those around us, but a lot of the times we (myself included) don't let the fact be known that we're a Christian. If asked, those around us might have no idea that we are Christ's followers. So, we need to do two things:

1. We need to act in a Christlike way and refuse to do things that are against biblical teaching. It's a great witness when we (politely) say, "Sorry, I can't do that because I'm a Christian and the Bible says for me not to do that."

2. It doesn't stop there! Living a Christlike life is a good witness, but it's not enough. We also need to share our faith with those around us. When you're still a teenager there aren't as many opportunities to do this, but you can ask your parents to help you with ideas. Think about the fact that you might be the only Christian your friends know. What if you are the only person who can tell them about Jesus?

Pray for boldness to speak up about God with your friends who aren't Christians. Ask Him to give you opportunities to share about Him, and pray that He will give you the words to say.

MICAH COOKSEY: *19, McMinnville, OR*
Valley Baptist Church, McMinnville, OR

HELP US!

"A wise man's instruction is a fountain of life,
turning people away from the snares of death." —*Proverbs 13:14*

We all get a lot of advice about what the church does and what the church should give its members. One good way to know what the church is supposed to do is to read the Epistles in the New Testament. But the most important thing the church should teach us is how to apply to our lives what we learn from the teaching we read in God's Word and hear from godly leaders. A lot of times we go to church and learn lots of new, interesting ways to help non-Christians, or even our other fellow Christians. Think about all of the lives we could change if we applied the truth we learn from the Bible! We could even show someone how to know the Lord! How awesome would that be? I have found that there are certain methods we all can learn that will help us witness to others. We need churches that teach us these methods, along with the already amazing messages we hear.

BRANDON CARROLL: *17, York, SC*
Hillcrest Baptist Church and York Comprehensive High School, York, SC

RUMORS

"You must not go about spreading slander among your people; you must not jeopardize your neighbor's life; I am Yahweh."

—Leviticus 19:16

Spreading rumors is as much a sin as engaging in gossip. They always hurt whomever they're about. The sad part is, for the most part, we don't ask if it's true or not, but instead we accept it as fact and even tell others what we have been told. The people hurt by the rumors suffer greatly and feel deep and sometimes lasting pain as a result. In the first part of today's verse we are told to not repeat what we hear. As born-again believers, we are all brothers and sisters in Christ, and we should not hurt each other with lies. In the second part of the verse we are told that we should not jeopardize another person's life. When we spread rumors we can hurt others to a point where they can't bear it. Some will even contemplate suicide, jeopardizing their lives or the lives of others. So, according to God's Word, we should not spread rumors about others or even listen to them. Remember, you can be the one where the rumor stops and where someone else's life actually begins.

DAVID JOSEPH DALESANDRO: *14, York, SC*

Hillcrest Baptist Church and York Comprehensive High School, York, SC

CHRIST THE CORNERSTONE (PART 1)

"So then you are no longer foreigners and strangers,
but fellow citizens with the saints, and members of God's household,
built on the foundation of the apostles and prophets,
with Christ Jesus Himself as the cornerstone." —*Ephesians 2:19–20*

Our culture exemplifies a me-centered approach to life. Our world revolves around ourselves. We stand at a crucial crossroad in life. As we begin to shape our lives by deciding what career field we will enter, which college we will attend, and who we will spend the rest of our lives with, the decision of taking on a me-centered approach to life or a Christ-centered approach is brought to light. A *cornerstone* is the stone that is placed on the corner of a building. It is the first stone that is put into position. Every other stone is laid in relation to the cornerstone. In terms of importance, no other stone can compare. Christ is the cornerstone of the church and the common bond between believers. The church must be Christ-centered. To live up to this, the members of the church must live with Christ as the cornerstone of their lives. Living with Christ as the cornerstone means that everything in our lives and our futures has to be put in its place by our relationship with Christ: our education, our career, our spouse, our giving. Our focus in life has to be radically impacted by Christ.

LUKE PERSTROPE: *17, St. Peters, MO*
First Baptist Church of St. Charles, St. Charles, MO; Fort Zumwalt East High School, St. Peters, MO

CHRIST THE CORNERSTONE (PART 2)

*"So then you are no longer foreigners and strangers,
but fellow citizens with the saints, and members of God's household,
built on the foundation of the apostles and prophets,
with Christ Jesus Himself as the cornerstone." —Ephesians 2:19–20*

As long as our focus on life occupation is based on the me-centered approach, we will never find our true potential and will never be able to lay the cornerstones that God ordains. We will find limitations at every front, and success will be hard to come by in every area of our lives. Sadly, we will have things so confused in our own hearts that everything God has purposed for us will be changed and always less than His highest. Those limitations will prove to be a hindrance to the kingdom work. We simply cannot try to reach a lost world while the gospel remains idle in the back of our minds! Given the vast resources that our nation has been blessed with, our generation can shake all nations for the cause of Christ and reach the billions who are on their way to an eternity apart from Him. We have to be intentional in our purpose of accomplishing the Great Commission! Christ is the foundation we build our lives upon and His glory must be at the forefront of our minds. Is He the cornerstone in your life?

LUKE PERSTROPE: *17, St. Peters, MO*
First Baptist Church of St. Charles, St. Charles, MO; Fort Zumwalt East High School, St. Peters, MO

WHAT WOULD JESUS DO?

"So God created man in His own image; He created him in the image of God; He created them male and female." —*Genesis 1:27*

Many people hear the question, "What would Jesus do?" and think to themselves, "Well I'm not Jesus, and I will never be perfect, so what does that have to do with me?" Well, it has everything to do with you and your life. One of the first things God did was create us. Genesis 1:27 says, "God created man in His own image." Now, this doesn't say that God created us in our own image, or the image the world gives us, but in His image. For us, this means that we should strive to do everything in our lives just as Jesus would. I know sometimes I come across the question of whether or not it is OK to do something. Oftentimes this question is about something that is right on the edge of what we think is OK. What has helped me is looking back to the life Jesus lived. This helps me to put the situation into perspective. The easiest way to do this is to open up the Bible. The Bible is the Word of God and shows the perfect, sinless life that Jesus lived as an example for us and, ultimately, to assure our salvation. This fact should be extra motivation for us to live our lives to the standard Jesus set. I mean, if you think about it, God didn't really have to send Jesus to bring us salvation. He created us so why couldn't He just start over? But the fact is, He loves us so much that He gave us a second chance. We need to do everything we can to thank Him for that. The best way to do that is to live the lives He created us for.

JESSE NIEMAN: *18, Ocala, FL*
Church @ The Springs and Forest High School, Ocala, FL

WAITING FOR THE MRS. RIGHT! (PART 1)

"Husbands, love your wives, just as Christ loved the church and gave Himself for her." —*Ephesians 5:25*

When teen guys think about dating and getting married, we selfishly spend much of the time thinking about trying to find that one person that will meet our needs, and even our wants, then falling in love with them will hopefully come later. However, the relationship that is to last "until death do us part" is not about finding a woman who will spend her married life meeting our needs! That "until death do us part" relationship is so much more than that. It's true that we need someone with the same beliefs and values. And it is true that we even need someone who will complement us and meet our needs, and someone that we will love and will love us. But, there is something a whole lot bigger than the love you will have for the woman you marry, and that is your love for Christ. The love you have for Christ, and share with her, comes before anything else. The woman you marry, that you will spend the majority of your life with, should have the same depth of love for Jesus that you do. And your love for her should always be about loving her more than you love yourself. If the relationships that you are in as a teen are not based on what God says a marriage is to be, then you might want to step back and ask God to help you love Him more, so that you can love the woman He is preparing for you the right way.

BRANDON CARROLL: *17, York, SC*
Hillcrest Baptist Church and York Comprehensive High School, York, SC

WAITING FOR THE MRS. RIGHT! (PART 2)

"Husbands, love your wives, just as Christ loved the church and gave Himself for her." —*Ephesians 5:25*

Marriage is about loving and serving your spouse. You cannot out-love or out-serve the person God lets you marry, and she cannot out-serve you! When you love your wife the way God wants you to, she will want to be there for you and will help you when you need it. She will also be someone you can trust with every detail of your life, no matter how painful or exciting. The two of you will feel comfortable around each other all the time! She will help keep you on track with your walk with Christ, just as you will do for her. You will want to nurture her and help to guide her in the ways of God. She will remind you that everything the two of you do is through and for Christ! She should be someone that God has put in your life. So don't get caught up in finding the prettiest, smartest, funniest woman ever. Trust God to have control of your life, and He will bring you the perfect wife; and she will be more beautiful, smarter, and funnier than you could have even picked out on your own! She will cause your heart to swell every time you see her or even think about her. God delights in giving His children the desires of their hearts! That's something to look forward to, right? Not just a wife, but a woman who loves God and can love you because of that!

BRANDON CARROLL: *17, York, SC*
Hillcrest Baptist Church and York Comprehensive High School, York, SC

DREADED HOMEWORK!

"Therefore, whether you eat or drink, or whatever you do, do everything for God's glory." —*1 Corinthians 10:31*

There's one thing in the world that I absolutely dread. I have hated this one thing ever since I started doing it. Yes, the very thing I am referring to is homework! I can't stand it! If school was just going there and doing classwork and coming home, I'd be a straight-A student! As much as I don't like doing homework, I know that I need to do it because it is required and I need to be obedient in everything that I do. And, I need to do it for the glory of God. So, if there's one thing that you can't stand to do—such as washing the dishes, cleaning your room, grocery shopping for your mother, or like me, doing your homework—always remember that whatever you do, you're doing it for the glory of God. So pick up your pencil or pen, read that book you're supposed to be reading, and just get your homework done! Remember, that if you don't do what you are supposed to do, your life won't be pleasant. We will always have people in authority over us, so we need to learn to obey and do what is required; and for some of us that begins with homework!

CHRISTIAN SMITH: *17, New Orleans, LA*
Franklin Avenue Baptist Church and New Orleans Charter Science and Mathematics High School, New Orleans, LA

I'LL SEE YOU AGAIN!

"In my Father's house are many dwelling places; if not, I would have told you. I am going away to prepare a place for you." —*John 14:2*

My grandmother and I were very close. She suffered a very long battle with illness during the last year and a half of her life. It killed me inside to see her going through all of that, almost like someone was squeezing my heart. She tried to go home to heaven a couple of times, but God told her it wasn't her time yet. Then one day, through the pain she was experiencing and my emotional pain, God finally told her that it was time for her to come home. And so she went with Him to that mansion He had prepared for her. As anyone can imagine, I was so upset for a while. Then I realized that my grandmother was a godly woman and that she is in heaven with Him. One day I will be able to see her again! If you struggle with grief from the loss of a loved one, just remember that God is always with us and will never give us a challenge we cannot overcome. He will take care of our loved ones in heaven and us here on the earth. And you will be able to see them again one day too. How great that day will be!

BRANDON CARROLL: *17, York, SC*
Hillcrest Baptist Church and York Comprehensive High School, York, SC

LOVE, BECAUSE GOD LOVED US FIRST

"If I speak human or angelic languages but do not have love, I am a sounding gong or a clanging cymbal. If I have the gift of prophecy and understand all mysteries and all knowledge, and if I have all faith so that I can move mountains but do not have love, I am nothing. And if I donate all my goods to feed the poor, and if I give my body in order to boast but do not have love, I gain nothing."

—1 Corinthians 13:1–3

Love is what drives the lives of Christians. God loved us first so that we could love; but without love, everything we do means nothing. Love is supposed to be important to us as Christians, intimate love with Jesus that we show others by our actions. Without love, we become a people who do not know how to show compassion, tenderness, respect, and honor. We can give all our money to the poor and all our possessions to the less fortunate; but if we do so without love, it means absolutely nothing. We are simply making noise that resembles sounding brass clanging together, with no benefit to it. We could be missionaries to all ends of the earth, but without love, it is pointless. We could be martyred at the stake for Christ; but if we do so without love, it is worthless. Love has to be the driving force behind our actions. God is love, and thus, we must love. Jesus commands us to love. Pray: Lord, help me to live my life in a loving way. A way that in everything I do, I am going to love You and love the people around me with Your love. Let my life be centered on Your love.

ZACH WATKINS: *16, Henderson, NV*
Highland Hills Baptist Church and Green Valley High School, Henderson, NV

THE TWELFTH MAN

"The Lᴏʀᴅ of Hosts has sworn: As I have purposed, so it will be; as I have planned it, so it will happen." —*Isaiah 14:24*

Sports can be very frustrating at times. Sometimes you feel that you have more potential than the guy your coach puts in before you. You may be that person who gives 100 percent at practice, but coach doesn't put you in until the team is getting blown out or vice versa. I've been through many instances where I've never been put in the game, and I think to myself, *What is wrong with coach? I'm better than who he put out there.* The real question is, was the role that you play on the team needed tonight? The coach usually knows more than you do, and that was a lesson I had to learn. Everyone on the team has a certain role that they play, and maybe they don't need it that game, or maybe someone else was stepping up at the time. Just because you're not in the game doesn't mean your purpose on the court is not being fulfilled. That goes both ways, on and off the court. A complete player is someone who fulfills his duties on the court, in the classroom, and in Christ. God has a plan for your life, just like the coach has a plan for you in the game, and you must execute it. We have to trust that God's plan is what is best for us and learn that as long as our purposes are being fulfilled, we should be satisfied with our lives.

CHRISTOPHER COLEMAN BAILEY: *17, Albany, GA*
Greater Second Mt. Olive Baptist Church and Sherwood Christian Academy, Albany, GA

CHOOSING A WIFE

"Charm is deceptive and beauty is fleeting, but a woman who fears the LORD will be praised." —*Proverbs 31:30*

Everyone wonders about whom they will marry and what their family will be like. We can dream about a beautiful wife, cute kids, a dog, a pickup truck, and a nice house with a picket fence in the future. Choosing a wife is one of life's most important decisions and needs to be made with wisdom, prayer, and the wise counsel of trusted parents and other believing friends. I think there are two aspects to making the wise choice of a mate:

1. We need to be the right person walking with God, living in the Spirit, and staying in God's Word. Men should be faithful to God, commit to love our wives sacrificially, and lead our families to pursue a relationship with Christ; and

2. We need to choose the right person. Looks are deceiving, and beautiful girls are a temptation for many guys. Our mates need to have a heart for the Lord.

In order for a house to have stability, it must have a solid foundation. The foundation of the guy and girl must be the same before marriage so that they can stand and work together on one united foundation. The foundation should be built on a relationship with God and a desire to follow His will. Luke 11:17 reminds us that "a house divided against itself falls." Trying to combine two different foundations can bring instability. The family is the basic unit of society, and we all naturally desire strong families. We should make wise choices before we get married to ensure that our marriages will last till death do us part. "Husbands, love your wives, just as Christ loved the church and gave Himself for her" (Ephesians 5:25).

LUKE PERSTROPE: *17, St. Peters, MO*
First Baptist Church of St. Charles, St. Charles, MO; Fort Zumwalt East High School, St. Peters, MO

ENJOYING YOUR FAITH

"But godliness with contentment is great gain." —*1 Timothy 6:6*

In a world where it is not popular to follow Christ, I find it difficult to find contentment in my faith at times, as I'm sure you do. Sometimes I feel like Christians can't have fun or that we are restricted far too much. Over the years, I've learned that I have more freedom as a believer in Christ. I've been called goody-goody and "one of the lame ones." Although it hurt for a little while, I've learned that, in the long run, I will be enjoying my life in Christ a lot more than they will enjoy life if they don't turn to Christ. Guys, it may not be cool to be a Christian right now, but God is enough. He can and will sustain you. He will give you joy no matter what circumstances you face. One important thing to remember is that the fun nonbelievers are having or seem to be having is only temporary. The joy you have in Christ is everlasting and can be spread to other believers and nonbelievers. I am learning how to be content in my faith and find joy, no matter what others say. Be your own man in Christ, and spread His love to all of your peers.

CHRISTOPHER COLEMAN BAILEY: *17, Albany, GA*
Greater Second Mt. Olive Baptist Church and Sherwood Christian Academy, Albany, GA

SPEAKING WISDOM

"The mouth of the righteous utters wisdom; his tongue speaks what is just." —*Psalm 37:30*

I believe our verse for today has two meanings: 1) God will speak through us, and 2) we need to speak words of truth. We should never worry about what to say when the time comes to witness, because God will speak through us what He wants to say, provided we have been in prayer and are learning from Him in Bible study. We can memorize tactics for what to say when someone asks us questions, but we should rely on God, not our own words, to minister the truth of the gospel to others. We also need to speak words of truth: the clean and perfect words of God. No unclean thing should proceed from our mouths, but just the opposite. Every day I hear Christians use the Lord's name in vain, and it is very sad the lack of remorse they feel for doing it. Yet, when they are confronted, they will either deny having said it or try to justify it. Not only is speaking it wrong, but to hear it and not speak against it is also wrong! Not speaking up against it or turning off the television when we hear it is not showing our protest against it. I have seen people, even friends, ignore hearing it, or simply filter it out. But if you confront someone about this matter, be sure that you are holding yourself accountable to the same standard you are holding them to.

JESSE D. SANDO: *13, Pleasant Hill, OH*
First Baptist Church, Vandalia, OH; Homeschooled

FAMILY NICKNAMES

"But you are a chosen race, a royal priesthood, a holy nation, a people for His possession, so that you may proclaim the praises of the One who called you out of darkness into His marvelous light." —1 Peter 2:9

Our family loves to call each other nicknames. We call my older brother "The Captain." My younger brothers are called "General" and "Mister Beast." I am affectionately referred to as "Mr. Incredible." When I played baseball my dad called me "Joel-man." Whenever I would make a good play or strike someone out, he would shout things like, "Way to go, Joel-man!" We call each other names to show our appreciation, friendship, encouragement, and love for each other. In this verse, God tells us who we are: We are a "chosen race"—that means that God has chosen us specially for Him. We are a "royal priesthood." God tells us that we can pray directly to Him. We are a "holy nation" through Jesus' sacrifice on the cross. And we are a "people for His possession." He not only tells us who we are in this passage, but He tells us what we are supposed to do. We are to proclaim His praises. God deserves all of the praise for sending His Son to provide our salvation. Even though we didn't deserve His love and His sacrifice, He sent Jesus to die on the cross for our sins. The Bible portrays sin as darkness and Jesus as being the ultimate light of the world (John 8:12). The Bible also says that Christians are to be the "light of the world" (Matthew 5:14). "You are the light of the world. A city situated on a hill cannot be hidden." Our life and our praise should give glory to God for rescuing us from darkness and testimony to those in the dark world. As believers we are to shine our light!

JOEL PERSTROPE: 15, St. Peters, MO
First Baptist Church of St. Charles, St. Charles, MO; Fort Zumwalt East High School, St. Peters, MO

DOES GOD EVER SEEM DISTANT TO YOU?

"Compassion and forgiveness belong to the LORD our God, though we have rebelled against Him." —*Daniel 9:9*

Do you ever feel like God is distant? The truth is that He never moves, but we do! Believers go through daily trials that test our faith. Sometimes we win the battles, but sometimes we fail. Even though we're forgiven, sometimes we feel as if God has turned His back on us. Let me tell you right now, God will never turn His back on you. You will always be His child, whom He loves dearly. Sometimes, though, we turn our backs on Him and don't even realize it. This is because we put other things in our lives that distract us. What distracts you from God? We all deal with this, especially in the world we have grown up in with all the technology. We always feel like we have to be entertained with something. This makes it very hard for God to be our center focus. Yet, it doesn't matter how many times we get distracted or turn our backs on God, He still loves us. His mercy and grace are always there for us to hold on to. He is always watching over you even when you mess up, because He is our Father. And, like any good father, He never stops loving or forgiving. Because He is our father, He also disciplines us. He does this because He loves us and wants to bring us back to His will. He loves you more than you could ever fathom, and He is always there for you. Take time to pray that God would reveal Himself to you, and thank Him for being there even when you turn your back on Him. Ask Him to let you feel the warmth of His love and forgiveness so that you may share it with others.

TREY SUEY: *16, Mt. Juliet, TN*
The Fellowship at Two Rivers, Nashville, TN; New Life Academy, Mt. Juliet, TN

HOMOSEXUALITY

"You are not to sleep with a man as with a woman; it is detestable." —Leviticus 18:22

Homosexuality is probably one of the most conflicting parts of life, especially for teens today. Hollywood wants to portray it as normal, and this sinful lifestyle is elevated even by men and women who make decisions for us: in schools, in politics, and in our communities. Trust me, at some point we will need to ask ourselves if it is a choice or not—and truthfully, it is. The Bible says that "You are not to sleep with a man as with a woman; it is detestable." This verse makes it clear that homosexuality is a sin. The choice is one more people today face than at any other time in history. The choice for those of us who know Jesus has to be that homosexuality is a sin against Him. People say they were born that way, but there must be a choice made to never give in to anything that will bring sin into a relationship with Jesus. We must decide to obey the Bible by forsaking every sin. By giving our lives to Jesus and asking Him to right all the wrongs in our lives by the blood that He shed for us on the cross, we know that He will protect us and help us to overcome these sins. God is all-loving and His grace is for us, so that we can live our lives for Him, even if we have been unfaithful to Him. He forgives His children and offers us hope for a future without depraved sin. God will forgive us, which gives us that much more to love about Him. We can trust Him with everything, even the stuff that confuses us.

DAVID JOSEPH DALESANDRO: *14, York, SC*
Hillcrest Baptist Church and York Comprehensive High School, York, SC

TATTOOS

"The law, then, was our guardian until Christ so that
we could be justified by faith. But since that faith has come,
we are no longer under a guardian." —*Galatians 3:24–25*

Tattoos and other types of marking of the body have become quite a debate in Christian circles. Many people see tattoos and think that it is a sin and not something Christians should have on their bodies, but I think the Bible teaches us something very different. In the Old Testament, Leviticus 19:28 reads, "You are not to make gashes on your bodies for the dead or put tattoo marks on yourselves; I am Yahweh." According to this passage, God says no tattoos at all, but early in the Bible God is trying to lead the Israelites away from the religious practices of the surrounding people. He set up laws to protect them from those practices. They had to be holy to be in God's favor. But Paul tells us we are under the law of the New Testament and of Jesus; we are not bound by laws of the Old Testament to gain or regain a right relationship with God. Tattoos worn by today's Christians have meaning. They are not pictures of demons or the Antichrist, but images to show love, glorify God, and to bring up questions of faith so that they can share the gospel.

ZACH WATKINS: *16, Henderson, NV*
Highland Hills Baptist Church and Green Valley High School, Henderson, NV

LIVING FOR GOD

"How happy is the man who does not follow the advice of the wicked or take the path of sinners or join a group of mockers!" —*Psalm 1:1*

Have you ever walked into a place and the first thing you hear is profanity? God's name being taken in vain? Gossip? These are sins that are in our world and in the everyday lives of many! It's so hard to believe, yet it is so true. It is very easy to slip ourselves and to not only hear these obscenities but to sometimes pick them up as a part of the way we talk. The truth is, there are many things that we all do that are sins, but we tend to consider them small and unimportant. We count ourselves as Christians because we go to church, read our Bibles, listen to Christian music, etc. What most of us don't realize is that there is so much more to being a Christian and we are missing out every day. Being a Christian is truly living for God! But living for God is so much more than just following the original routine. Instead of just going to church, we can take what we learned at church and allow God to apply it to our everyday lives. Instead of just listening to the tune of a song, we can actually hear the message through the lyrics. Once we make this a part of our routine and begin to live the life of a real Christian, others will start to see the difference in us. Before long, you might just end up bringing someone to Christ yourself!

BRANDON CARROLL: *17, York, SC*
Hillcrest Baptist Church and York Comprehensive High School, York, SC

RESIST

"Be serious! Be alert! Your adversary the Devil is prowling around like a roaring lion, looking for anyone he can devour."

—*1 Peter 5:8*

Satan is the adversary of every believer; appearing as an angel of light, casting illusions in every direction of happiness, satisfaction, and security. He takes advantage of joy and tries to make it sorrow, of relationships to create discord, of godliness and tempts us to sin. If we accept Christ as Lord of our lives, then we are saved; but Satan will take every opportunity to cripple us spiritually and make us not be dedicated or useful to God. John 8:44 calls Satan the father of liars. We must test everything against what we know God's will is through His Word. If we don't, Satan will try to deceive us, promising fulfillment from one side of his mouth and spewing emptiness, sadness, and loneliness from the other side. Satan never keeps his word! He will offer you things that are against God's will or something you want. But you will not experience fulfillment, you'll be drawn away from God! It is only through the sacrifice of Jesus Christ that we have the power to overcome Satan and choose to say no to the temptations he presents to us. Despite this power, I still falter and give in to the temptations of this world. Jesus is the only One who will never mislead us. God's Word and prayer are our defenses against the Devil. James 4:7 says, "Submit to God. But resist the Devil, and he will flee from you." Psalm 31:24 says, "Be strong and courageous, all you who put your hope in the LORD." And 2 Corinthians 10:5 tells us to take "every thought captive to obey Christ." Resist the devil and live a victorious life for God! Amen.

LUKE MERRICK: *15, Springdale, AR*
Immanuel Baptist Church and Shiloh Christian School, Springdale, AR

TRIALS OF LIFE

"A man who endures trials is blessed, because when he passes the test he will receive the crown of life that God has promised to those who love Him." —James 1:12

We all face hardships throughout our lives. At times it seems like God just won't give you a break, and sometimes life might be going pretty smooth for you. Although difficult trials seem overwhelming sometimes, we need to realize that life isn't easy, and God sends trials in our lives to test us. God tests all of His children. Two people in the Bible who went through many hardships were Job and the apostle Paul. Job was such a great servant of God that Satan bet God that Job would crack and blaspheme Him if He took away his possessions, family, and health. But Job passed every test and never blasphemed God, although he did question Him. Then God gave Job back two times what he had owned before. He also gave him seven more sons, three more beautiful daughters, and a long life. Paul, who used to be a persecutor of Christians, became a Christian himself and lived to serve the Lord. Paul went through many trials, but still served God unwaveringly. Paul was continually thrown into prison, shipwrecked three times, and even survived a stoning! And those are only a few of the many horrendous things he endured for the cause of Christ. God tested these two individuals to keep them relying on Him and to show their devotion and love for Him. The same goes for you. Look how the lives of Job and Paul continue to help Christians today to live their lives for God. Whatever you are going through, know that you can go to God for help and comfort, and He will help you through it.

WYATT CHAPMAN: *17, Pageland, SC*
South Pointe Fellowship and South Pointe Christian School, Pageland, SC

JULY

Avoid Seduction

My son, pay attention to my wisdom; listen closely to my understanding so that you may maintain discretion and your lips safeguard knowledge. Though the lips of the forbidden woman drip honey and her words are smoother than oil, in the end she's as bitter as wormwood and as sharp as a double-edged sword.

Her feet go down to death; her steps head straight for Sheol.

She doesn't consider the path of life; she doesn't know that her ways are unstable.

So now, my sons, listen to me, and don't turn away from the words of my mouth.

Keep your way far from her. Don't go near the door of her house.

Otherwise, you will give up your vitality to others and your years to someone cruel; strangers will drain your resources, and your earnings will end up in a foreigner's house.

At the end of your life, you will lament when your physical body has been consumed, and you will say, "How I hated discipline, and how my heart despised correction.

I didn't obey my teachers or listen closely to my mentors. I am on the verge of complete ruin before the entire community." (Proverbs 5:1–14)

ENEMIES

"But I tell you, love your enemies and pray for those who persecute you, so that you may be sons of your Father in heaven. For He causes His sun to rise on the evil and the good, and sends rain on the righteous and the unrighteous." —*Matthew 5:44–45*

Enemies. We all have them. They're people who dislike us, and we feel the same way about them most of the time. Most of our enemies are bullies. I know I should return their actions with kindness, but sometimes I can't do it by myself. I need God's help. We all need to be a good example to our enemies. What if they don't like you because you're rude to them? When I would rather pummel a kid, I instead return their fire with water. I don't return the attack; I send back coolness to the heat. I was not always like this. I experienced something like this once when, for some reason that was beyond me, a guy hated me. I was called names and other offensive things were said about my family and me. I was fed up with the constant attacks, and one day I snapped at my family and my pets. Then I realized that I should not take out my anger on them, but instead spill out all my feelings to God. As I prayed, I felt that God told me not only to forgive, but also to love. I went and forgave and asked for forgiveness. I then offered to be a friend. He didn't want to, but he never bothered me again. I knew that I had obeyed God. And I continued to pray for the guy. Only God can change a heart, even those who are using you as a verbal punching bag.

TERRELL STRAIN: *13, Spokane, WA*
Airway Heights Baptist Church, Airway Heights, WA; Medical Lake Middle School, Medical Lake, WA

DATING

"Do not be deceived: 'Bad company corrupts good morals.'"
—*1 Corinthians 15:33*

Dating is one of the most widely discussed topics among teenagers and young adults. I mean, come on. Who doesn't like telling their friends about that cute guy or girl they met at the mall the other day or about finally asking the girl you've liked for months out on a date? But you have to ask yourself one question: Am I glorifying God? Every relationship should have God at the center, especially dating. Nothing works without God's help and interaction. Would you be able to live if you didn't have God? Would anything be able to survive without God (see Ephesians 2:1–10)? If life is impossible without God, what makes dating any different? Now everyone's parents have a different set of rules for dating. Some might say, "Go for it." But if your parents are anything like mine, there are a lot of guidelines. I've tried several times to date someone, but all it ever brought me was a broken heart and frustration. God has someone special for everyone, and He gives us guidance about relationships in His Word. Dating is meant to be something special and pure with thoughts of a future. If that's not the case, then what's the point? The less you date the better. That way you save yourself for your future spouse and can give her something no one else has had. Don't feel frustrated and pressured into getting into a relationship because all your friends are. God has someone special out there just for you. There is a perfect time and place for you to meet that perfect person. And in the end, it will be well worth the wait.

NICHOLAS BERGER: *15, Fairchild Air Force Base, Airway Heights, WA Airway Heights Baptist Church, Airway Heights, WA; Homeschooled*

PRAYER FROM THE HEART

"Therefore I tell you, all the things you pray and ask for-believe that you have received them, and you will have them." —Mark 11:24

Sometimes I have a week filled with activity and find that I tend to forget about GOD. I have short quick prayers in the morning that hold little meaning. I'm not really thinking about those prayers and how to praise Jesus through them. I ask Him for things, not really having faith in those requests and remembering Mark 11:24: "Therefore I tell you, whatever you ask for in prayer, believe that you have received it, and it will be yours." When this happens, I try to remember how great a blessing it really is to be free to have a personal conversation with God, especially when many around the world cannot do that for fear of persecution. In the Old Testament, only the special priests could enter into the holy room where God lived. If anyone else did, they died. And now, we get to talk to Him whenever we like! This is not an opportunity to waste or to take lightly. It's important for us to remember to pray when our hearts are in tune to our relationship with Jesus. It's not just a time for us to check things off our list that we are asking Him for. God has given us this wonderful opportunity, because He loves us. Let's not waste it.

MATTHEW COOKSEY: *13, McMinnville, OR*
Valley Baptist Church, McMinnville, OR; Homeschooled

LOVING ONE ANOTHER, FORGIVING OTHERS, AND BULLYING

"Then Peter came to Him and said, 'Lord, how many times could my brother sin against me and I forgive him? As many as seven times?' 'I tell you, not as many as seven,' Jesus said to him, 'but 70 times seven.'"

—*Matthew 18:21–22*

It's a tough command sometimes. Have you ever been somewhere, say school, and someone called you a name or maybe they are spreading rumors, or picking on you. Whatever they are doing or have done, you can forgive them! Jesus did not say "Oh, I can't forgive that one because he committed such a painful sin and it hurt me and others to the core. Did He? No! We also need to love one another. Let's look to God's Word for help by looking deeply at the verse for today that deals with forgiving others. Jesus is telling us that even though someone might commit a horrible sin against you, then continues to sin over and over again, and, well, you get the point. But you can forgive! Just remember what Jesus said to Peter in Matthew 18:22 and let Him teach you how to forgive even the worst offender. After all, that is what God did for us when He sent His Son, Jesus, to die on the cross!

HANK F. GRIFFIN: *14, Pageland, SC*
White Plains Baptist Church, Jefferson, SC; South Pointe Christian School, Pageland, SC

UNASHAMED

"For I am not ashamed of the gospel, because it is God's power for salvation to everyone who believes, first to the Jew, and also to the Greek." —Romans 1:16

Am I ashamed of the gospel? This is a question I recently asked myself. God has been teaching me about being more bold and living out my faith, no matter where I am or what the situation is. Last year, I went to my local tech school for a class. I eventually figured out that I and one other student were the only Christians in the class. Throughout that whole year, I don't think I ever made it clear that I was a follower of Christ. I mean, I was a good kid, who they knew didn't curse, do drugs, or anything else like that. However, I never mentioned God around them. I wanted to be a good example but still wanted to fit in with all the other kids there. I was afraid that if I talked about God, they would think of me as a religious nut. God convicted me about my behavior. We shouldn't be ashamed or afraid to speak out for Christ or to stand up for Him. Our lives should show that we're living differently and preparing for eternity, not that we're caught up in the things of this world. We need to desire praise from God more than we desire praise from man. Our lives should clearly reflect that we've been changed and that there's something different about us. Let me challenge you with this quote from Francis Chan: "Having faith means doing what others see as crazy. Something is wrong if your life makes sense to unbelievers" (Francis Chan, *Crazy Love*, Colorado Springs: David C. Cook, 2nd ed. 2013). Finally, pray for courage and boldness. Sometimes the best way to take a stand is by getting on our knees. Always remember what 2 Timothy 1:7 says: "For God has not given us a spirit of fearfulness, but one of power, love, and sound judgment." Let's live our lives unashamed of the cross of Jesus Christ!

AUSTIN CANFIELD: *18, Tulsa, OK*
Evergreen Baptist Church, Bixby, OK; Homeschooled

POWER IN WORDS

"Then Peter came to Him and said, 'Lord, how many times could my brother sin against me and I forgive him? As many as seven times?' 'I tell you, not as many as seven,' Jesus said to him, 'but 70 times seven.'" —*Matthew 18:21–22*

Let me start off by asking you a question: Has someone ever done something to you that you couldn't forgive them for? After Jesus had come to the earth to preach the message of God's Word and save the lost that would believe and receive Him, He was arrested, beaten, and tortured beyond recognition. And as if that was not enough, Jesus was nailed to a cross to suffer pain like we have never known, and He did so for hours. This was, of course, all part of God's plan for Jesus. The reason He came in the first place was not just to be born and live on the earth like a man for thirty-three years, but He came to die for us! But at the end of it all, while He was hanging on the cross, Jesus said, "Father, forgive them, because they do not know what they are doing" (Luke 23:34). So after all of the mocking, humiliation, and horrible suffering, Jesus was able to forgive them. He forgave each person. And He is ready to forgive you, no matter what sin you have committed.

JACOB LAVALLEY: *16, Pageland, SC*
Mount Moriah Baptist Church and South Pointe Christian School, Pageland, SC

UNABLE TO FAIL

"My flesh and my heart may fail, but God is the strength of my heart, my portion forever." —*Psalm 73:26*

Do you ever feel like a failure? Like you just can't go on anymore? Do you ever feel like everything you do just never goes your way? I tend to feel like this a lot, and I think a lot of teenagers do. Are we just scared of failure? Scared of messing up? I know it is a huge problem when everything seems so crucial with school and sports and just life itself. It seems everything has to be done with perfection and at a certain time without any questions or leeway; and when that's the case, it seems almost impossible not to fail. But, what if we had the mind-set where we physically and spiritually could not fail? Why don't we start telling ourselves this: "Hey, today God is with me wherever I go; therefore, I cannot fail." What in the world would you want to do if you knew that, no matter what, you could not fail? Think of all the things you could do for God; you could bring an entire continent to Christ! So, when life just seems so hard and it looks like our only option is failure, let's tell ourselves that we can't fail because we have Jesus in us, and Jesus never fails! Let's think to ourselves, Today, I cannot fail, for I have God and I will do whatever it takes to bring glory to Him.

KORD OFFENBACKER: *16, Springdale, AR*
Cross Church Springdale Campus and Shiloh Christian School, Springdale, AR

LYING

"Do not lie to one another, since you have put off the old self with its practices." —*Colossians 3:9*

It is, sadly, a common misconception among even Christians that lying and deception are justifiable in certain situations. But we must always remember Colossians 3:9. This verse doesn't say, "Don't lie unless . . ." When I first heard this I thought, But, it's OK to lie when protecting someone or doing it for a good reason, right? But according to this passage, I guess not. I mean, God has enough power to accomplish His plans without having us sin in the process, right? Psalm 24:4–5 says, "The one who has clean hands and a pure heart, who has not set his mind on what is false and who has not sworn deceitfully. He will receive blessing from the LORD, and righteousness from the God of his salvation." The Lord takes promises and swearing very seriously, and if we swear deceitfully He hates it. God also says He'll bless those who keep themselves completely far and free from dishonesty and who say: "My lips will not speak unjustly and my tongue will not utter deceit" (Job 27:4). And, when God says that He's going to bless us, He means it, and a blessing from God is far better than any temporal thing of this world that could be gained by lying. And non-Christians see honesty and want to know why we don't ever lie, giving us opportunity to be a witness and an example of the true change Christ can make.

MATTHEW COOKSEY: *13, McMinnville, OR*
Valley Baptist Church, McMinnville, OR; Homeschooled

THE TASK
(PART 1)

"My mouth will tell about Your righteousness and Your salvation all day long, though I cannot sum them up." —*Psalm 71:15*

Have you ever thought that you did not have a good enough testimony to share the gospel? Sharing your testimony is a essential for ministry. Ministry is not an easy task, because the devil will use anything to tear you down or make you scared about sharing. If you ever have that feeling, remember that Christ is in you. Where you go He goes, and where Christ goes, the evil powers that surrounded you have to retreat. You don't have to be a missionary overseas, sometimes just a smile or hello can go a long way with someone who is hurting. The key to sharing God's love is to "gossip the gospel." Acts 4:12 tells all of us that, "There is salvation in no one else, for there is no other name under heaven given to people, and we must be saved by it." Tell them that we are sinners, imperfect and selfish, and that a loving and perfect God made Himself available to us as a free blood offering for our sins. Explain what the cross means. Ministry feels really overwhelming in the beginning, but I can't tell you the joy and pleasure you get when you start sharing God's unconditional love. It will change your life, and others might come to know Jesus as their Lord and Savior.

COLLIN MICHAEL SEELEN: *18, Itami, Hyogo, Japan*
Emmanuel Baptist Church and Kansai Homeschooled Network, Itami, Hyogo, Japan

THE TASK
(PART 2)

"My mouth will tell about Your righteousness and Your salvation all day long, though I cannot sum them up." —*Psalm 71:15*

If you're an outgoing person, I want to encourage you to approach someone you know who is hurting and tell them about the deep hurting pain you, too, felt before you accepted Christ as your Savior, then explain the love that God has given you. It will be rough and sometimes uncomfortable, but when you do the Holy Spirit will overwhelm you with the words to say. Maybe you're a quiet person and not as outgoing as others, but if you see someone struggling stop right there and pray for them. The power of prayer is strong and it will speak volumes to them. When you know the time is right, approach them and let them know that you have been praying for them because you care. Then you can encourage them to feel better. There is hope in Christ. If you are still scared, consider going with a friend to witness. Our Father has given us a great task to tell the world about His love with help and encouragement from His Holy Word. As we read in Romans 1:16, "For I am not ashamed of the gospel, because it is God's power for salvation to everyone who believes, first to the Jew, and also to the Greek." God will give us His grace for the task, so let's do it for Him and for eternity.

COLLIN MICHAEL SEELEN: *18, Itami, Hyogo, Japan*
Emmanuel Baptist Church, and Kansai Homeschooled Network, Itami, Hyogo, Japan

MANAGE YOUR TIME

"Pay careful attention, then, to how you walk—not as unwise people but as wise—making the most of the time, because the days are evil. So don't be foolish, but understand what the Lord's will is." —*Ephesians 5:15–17*

Today's teens are juggling school, church, family, friends, hobbies, and it's difficult to maintain a relationship with God. He understands our busyness, but He also expects His children to not use that as an excuse to not stay in His Word and do His will. Too often we float through life and almost forget about what God has done for us until Sunday, when we refuel and think about Him and promise to live for Him. Then on Monday morning we forget all about Him because other things take over our desires and attention. God desires that we spend time daily reading His Word and praying to Him, so we will be in tune to His will for our lives. God is not opposed to you being busy. He wants to use you in every situation in your life to promote the gospel. I used to think that playing sports would challenge my spiritual life. I was worried that all the time I took up with sports would get in the way of time for discipleship groups and to read the Word. God is teaching me that sports are fine, but to use sports to be a light for Him. I had to cut out things that I believed were hindering my walk with Him: too much television or hanging out with the wrong friends. Pastor and author Max Lucado put it this way in a devotional on February 5, 2011: "Being busy, in and of itself, is not a sin but being busy on an endless pursuit of things that leave us empty and hollow and broken inside—cannot be pleasing to God" (UpWords © The Teaching Ministry of Max Lucado, http://www.crosswalk.com/devotionals/upwords).

WILLIAM DAVID ORR: *17, Albany, GA*
Sherwood Baptist Church and Sherwood Christian Academy, Albany, GA

TEMPORARY LIFE ON EARTH

"Oh, Lord God! You Yourself made the heavens and earth by Your great power and with Your outstretched arm. Nothing is too difficult for You!" —*Jeremiah 32:17*

American culture is heavily focused on self; we want it, and we want it when we want it! Our greed comes at the disadvantage of others or disobedience to God. It isn't always severe, though. Possessions, power, and money often distract from what is important. Fear, opposition, and heartache can seem too large to tackle. I think our failure to faithfully follow and trust God is a result of our diminished view of Him. We understand and are grateful that Jesus died for us, we know God is there, but sometimes we do not live or act like it. The right perspective on who our God really is would be helpful. This is the God who hung the heavens in the sky, the God who formed the universe out of nothing, the God who calms oceans with a spoken word, the God who sees beauty in ashes. How big must God be to create a universe that has an expanse that blows our minds? How much love must God have to sacrifice His own Son for the love of wretched sinners? There is no one before God. God is the essence of everything: His reign encompasses everything, His kingdom existed for an eternity past and will exist for all eternity. With the right view of God, our mountain-sized problems would melt away. Our service to Him would be an honor and not an obligation, and our fears would pass away. We would then be confident that if we fall—no matter how big the mountains, how hot the deserts, or how cold the winters—God is a loving Dad. Our new thinking will change the way we live.

LUKE MERRICK: *15, Springdale, AR*
Immanuel Baptist Church and Shiloh Christian School, Springdale, AR

PRESSURE FROM PEERS

"The one who walks with the wise will become wise,
but a companion of fools will suffer harm." —*Proverbs 13:20*

One May afternoon a few years ago I was at a high school graduation for my cousin. There is one thing I remember clearly from that day. Right after the ceremony, my family went to congratulate the graduate and take pictures. After taking more than enough pictures, one of my aunts turned to my cousin and said something intriguing: "Glad to see you, but I think right now you should go talk to your high school friends. Some of them you will never see after today." I thought, Wow, there are kids at my school that I spend 180 days a year with that I may never see again once I graduate. But in today's world, teenagers will spend their entire lives trying to impress people that will not matter to them at all once they get their diplomas. God does not want us to worry about how cool or popular we are, because He knows that if someone is trying to impress people all the time, they will not be able to live effectively for Him. Being sold out for Christ seldom means doing the popular thing. A good example is found in 1 Kings 18 when Elijah was the only outspoken Christian from the people of Israel at that time. Because of his faith in God, he was granted victory over the false prophets of Baal. If Elijah had wanted to be popular, he would not have declared God to be the one true God but would have gone along with whatever was said by the king. God wants us to trust Him. Because of Elijah's willingness to trust God, many became believers. How many people do you think would come to Christ if you forgot about being popular but let Christ shine through you?

WILLIAM DAVID ORR: *17, Albany, GA*
Sherwood Baptist Church and Sherwood Christian Academy, Albany, GA

THE POWER OF THE TONGUE

"The one who guards his mouth and tongue keeps himself out of trouble."
—*Proverbs 21:23*

The tongue is a powerful tool and one that is impossible to completely control. It is easy to say something out of habit or pressure that you immediately wish you could take back. Similar to not being able to put toothpaste back in the tube once you squirt it out, we cannot take our words back most of the time. And we all know that the phrase "Sticks and stones can break my bones, but words can never hurt me" is untrue. We have all been hurt by a friend who has said something without realizing the damage it caused. However, we can only control what we ourselves say. We must continually be aware of the situation we are in and decide how to speak accordingly. Ecclesiastes 3:7 says that there is "a time to be silent and a time to speak." This verse is one that must be on our hearts and minds to affect our choice of words. Also, an ancient proverb says, "It is better to be silent and people think you a fool than to open your mouth and remove all doubt." What we say around others often determines what people think of us. Do you like spending time with someone who is constantly bossy? How about someone who always argues? No, and the same goes for other people who use their tongues to tear down and destroy. Be aware of how you talk to others and always remember that things are easily taken the wrong way. So, as you go about your day, think twice before you speak and always respond in a way that glorifies the Lord.

JONATHAN DISMUKES: *17, Mobile, AL*
Redeemer Fellowship Church and Cottage Hill Christian Academy, Mobile, AL

WHOLLY HIS

"For it is written, 'Be holy, because I am holy.'" —*1 Peter 1:16*

To be holy is to be set apart, to be vastly different in a positive way. For Christians, being holy is usually considered an unreachable benchmark that we are to continue to strive for. For God, however, being holy is what He is. He is the Holy One, the Great I Am. The Bible says for us to be holy, because He is holy. This verse may seem cliché to some. But in all actuality, it is truly God's calling for how we should live our lives; just as Christ did, holy and blameless. Now obviously we cannot achieve such a goal, for we are innately sinners and simply cannot stop sinning. However, God didn't give such an impossible calling just to prove Himself better than all other beings but, rather, to give us a goal and a purpose in life and to convince us that there is no way to be completely blemish-free outside of His love. To give your entire self to God and to simply, as Carrie Underwood sings, let "Jesus take the wheel" of your life is the only way to be holy. I put it like this: We must be wholly His, for He is Holy.

BRADY FOWLKES: *16, Tuscaloosa, AL*
Valley View Baptist Church and Hillcrest High School, Tuscaloosa, AL

THE CHOICE TO PROCEED (PART 1)

"Woe is me for I am ruined because I am a man of unclean lips. . . . Then one of the seraphim flew to me, and in his hand was a glowing coal that he had taken from the altar with tongs. He touched my mouth with it and said: Now that this has touched your lips, your wickedness is removed and your sin is atoned for. Then I heard the voice of the Lord saying: Who should I send? Who will go for Us? I said: Here I am. Send me." —Isaiah 6:5–8

When my youth pastor talked with me about writing for a teen devotional, I was hesitant. I wasn't scared of what people might think, or even something I wrote would sound foolish or bad. I was concerned about other things. Let me explain it this way: Have you ever felt that you were right about something biblically or spiritually but weren't sure whether to say something due to that slight doubt in your mind that you could be wrong? Well, that's along the lines of what I was feeling. I was worried about saying something that was wrong or incorrect. After all, these are issues dealing with people's spiritual lives. I was being asked to offer encouragement and help to my peers! And, to add pressure to that, I had a short time to decide. I went home and talked with my parents about it, later prayed about it, thought about it, and then did the same things all over again. The decision weighed on my mind. Then, as you have likely done in your own life, I took out the Bible and read, hoping to find an answer. The reading that day (which is just like God!) was from Isaiah 6. God used those verses, written years ago, to guide me in my decision.

ROBBY D. LAND: *18, Gatlinburg, TN*
First Baptist Church and Gatlinburg-Pittman High School, Gatlinburg, TN

THE CHOICE TO PROCEED (PART 2)

"Now that this has touched your lips, your wickedness is removed and your sin is atoned for. Then I heard the voice of the Lord saying: Who should I send? Who will go for Us? I said: Here I am, Send me."

—Isaiah 6:7–8

A request to be a contributing writer for a devotional for my peers caused me to worry about telling others about spiritual issues, especially when I felt I wasn't doing the right things myself. I was concerned about speaking biblical truth. So was Isaiah, which is explained in Isaiah 6. Isaiah saw the Lord and was scared thinking about "his unclean lips." But a creature flew over to Isaiah with a coal in his hand and touched Isaiah's lips, telling him that his sin has been atoned for. This made me think that Isaiah was concerned and even scared like I was, but his sin was atoned for. But instead of a coal, Jesus atoned for my sin. Isaiah was freed and so was I. "Then I heard the voice of the Lord saying, 'Who should I send? Who will go for Us?'" Isaiah stepped right up. I, on the other hand, was still apprehensive. I always want things to be solidly set out. I doubt and fall short, second-guessing myself and even the facts. But God made that so clear to me and continued to guide me, and I decided that the right choice was for me to write. You may hear about your pastors, parents, maybe even your friends saying they found the answers to their questions in the Bible. It can happen for us teens too. Just pay attention and search. God says that He will be our teacher. Fact is, we have to allow Him to do that through prayer, through Bible reading, and by listening to wise godly counsel.

ROBBY D. LAND: *18, Gatlinburg, TN*
First Baptist Church and Gatlinburg-Pittman High School, Gatlinburg, TN

PROCRASTINATION

"You also be ready, because the Son of Man is coming at an hour that you do not expect." —Luke 12:40

Procrastination. It's honestly one of the worst things you can do. It's one of the two problems I have that make my life so much harder. Have you ever waited until the last minute to do something, anything? Every single time I have homework or a project to do, I always put it off to the side and say to myself, "I have time." You probably wouldn't be reading this right now because of my extreme procrastination; but by the grace of God, you are! Proverbs 13:4 tell us that, "The slacker craves, yet has nothing, but the diligent is fully satisfied." I also am lazy with sharing my faith. I say to myself again, "I have time" or "Someone else will get to them in church." I have to realize that I may be the only Bible in someone's life. If you're a major procrastinator like I am, please learn to discipline yourself and do your work, no matter how hard it is. If you're a Christian, and you procrastinate with your faith, please reach out to people with the gospel message. They could be on their way to hell, and you may be the only person they know who knows the truth. Don't put away progress, and you will have success! "I am able to do all things through Him who strengthens me" (Philippians 4:13).

CHRISTIAN SMITH: *17, New Orleans, LA*
Franklin Avenue Baptist Church and New Orleans Charter Science and Mathematics High School, New Orleans, LA

THE SHORT-LIVED PLEASURE OF SIN

"By faith Moses, when he had grown up, refused to be called the son of Pharaoh's daughter and chose to suffer with the people of God rather than to enjoy the short-lived pleasure of sin." —*Hebrews 11:24–25*

Everyone wants to live a happy, joyful life, filled with fun and laughter. They don't want to experience consequences, pain, and trouble. There are too many people out there living in the heat of the moment and making sinful choices. Then later, when consequences and afterthoughts begin to set in, it leaves them wondering, What was I thinking? People just get caught up in the present and do whatever is fun and cool without thinking about their future. When I was about seven years old a babysitter brought a whole can of frosting to my house. At the time, I, being a huge frosting fan, decided that I would eat as much frosting as I could. My babysitter tried to give me advice like, "Don't eat too much! You'll get sick!" But I had never gotten sick on frosting before, so why worry now? While I was eating the frosting, and for the next two or three hours, I was living the life. I was so happy, so full, so satisfied. I felt great. But, later that night my foolish decision haunted me as I had trouble sleeping and threw up not once, not twice, but eight times in the night. My failure to listen to the advice given to me, and my desire to satisfy my own wants without considering the consequences, took its toll. Sin is the same way. It can feel fun and you can enjoy the moment, but it ultimately brings consequences. Moses knew the pleasure of staying in Pharaoh's house would be short-lived. Sin can be fun for a moment, but it always costs.

JOEL PERSTROPE: *15, St. Peters, MO*
First Baptist Church of St. Charles, St. Charles, MO; Fort Zumwalt East High School, St. Peters, MO

GOD WASHES OUR SINS AWAY

"And from Jesus Christ, the faithful witness, the firstborn from the dead and the ruler of the kings of the earth. To Him who loves us and has set us free from our sins by his blood, and made us a kingdom, priests to His God and Father–the glory and dominion are His forever and ever Amen."

—Revelation 1:5–6

When we were children, we were dependent creatures. We couldn't provide for ourselves, feed ourselves or clean ourselves. One of my parents' favorite baby pictures of me is a bathtub shot that has my name, LUKE, spelled across my chest in small foam letters that I played with in the tub. Like all babies, my parents had to make sure that I was clean because I couldn't clean myself. This passage talks about how Jesus has cleansed us with His blood by dying on the cross for our sin. In the Old Testament, Isaiah 64:6 tells us that our "righteous acts are like a polluted garment." If this is what our righteousness looks like, imagine how horrendous our sins (all of our bad thoughts, all of our ugly words, and all of our disobedient deeds) look to God. Sin stains us worse than we can ever imagine. The effect sin has on our lives is much greater than we realize and stains us so deeply that we could never cleanse ourselves. You may be reading this book and feel like you do not know for certain that your sins have been forgiven. You can never earn your way to heaven by trying to clean up your own life or by doing good deeds. Jesus is the one who paid the penalty for your sins and washed them with His blood, so that you could enter God's kingdom. Call on Him for salvation, trust what He has done on the cross, and receive Him in your life.

LUKE PERSTROPE: 17, St. Peters, MO
First Baptist Church of St. Charles, St. Charles, MO; Fort Zumwalt East High School, St. Peters, MO

SHARING THE FAITH

"The 11 disciples traveled to Galilee, to the mountain where Jesus had directed them. When they saw Him, they worshiped, but some doubted. Then Jesus came near and said to them, 'All authority has been given to Me in heaven and on earth. Go, therefore, and make disciples of all nations, baptizing them in the name of the Father and of the Son and of the Holy Spirit, teaching them to observe everything I have commanded you. And remember, I am with you always, to the end of the age.'"

—*Matthew 28:16–20*

From around the world or to our neighbors, we should be fishers of men. Jesus calls us to share our faith, and to not only witness to people but to make disciples. We need to continue to teach them more after they ask Jesus to come into their lives. After someone is baptized, they need to learn as much as they can about Christ's commandments and to become disciples of Christ, so that they can make more disciples. There are two people in my small group Bible study that got saved, and it is awesome to watch the Great Commission in action. They have become disciple-makers and are making an impact for the kingdom. All believers should desire to bring people to Christ. It can be really hard to tell your friends and family about Christ, but I think it should be our biggest desire for them to come to Christ, because they are the ones we love most. When Jesus called Simon, Simon immediately went to his brother Andrew with the good news. We should do the same with the same urgency. Our goal should be to win lost souls to the Lord.

MICAH PERSTROPE: *13, St. Peters, MO*
First Baptist Church of St. Charles, St. Charles, MO; Dubray Middle School, St. Peters, MO

DEPRESSION

"The LORD is near the brokenhearted; He saves those crushed in spirit."

—*Psalm 34:18*

We all have our low days; sometimes those days tend to come in clusters. Sometimes those days turn into weeks and even months, with seemingly no end in sight. When we get depressed we can find ourselves hardly able to function or to move. So what do we turn to? We all have something that will allow us to move on: music, drawing, sleeping for long periods of time, and many other things come to mind. What about God, where does He find a place on that list? Psalm 34:18 tells us "The LORD is near the brokenhearted; He saves those crushed in spirit." So, when we find ourselves depressed for whatever reason, God is near to us and can reach us in spectacular ways. All we have to do is turn to Him, but this isn't what many of us do first. We often try many other helps and ignore Him and block the world out with whatever we turn to. Maybe you're not the one depressed; maybe it's a friend, or a family member. As Christians, we need to try to lead them to God and help them in their time of need. Sometimes we all need a friend to pick us up; we shouldn't be ashamed of being depressed. If you feel all alone, just remember: God always stands with you and He will always comfort you in your time of need. He graciously makes Himself available to us, when we feel on top of the world and when we feel terribly brokenhearted. No matter what the situation, we can trust that God is there for us.

DAVID JOSEPH DALESANDRO: *14, York, SC*
Hillcrest Baptist Church and York Comprehensive High School, York, SC

MOVING TO A NEW CITY

"'For I know the plans I have for you'-this is the Lord's declaration-'plans for your welfare, not for disaster, to give you a future and a hope.'" —*Jeremiah 29:11*

Change is hard. For ten years I lived in Panama City, Florida. I had a great home, a church I was comfortable in, and a school that I loved. I definitely can't forget my friends—I had tons of them! One day I got the news from my parents that we were going to move to Albany, Georgia. At first, I didn't like the idea at all! I didn't want to leave all the things I had grown up with. As I talked to my parents, though, it became obvious that God had a plan for me. My dad told me we would be going to a church called Sherwood Baptist Church, which was the church that made the movies called *Courageous, Facing the Giants,* and *Fireproof.* At first I was nervous about going there, because it was a huge church! But the moment I stepped into my Sunday school class, all of the people welcomed me and I felt wanted. Three and a half years have passed, and all those people in that first class are still my closest friends. Last year I went to a camp and felt God calling me to be a pastor of a church. The move was part of God's plan for me. I now realize that if none of these changes had happened, I would never have met all of my friends and would not have attended the camp where God called me to be a pastor. My story is a perfect example of how God has a plan for your future. If you struggle with change, just remember that it's all part of God's plan, and His plan is what's best for you!

ANDREW CLEM: *13, Albany, GA*
Sherwood Baptist Church and Sherwood Christian Academy, Albany, GA

YOUR FRIENDS

"How good and pleasant it is when brothers live together in harmony!"
—*Psalm 133:1*

Pretty much everyone has friends, but it's good to know how to be with friends. Your friends probably already like you, but if you're really good to them it will reward you later. My friends could tell you I'm not all there yet. If you give your friends priority, they will enjoy being around you more. And later they will give you priority. If you talk all the time, they will prefer to talk with other people. But if you listen a lot, they will like talking with you. You don't have to be super formal, just be nice and don't take over conversations. Sports are fun to play, especially with friends. And it's easy to get competitive, which isn't necessarily bad. But being too competitive can be annoying to other people, especially when you argue. I like to play foursquare with my friends after church. Sometimes they'll say I'm out when I'm sure I'm still in. But when you're a good sport you will get respect. I used to never admit I was out, and I'm sure I was biased. People got really annoyed. I eventually learned that it's really not that big of a deal to go to the back of the line. Your friends will probably be around your age. But that doesn't mean you can't be nice to people that aren't near your age. I'm fifteen, and I enjoy playing Ping-Pong, basketball, volleyball, and foursquare with kids from nine to eighteen. Sometimes adults play too! Good friends will be there for you later. This week I could not play outside because of an injury, so my friends played cards with me inside. If you are a good friend, you will find your friends to be rewarding in the end.

JOSHUA COOKSEY: *15, McMinnville, OR*
Valley Baptist Church, McMinnville, OR; Homeschooled

GIVING OUR ALL TO GOD

"Because they disregarded the righteousness from God and attempted to establish their own righteousness, they have not submitted themselves to God's righteousness." —*Romans 10:3*

Why do I refuse the Lord and not submit to Him everything within me? Our verse for today is telling us that man, you and I, are simply ignorant to the will of God, and we do not submit to His righteousness. I tried to establish my own righteousness through works and did not submit to God's authority. I think that I refused God in certain areas of my life because I was afraid He might take my life in a different direction than I wanted. And sure enough, once I submitted that area to Christ, He took it and spun me around in a completely different way. That automatically forced me to realize that my idea was obviously not what God wanted for my life, and that I wasn't following what God intended for me. As Jeremiah 29:11 says: "'For I know the plans I have for you'—this is the LORD's declaration—'plans for your welfare, not for disaster, to give you a future and a hope.'" The way I take this verse is this: God's ways are better than my own. My plans are a straight road to disaster and destruction, but God's plans are prosperous. His plans will not harm me but, ultimately, my plans will. If you are willing to follow Him, give all you have for Him, He will never disappoint you. So next time you are struggling to submit an area of your life to Christ, remember that His plans are going to make you prosperous, but only if you are willing to follow them.

JESSE D. SANDO: *13, Pleasant Hill, OH*
First Baptist Church, Vandalia, OH; Homeschooled

THE POWER OF THE GOSPEL

"For I am not ashamed of the gospel, because it is
God's power for salvation to everyone who believes,
first to the Jew, and also to the Greek." —*Romans 1:16*

One of my friends started to regularly attend church and our guy's small group a few months ago. He started asking questions about salvation. After a Bible study one night, at our dining room table, he prayed to receive Jesus Christ. His salvation was a great joy to all of us! His life was eternally changed. He then wanted to be baptized. By going to church and digging into the Word, he grew in knowledge of the Scriptures and became passionate about the Word. He didn't keep this to himself! He invited friends and he brought other friends. A few months later, one of my friend's friends was saved and baptized. Both of these guys are pursuing Christlikeness and are being lights in a dark world. Everyone said that these guys were completely different than they were in their presalvation days. We sometimes forget about the power of the gospel. People around our schools try to push it out of the picture; they call it irrelevant and outdated. The gospel's power changes lives, which gives us great encouragement as we live for God by witnessing to others. God is powerful! God is at work! We have a great power inside of us, we must not take it for granted. The gospel cannot be quenched. We must not hide it within ourselves, but we should preach this power to everyone around us!

LUKE PERSTROPE: *17, St. Peters, MO*
First Baptist Church of St. Charles, St. Charles, MO; Fort Zumwalt East High School, St. Peters, MO

DOING LIFE FOR GOD'S RIGHTEOUSNESS

"My dearly loved brothers, understand this: Everyone must be quick to hear, slow to speak, and slow to anger, for man's anger does not accomplish God's righteousness." —James 1:19–20

Like a lot of people, I love to hear myself talk. I like people to listen to me, and I like to be in charge. I find myself frequently overlooking the verse for today, or dismissing it as not a very big deal. I have to be intentional about being quick to hear and slow to speak. While that is difficult in and of itself, and probably more difficult for teens than any other age group, the more challenging part of the verse is the second part. Whenever we are wronged or hurt, it is so hard not get angry. God is clear in His command to be slow to anger, and it is necessary to pray for His strength to keep our tempers in check. God is on our side to always encourage us to not do wrong. He wants us to do right, and He is available to help us if we'll just ask. If we truly want to accomplish God's righteousness, we will seek to accomplish these three things God has commanded: Be quick to hear, slow to speak, and slow to anger. It is up to us. Are you willing to do it God's way?

CHANDLER SMITH: *16, Springdale, AR*
Cross Church Springdale Campus and Shiloh Christian School, Springdale, AR

PEER PRESSURE

"A man with many friends may be harmed, but there is a friend who stays closer than a brother." —*Proverbs 18:24*

I was at a friend's house one afternoon, along with three more of her friends, and we never really talked the whole time. We had had a great day so far, going crazy to music, swimming, watching a movie, and just hanging out. In the midst of all of this, a very ungodly substance was introduced into the picture. As I stood there, I didn't want to be made fun of or be called a chicken. You can guess what happened from there. We must be careful in choosing our friends. It turns out a lot of them end up just pulling us away from our walk with Christ. I know it is shocking that some of those that we think we can trust will also do things, and even want us to do things, that are sinful! The Bible tells us to be happy when we resist sin, even when people are laughing and making a mockery of us, because great joy awaits us in heaven! We do need to make a choice to do the right thing. In the end, even when we are laughed at by those we thought were our friends, God will bless our decision to do the right thing. He has given us what we need to do the right things in life: His Word, prayer, and helpers like our parents and Christian leaders at church and school whom we can call upon for guidance. Are you willing to take a stand for God, even if it means you get laughed at or that you can't have certain friends? It's your choice, so choose wisely and choose what has lasting value!

BRANDON CARROLL: *17, York, SC*
Hillcrest Baptist Church and York Comprehensive High School, York, SC

GRACE

"For you are saved by grace through faith, and this is not from yourselves; it is God's gift." —*Ephesians 2:8*

We often hear about God's grace. We sing "Amazing Grace" in church and at other functions, and sometimes maybe miss the timeless truths: "Amazing Grace, how sweet the sound that saved a wretch like me!" Hmm, you might ask what a wretch is or you may declare that you are definitely not a wretch. A wretch, as defined by *Merriam Webster* is: "A miserable person, one who is profoundly unhappy or in great misfortune." This does apply to all of us in Christ. Let's break this down for what this means to the Christ follower. Christ is the essence of grace. We were here on the earth dying in our sin, drowning in our despair. We had no way out. We were destined to a lifetime of misery and an eternity in hell. But then Jesus burst onto the scene! He left perfect heaven to come live with debased humanity. He could've had the angels take Him off the cross. He didn't have to do it, but He willingly chose to put yours and mine and everybody else's sin upon Himself on the cross! He removed it as far from us as the east is from the west! Praise God! We have no hope aside from Him. Amazing grace is not just an old church hymn, it is everything we are and He is. It is the very heart of God! "I once was lost, but now am found, was blind but now I see!" Do me a favor, go find a blind person and make them see. That's ludicrous—you can't! Jesus alone can save us from our spiritual blindness and hopelessness. Therefore, let us take to heart the words of John in Revelation 5:12: "The Lamb who was slaughtered is worthy to receive power and riches and wisdom and strength and honor and glory and blessing!"

LUKE MERRICK: *15, Springdale, AR*
Immanuel Baptist Church and Shiloh Christian School, Springdale, AR

THANKFULNESS

"Give thanks to the LORD, for He is good;
His faithful love endures forever." —*1 Chronicles 16:34*

Have you ever put a lot of thought into something that you have given a friend, only to see them receive it without ever thanking you? Even though you shouldn't seek praise, it makes you question whether it was worth the effort. Now, what about what God has given us? Do you thank Him enough, or do you take Him for granted? It's easy to become complacent and not realize all the things we have, as small as the breaths we take. As we go about our lives, we should constantly remember the sacrifice God made in giving us His Son so that we might spend eternity with Him. We must remain thankful that we have been chosen and set apart as children of God. We are all guilty of getting caught up in our own lives and not realizing why we are here, to give glory and honor to the Lord. Also, if we are truly thankful for the gift of salvation, wouldn't we want to share it with others? We are to search for opportunities to share the gospel with others and proclaim the goodness of our Lord and Savior. So, continue to dwell on the gifts we are given and be thankful. Take some time today to write down what you are thankful for. You will be amazed by all you have been blessed with.

JONATHAN DISMUKES: *17, Mobile, AL*
Redeemer Fellowship Church and Cottage Hill Christian Academy, Mobile, AL

AUGUST

Wisdom's Appeal

Doesn't Wisdom call out? Doesn't Understanding make her voice heard? At the heights overlooking the road, at the crossroads, she takes her stand. Beside the gates at the entry to the city, at the main entrance, she cries out: "People, I call out to you; my cry is to mankind. Learn to be shrewd, you who are inexperienced, develop common sense, you who are foolish. Listen, for I speak of noble things, and what my lips say is right. For my mouth tells the truth, and wickedness is detestable to my lips. All the words of my mouth are righteous; none of them are deceptive or perverse. All of them are clear to the perceptive, and right to those who discover knowledge. Accept my instruction instead of silver, and knowledge rather than pure gold. For wisdom is better than jewels, and nothing desirable can compare with it. I, Wisdom, share a home with shrewdness and have knowledge and discretion. To fear the Lord is to hate evil. I hate arrogant pride, evil conduct, and perverse speech. I possess good advice and competence; I have understanding and strength. It is by me that kings reign and rulers enact just law by me, princes lead, as do nobles and all righteous judges. I love those who love me, and those who search for me find me. With me are riches and honor, lasting wealth and righteousness. My fruit is better than solid gold, and my harvest than pure silver. I walk in the way of righteousness, along the paths of justice, giving wealth as an inheritance to those who love me, and filling their treasuries. (Proverbs 8:1–21)

BULLYING

"For if you forgive people their wrongdoing, your heavenly Father will forgive you as well. But if you don't forgive people, your Father will not forgive your wrongdoing." —*Matthew 6:14–15*

When one person harms another for no good reason it's called bullying. Whether as a victim, bully, or bystander, we have all been a part of it. Sometimes the target of bullies is physically injured, other times we are injured emotionally. The most important help during these times is God. He tells us in the Bible to return the hate with forgiveness. Christian parents are the biggest part of leading us to God's help. When we would rather go to our rooms and do nothing, they will pray with us and help us see that God will help through prayer. Let me tell you, He sure does! God tells us to forgive the people who hurt us. When we do, a huge load will be lifted from our chests. After we forgive the bullies, they will often be convicted and will actually apologize, and we need to be willing to forgive. One of the lessons that keeps coming up from my own parents is that most bullies bully to make themselves feel better. They are wrong to use bullying for any reason, whether they feel it's right or not. They need help, they need friends, they need you, and for sure they need God. It is up to you and me to make sure that these poor people get help. Without us pointing them toward God, they will most likely keep on doing what they are doing. Both bullies and victims need help from the one and only One who can help, God.

TERRELL STRAIN: *13, Spokane, WA*
Airway Heights Baptist Church, Airway Heights, WA; Medical Lake Middle School, Medical Lake, WA

FAITH TAKES ACTION

"What good is it, my brothers, if someone says he has faith but does not have works? Can his faith save him?" —James 2:14

Imagine a rope extended across a deep valley and crowds watching a man tightrope across it. After walking across several times, he decided to push a wheelbarrow across it, and the crowd cried out, "Do it!" He successfully accomplished it several times. Then he asked for someone to get inside the wheelbarrow, and silence swept through the crowd! This story illustrates the incredible difference between intellectual assent and saving faith. To trust, we need to focus on God by reading the Bible, praying, listening, and putting Him in the center of our lives. This is like the people trusting the guy to walk across the tightrope without the faith to get inside the wheelbarrow. God says with faith anything is possible, but we must exhibit this through our actions. I've experienced the fear of getting inside the wheelbarrow, like when I go out into a city of eight million people to talk to college students about Christ. It's tough, but when I did it, I saw God work through me to share with people who had never heard before. I wanted to stay in that wheelbarrow all day long. James 2:26 says, "Faith without works is dead." God shows us how to take action in Matthew 28:19: "Go, therefore, and make disciples of all nations, baptizing them in the name of the Father and of the Son and of the Holy Spirit." The action is when we go and share God's love with the nations. I encourage you to trust God, step out on faith, and climb in the wheelbarrow. Enjoy the ride!

COLLIN MICHAEL SEELEN: *18, Itami, Hyogo, Japan*
Emmanuel Baptist Church and Kansai Homeschooled Network, Itami, Hyogo, Japan

A LIGHT AT THE END OF THE TUNNEL

"I will lead the blind by a way they did not know; I will guide them on paths they have not known. I will turn darkness to light in front of them and rough places into level ground. This is what I will do for them, and I will not forsake them." —*Isaiah 42:16*

The verse for today has been special to me for the past five years. When I was in the fourth grade, my father took his own life. Before he died, he cheated on my mom, and when he confessed this there were some obvious issues. The week before he died, he moved out of the house. The last time I saw him we were throwing the football together. I had no idea why all of this had happened to me. I still don't understand why he had to go. The only way I can keep going on with some peace is because I know that God is in complete and total control of everything going on around me. My mom is now remarried, and I have a fantastic relationship with my stepdad. I do not know what my life would look like right now if my dad was still alive. It could look completely different, or very similar, but I just wanted to encourage you guys who are going through extremely tough times that there is a light at the end of the tunnel. Though you may not know where the tunnel is leading, it will get better all because of Jesus. Don't misunderstand; everything will be worked out in the Lord's timing. You just have to trust whatever He is going to do. Be strong, have faith, and don't lose hope!

REED REYNOLDS: *15, Albany, GA*
Sherwood Baptist Church and Sherwood Christian Academy, Albany, GA

COURAGE

"Be strong and courageous, all you who put your hope in the LORD."
—*Psalm 31:24*

Courage is something all of us have but not all of us use. A lot of us think people with courage are just tough people who get in fights and don't fear anything. But courage is actually tons more than that. People that have courage are people who can stand up for what they believe in and aren't afraid to be different than those around them. For example, one time some friends of mine went to see a movie that wasn't the nicest movie in the world. So I told them I didn't want to see a movie with material in it that is not decent. My friends now understand that I have limits, which I will not cross, just because they or anyone else want me to. Now, let's take a look at two passages that speak of courage. "Be strong and courageous; don't be terrified or afraid of them. For it is the LORD your God who goes with you; He will not leave you or forsake you" (Deuteronomy 31:6). "Above all, be strong and very courageous to carefully observe the whole instruction My servant Moses commanded you. Do not turn from it to the right or the left, so that you will have success wherever you go" (Joshua 1:7). You have to realize that you don't have to be a tough person to have courage, but you have to be willing to take criticism and be ready to stand up for what you believe is right.

JOSH DANIEL: *14, Troy, OH*
Two Rivers Community Church, Vandalia, OH; Homeschooled

THE TREASURE AT THE FINISH LINE

"Therefore we do not give up. Even though our outer person is being destroyed, our inner person is being renewed day by day. For our momentary light affliction is producing for us an absolutely incomparable eternal weight of glory." —*2 Corinthians 4:16–17*

Following Christ can be difficult. Christians are subjected to mockery, rejection, and disrespect. Christ experienced all of these things. We see that there is a reason to live this kind of life with gratefulness. We are torn down by enemies, encountering verbal attacks and mean jokes from unbelievers, but our present suffering is just a momentary light affliction It is nothing compared to the joy we will experience in eternity! You've heard the phrase "no pain, no gain." We will experience pain, but we will gain much more than we ever could imagine because of what Christ did on the cross. Jesus told the parable of the man who found a priceless treasure and buried it in a field. He then sold everything he had to acquire that field. People must have thought the man was crazy, likely encountering ridicule and mockery for his decision. However, the man knew what he had found was so much greater than anything else he could have experienced. Smiling, the man walked out with a field and the treasure. If you are experiencing tough times remember that heaven is the ultimate! Christians must realize that we live for a kingdom not of this world but one that is to come. Our kingdom is vastly superior to anything the world can offer. Though there may be pain and hardships in going to heaven, we know that it is all for the most amazing treasure when we reach the finish line.

LUKE PERSTROPE: *17, St. Peters, MO*
First Baptist Church of St. Charles, St. Charles, MO; Fort Zumwalt East High School, St. Peters, MO

HAVING FAITH

"Now faith is the reality of what is hoped for,
the proof of what is not seen." —*Hebrews 11:1*

So what is faith, and what does it do? Hebrews 11:1 clearly states what it is and what it does. Most people, including me, put their faith in things of this world. For instance, we put our faith in a chair to hold our weight as we sit down. We have faith that we will go to sleep at night and wake again in the morning in time for school. We have faith that once we flip a light switch, the room will be filled with light within a split-second. However, our faith in Christ is a bit different. Our faith in God does not involve sitting around and waiting for an opportunity to share our faith with others; it involves rising to the occasion and stepping up for the name of Christ. Granted, God does not need us to do this for Him, but it is a great part of being a Christian. Matthew 16:24 says, "If anyone wants to come with Me, he must deny himself, take up his cross, and follow Me." This means that to begin our faith in Christ, we must deny ourselves, our flesh and desires, and follow the One who gives life. This is not a one-time deal. Jesus wants us to deny ourselves and ask for His forgiveness day after day. Jesus referred to picking up our crosses so that we would expect that we will be persecuted for our relationships with the Father, and so that we will be aware that we will have to give up everything for God.

JESSE D. SANDO: *13, Pleasant Hill, OH*
First Baptist Church, Vandalia, OH; Homeschooled

PREPARE FOR PURITY (PART 1)

"But each person is tempted when he is drawn away and enticed by his own evil desires. Then after desire has conceived, it gives birth to sin, and when sin is fully grown, it gives birth to death." —James 1:14

It's easy to fall into the trap of immorality. Every man deals with this at some time in his life. It's one of the devil's traps for young men, and God hates it. Unfortunately, even grown Christian men fall into this trap, even though they know it's wrong. So if it's wrong and we know it, then why do we sometimes fail at being moral? When we're alone at night the devil tempts us and we feel like lust is the greatest thing ever. But after we sin, we have guilt, and the devil shames us. Then we ask the question: Why? We knew it was wrong, then we forgot how much we really hate sin. The answer is to work hard to prepare yourself in the daytime, when we're not under temptation. The more time you spend preparing, the more you will remember how hard you worked. When you are tempted, you will remember what you did to prepare. First the devil tempts you into thinking that you want to sin, but you don't! God will give you His strength to overcome the temptations that Satan throws at you. Have verses in your heart and mind that you can call on to block the onslaught of the enemy. God is greater, and He wants to aid us in all areas of temptation. Call on Him, day or night.

JOSHUA COOKSEY: *15, McMinnville, OR*
Valley Baptist Church, McMinnville, OR; Homeschooled

PREPARE FOR PURITY (PART 2)

"But each person is tempted when he is drawn away and enticed by his own evil desires. Then after desire has conceived, it gives birth to sin, and when sin is fully grown, it gives birth to death." —*James 1:14*

When temptation comes we need to be prepared. I have found that there are steps young men can take to help when the enemy tries to overtake our hearts and minds, even our dreams.

I like to use the following steps to help me to be prepared:

1. Memorize Scripture. 1 Peter, 5:8–9 says, "Be sober! Be on the alert! Your adversary the Devil is prowling around like a roaring lion, looking for anyone he can devour. Resist him and be firm in the faith, knowing that the same sufferings are being experienced by your fellow believers throughout the world." Say these verses to the enemy the next time you're tempted.

2. Be accountable. Get with your dad or a friend and talk each night before bed about how you strived against evil. How did you handle temptation that day? When you did not handle the temptation? Then pray together asking God to forgive you and that He would give you the strength to do better next time.

3. Destroy all stumbling blocks: TV ads, books, movies, the Internet, literature, and other stuff. Remember the world is out to seek and to destroy, and there is much evil in the world. Use ad blockers and filters for the Internet and Safe Eyes and limit which websites you can go to. Don't believe the devil's lies when he tells you you're doomed to failure. You are not alone, and you can do this. God is always available to help you make it!

JOSHUA COOKSEY: *15, McMinnville, OR*
Valley Baptist Church, McMinnville, OR; Homeschooled

FOLLOW ME

"'Follow Me,' He told them, 'and I will make you fish for people!'"

—Matthew 4:19

"Follow Me" are the words Jesus spoke to Simon and Andrew as a simple command, but it offers a challenging course. Following Christ isn't always easy. In many nations people make great sacrifices to follow Christ. What does following Christ mean? The easy answer is to submit to His will. By submitting to His will, we acknowledge that God's plan is best for our lives. While in high school, our lives are being shaped for the rest of our lives. When choosing our college and vocation, we must pray to ask if this is God's will. Everyone has a different calling. Our goal should be to discover and to complete God's will. Jeremiah 29:11 tells us that He "has plans for your welfare, not for disaster, to give you a future and a hope." The Bible makes it clear that God's will is not a mystery, but it is distorted by our sin. We should follow Christ's will because He is all-knowing. Though we don't always understand things in the midst of the storm, we are confident that, in His omnipotence, God knows best. He sees the whole picture! We focus on the struggles of today. Simon and Andrew had priorities. As fishermen, they were committed to fish. However, they immediately left everything they once knew for an unknown journey. We don't know the journey ahead. However, we do know that if we are following God's will we are on the right path!

LUKE PERSTROPE: *17, St. Peters, MO*
First Baptist Church of St. Charles, St. Charles, MO; Fort Zumwalt East High School, St. Peters, MO

LESSONS LEARNED THROUGH LONELINESS

"Finally brothers, whatever is true, whatever is honorable, whatever is just, whatever is pure, whatever is lovely, whatever is commendable—if there is any moral excellence and if there is any praise—dwell on these things. Do what you have learned and received and heard and seen in me, and the God of peace will be with you." —*Philippians 4:8–9*

Loneliness is a place of comfort for some and darkness for others. While living overseas, loneliness can be hard to overcome because the people around you think, speak, and even look different. I have struggled with this, because I am a very outgoing person and Japanese culture is very private. It's hard to break that barrier. All of us feel lonely sometimes in our life, and we have to remember to find people that encourage us and help us in our walk with God. One year I was vacationing at the lake, and I made a few friends. We had a great time, but the time came when my loyalty to them was tested. It was late, and they all decided to go to a convenience store to purchase alcohol. Because I was dealing with loneliness, I was tempted to go along. They told me it would be loads of fun, but I knew it would be a mistake. I felt crushed because I thought these people would be an encouragement to me. Instead, I was left feeling lonely again. God was faithful and put incredible friends in my path who have encouraged me and challenged me to know God better. We must remember that God uses our families and friends to fill the loneliness by encouraging and challenging us. Think on the good things you have in your life, and you will never be alone again.

COLLIN MICHAEL SEELEN: *18, Itami, Hyogo, Japan*
Emmanuel Baptist Church and Kansai Homeschooled Network, Itami, Hyogo, Japan

JESUS

"But He was pierced because of our transgressions, crushed because of our iniquities; punishment for our peace was on Him, and we are healed by His wounds." —Isaiah 53:5

What does the name *Jesus* mean? It is used as an expletive and as the final expression in a sacred prayer. To some Jesus is salvation; while to others, He is a good prophet; and to yet another group, He is part of a mythological Jewish fairy tale. Who is this Jesus? Those who believe He didn't exist clearly don't believe God's Word or documented secular history. If He was a prophet, what would drive Him to endure torture for a cause in which He was only a messenger? Why did He not cry out to God for rescue when the nails were hammered through His wrists? Why did He leave the glory of heaven to save dirty sinners like us? The Prince of Glory gave up everything for what? Love! Love like an overwhelming flood through the galaxies. Love with volcanic force, rushing through the veins of creation. Love is undeserved, unsuspected, and unprecedented. Love is unlike that shared by humans, but the love it takes to look your enemies in the face as they crucify you, when all you are trying to do is help them. This love is the foundation of everything. Life is fleeting, and the only hope we have for eternity is Jesus' unconditional love. Let your life be consumed with the holy fire of Jesus' unfathomable love and sacrifice, for only what is done for Him will last.

LUKE MERRICK: *15, Springdale, AR*
Immanuel Baptist Church and Shiloh Christian School, Springdale, AR

AWAKE

"Stay awake and pray, so that you won't enter into temptation. The spirit is willing, but the flesh is weak." —*Matthew 26:41*

What does Jesus mean when He says in the verse above to, "Stay awake and pray"? The disciples are falling asleep around Jesus when He needs them most. Why is that? Why can't they stay awake for Jesus? Jesus says this in physical terms to His disciples, but He also uses it spiritually. What does being awake for Jesus really mean? Well, it means that you are completely in love with and on fire for God. Jesus just wants you to spend a little time with Him; He wants you to stay awake with Him for a little bit! He wants you to read His Word and talk to Him for a while! A lot of times in life, you can say you've fallen asleep on Jesus. You might've gotten a little lazy in your quiet times. The disciples fell asleep on Jesus in the garden when He asked them to stay awake. He wants us to know Him so deeply that we will want to be close to Him in Bible study and in prayer. This is how we learn to live the life of a Christian. This is how we learn about Him, our Lord and Savior. So, are you going to fall asleep on Jesus when He asks you to stay awake?

KORD OFFENBACKER: *16, Springdale, AR*
Cross Church Springdale Campus and Shiloh Christian School, Springdale, AR

BE DIFFERENT

"Do not be conformed to this age, but be transformed by the renewing of your mind, so that you may discern what is the good, pleasing, and perfect will of God." —Romans 12:2

Today's verse has been a comfort to me throughout the past few years. It keeps me in check. I'm constantly seeing things around me that I do not really want to do, but I know I need to because they are the right things to do. For example, if you see someone sitting by themselves, just go talk to them. Learn about their stories. You have no idea the pain some people have been through. They just want someone to talk to, have someone listen to them, or just have someone show them they care. I understand this may not be the popular decision, but we are called to make disciples in Matthew 28:19. Another thing Romans 12:2 has shown me to that I shouldn't worry about what others think about what I'm doing, as long as it is the right thing to do. I know how tough it is to reach out to people with the gospel, because I am in the same boat you are. I know that there is that one guy who when you think of him you think, No, I can't do that or Bob is going to make fun of me, and if he makes fun of me then Jimmy, Fred, and Matt will too. I have an illustration to show you how little Bob matters in your life. If you had an 800-foot rope representing your entire life, assuming you live to be about 70 or 80, those years would only take up about half a foot of that rope. The rest of that rope you will be in either heaven or hell, so who cares what Bob thinks? Continue to be different from this world, spread the gospel, and pray for your enemies like Bob.

REED REYNOLDS: *15, Albany, GA*
Sherwood Baptist Church and Sherwood Christian Academy, Albany, GA

GOD'S PLANS REVEALED THROUGH THE LIFE OF JOSEPH

"You planned evil against me; God planned it for good to bring about the present result—the survival of many people."

—Genesis 50:20

Like Joseph, we will go through tough times as Christians. Joseph's brothers were jealous of him, which led them to sell Joseph into slavery. While in slavery, Joseph was wrongly accused of coming on to Potiphar's wife. He was sent to prison for at least two years. Eventually, Joseph was able to interpret the dream of Pharaoh and made second in command of all of Egypt. What man tries to set up as a trap, God sets up as a platform to elevate and to glorify Himself. The intention of Joseph's brothers was evil. God made good out of bad. The discernment God gave to Joseph enabled him to know to stockpile food to be prepared for a famine. I'm sure Joseph asked the question Why? when he was rotting in the jail cell for a crime he didn't commit. We don't always understand God's purpose for allowing us to go through tough times, but we do know that God's plan is always superior to any scheme we could draw up. Jeremiah 29:11 says, "'For I know the plans I have for you'—this is the LORD's declaration—'plans for your welfare, not for disaster, to give you a future and a hope.'" God's plans have a purpose. You may feel like your life has no purpose. Perhaps a friend turned his back on you or you are struggling with a family situation. Though we may go through tough times, we are reminded that God's plan for us gives us a purpose! We are to submit to His will to accomplish greater things for the kingdom! There is no greater joy than to serve the Lord and glorify His name.

LUKE PERSTROPE: *17, St. Peters, MO*
First Baptist Church of St. Charles, St. Charles, MO; Fort Zumwalt East High School, St. Peters, MO

BE SEPARATE

"Therefore, come out from among them and be separate, says the Lord;
do not touch any unclean thing, and I will welcome you."

—*2 Corinthians 6:17*

In high school and in middle school, most of us go through a stage where we tend to want to be like everyone else. In other words, we follow the crowd. Sometimes all the guys want a certain kind of shoe, the newest phone, the latest video game, or the newest album off iTunes. "My friend has it, so I want it too" is our mind-set. But if we look at the verse above, it says to "come out from among them," or, in other words, we have to take a bold step and separate ourselves from being just like everybody else. We don't have to do what they do or have what they have. Taking this bold step of faith and separating from the crowd will be hard, but we have to look to God in this situation. We cannot do it on our own. The verse says to "be separate," so we must ignore what everyone is doing and spend time focusing on our walk with God. If we choose to follow God instead of the world, it will be a huge blessing in our lives. Think about the story of Noah in the book of Genesis. Because of the wickedness in the world, God was going to destroy the whole world by flood. Noah was not like everyone else. He listened to God and was "separate," which led to God letting him and his family live. So what we can learn from this is that if we choose to be separate from the world, God will bless and protect us. Just remember, sometimes it all starts with not following the crowd.

ANDREW CLEM: *13, Albany, GA*
Sherwood Baptist Church and Sherwood Christian Academy, Albany, GA

GOD REMAINS FAITHFUL

"For I will be merciful to their wrongdoing, and I will never again remember their sins." —Hebrews 8:12

It's very good for us to remember just exactly how others got to the position they're in today. Where they came from, and who helped them along the way. It's especially important for us as Christians to understand these questions and to know the answers for our own lives. I think it can be easy for us to forget a life not worth remembering, but should it be so easy, so right, to forget how we got here; and, even more so, who got us here? Too quickly one forgets the faithfulness of God and His graciousness in forgiving our wretched crimes against Him. And too quickly we forget our faithlessness, which is all we have to offer when left on our own. Yet, by the wonderful grace of God, He gave us the faith to believe. He continues to forgive us when we, like the Israelites, are so quick to forget. And He is quicker still to "never again remember their sins." Would we only be so apt to remember as He is to forget. He might just have less to forget! We should remind ourselves daily that God, in His own pleasure, saw fit to save our wretched souls, in order that He might find glory in our salvation. If we take time to remember, I hope we would be less likely to get angry at our siblings or parents. If God can forgive us, why can't we forgive others? The Lord will always remain faithful even when we are faithless.

JOSHUA JOHANSEN: *18, Shrewsbury, MA*
Bethlehem Bible Church, West Boylston, MA; Quinsigamond Community College, Worcester, MA

DEVELOPING A HEAVENLY MIND-SET

"Set your minds on what is above, not on what is on the earth."
—*Colossians 3:2*

Our lives get hectic and stressful as we try to balance a schedule of school, church, and friends. We can get burned out by running around all of the time. Though being active isn't bad, we need to be cautious to not get too busy for God. I once heard the saying, "If Satan can't get you to do bad things, he will get you busy." This is so true. For many Christians, we avoid the "big sins," but we pour hours of our lives into things that aren't necessarily advancing the kingdom. I see Christians who are totally committed to sports, music groups, or school. Though these things aren't bad, many fall away from Christ as a result of the time that these activities require. I was in marching band at my old school. If you were ever in band or a sport, you know that it takes a good chunk of time out of your schedule. I was becoming so busy with band practices, church events, and school work that my head felt like it was going to explode. My relationship with Christ grew weaker as a result of these idols in my life. When we moved, I was careful not to overindulge in activities, so that I could still have adequate time to focus on the most important thing: my relationship with Christ. Remember that we are just passing by in this world. We look forward to our ultimate destination: heaven. Our mission here on Earth is to glorify God and to spread His name to a lost and dying world. Our mind-set and focus can be polluted by things that pull us away, instead of propelling us toward Christ. Maybe you are stressed out. Prayerfully consider what is getting in the way between you and Christ.

LUKE PERSTROPE: *17, St. Peters, MO*
First Baptist Church of St. Charles, St. Charles, MO; Fort Zumwalt East High School, St. Peters, MO

RESPECT

"Pay your obligations to everyone: taxes to those you owe taxes, tolls to those you owe tolls, respect to those you owe respect, and honor to those you owe honor." —*Romans 13:7*

It is hard to respect those that you may not like. Yet, we are to obey and honor those who have been given authority in our lives. Most important, we are to respect our parents. Exodus 20:12 commands "Honor your father and your mother so that you may have a long life in the land that the LORD your God is giving you." God has placed us in their control, so that we might learn and mature from their knowledge. How we act toward their instruction is a direct insight into the respect we have for our Creator. Also, our parents' teachings are for our benefit. Consider yourself an athlete playing football. Wouldn't you first like to have a general knowledge of the game and how it's played, before playing yourself? Likewise, we need the teachings of our parents before trying to be independent in a world full of temptations. Furthermore, we are being watched by those around us and our actions determine their opinions of how we are supposed to act as Christians. If they see a professing Christian arguing with his parents, wouldn't they question how they are being taught in the church? Your life is a testimony of your faith, so remain aware of how you act toward those in authority, and honor God in everything.

JONATHAN DISMUKES: *17, Mobile, AL*
Redeemer Fellowship Church and Cottage Hill Christian Academy, Mobile, AL

OUR IDENTITY IN CHRIST

"But you are a chosen race, a royal priesthood, a holy nation, a people for His possession, so that you may proclaim the praises of the One who called you out of darkness into His marvelous light." —1 Peter 2:9

Teen boys tend to lose their identities in Christ. I remember when I was a sophomore in high school. I constantly tried to fit in and make as many friends as I possibly could, just to be popular. However, what I was doing was ignoring God, who saved me from my sins, which is way more important. What caused me to stumble during this period of my life was the fact that I kept trying to compare myself to everyone else, and I felt completely insecure about who God had made me. I was not looking at who God actually made me to be. God continually shows us who we are in Christ. For example, in Psalm 139:13–16 says, "For it was You who created my inward parts; You knit me together in my mother's womb. I will praise you because I have been remarkably and wonderfully made. Your works are wonderful, and I know this very well. My bones were not hidden from You when I was made in secret, when I was formed in the depths of the earth. Your eyes saw me when I was formless; all my days were written in Your book and planned before a single one of them began." God knows who we are and He wants us to be who He created us to be. We are a chosen people, and God loves us even if the world does not. John 15:20 stays, "Remember the word I spoke to you: 'A slave is not greater than his master.' If they persecuted Me, they will also persecute you. If they kept My word, they will also keep yours." Our identity in Christ is to be who God called us to be: men of God.

CALEB PAYNE: 18, White House, TN
Long Hollow Baptist Church, Hendersonville, TN; Volunteer State Community College, Gallatin, TN

TO DIE IS GAIN
(PART 1)

"My eager expectation and hope is that I will not be ashamed about anything, but that now as always, with all boldness, Christ will be highly honored in my body, whether by life or death. For me, living is Christ and dying is gain." —*Philippians 1:20–21*

I asked a elderly man once if I had to do something. He responded, "All you've really got to do is breathe 'til ya die, I guess." Breathing until you die, that sure sounds eventful, doesn't it? Believe it or not, a lot of Christians do just that as far as God is concerned in their lives—they just breathe! They know they are saved so they have no desire to be used by Christ, the one who went to the cross for them. They say the sinner's prayer, get baptized, then kick back and take it easy until they die, without ever realizing that the Word of God teaches them to be used to minister to the lost and to reach out in a lot of ways to those in need. They believe that everything is now set for them to enter eternity. These people, though not on purpose, are very misguided in their perception of how to live the Christian life. The Bible gives us guidance on how to live our lives for Him once we are saved. However, there are other people who are the exact opposite of the nonchalant Christians. They feel that no matter how hard they try, no matter what they do, God will not be sufficiently pleased with their lives and all of their efforts. So they try to work for eternal life.

BRADY FOWLKES: *16, Tuscaloosa, AL*
Valley View Baptist Church and Hillcrest High School, Tuscaloosa, AL

TO DIE IS GAIN
(PART 2)

"My eager expectation and hope is that I will not be ashamed about anything, but that now as always, with all boldness, Christ will be highly honored in my body, whether by life or death. For me, living is Christ and dying is gain." —*Philippians 1:20–21*

The solution to both situations mentioned previously, being lazy about the Christian life or working to keep salvation, can be found in the verse for today. We are not ever going to be perfect on this earth, but we are to aspire to be as much like Christ as possible. Being like Christ will only come from knowing Him personally and from obeying His Word. The verse goes on to say that our living should be Christ, and dying is gain. When we do live our lives for the glory of Jesus Christ, why should we fear death? Our life should glorify Christ in all its aspects and, in this, death has no sting. Typically, death isn't something one should look to gain, but in this situation, it is all gain and no loss. What Paul is saying is that, in all boldness and with all his possible power, he will live to glorify Christ, and so should we.

BRADY FOWLKES: *16, Tuscaloosa, AL*
Valley View Baptist Church and Hillcrest High School, Tuscaloosa, AL

CHRISTLIKE IN FORGIVENESS

"Then Peter came to Him and said, 'Lord, how many times could my brother sin against me and I forgive him? As many as seven times?' 'I tell you, not as many as seven,' Jesus said to him, 'but 70 times seven.'"

—*Matthew 18:21–22*

One of the greatest gifts we can give to another is our forgiveness. Everyone messes up at some point and there is nothing better than to know that you are forgiven and to receive a second chance. Likewise, we are called to be holy and Christlike in our character. Did not Christ teach us to forgive and forget? This is one of the hardest parts of living to glorify God. We are prone to search for ways that we can attack someone just because they failed at a task. We love to be better than others and are quick to judge their actions, even if we have done the same. However, we must remain conscious of the forgiveness we have received for our sins. The punishment for sin is death (Romans 6:23), and nothing we can do can justify our transgressions in the midst of a perfect God. Before Christ, sinners relied on the blood sacrifice of animals as a picture of the forthcoming death of Christ on the cross. Once Christ died at Calvary He became the sacrifice for our sins and we are free from our transgressions if we are children of God. As believers, we are to share this love of Christ with others simply by forgiving them no matter what they have done. As you live your life, remember the love of God, the sacrifice of His Son, and remember that we were once in sin but have been forgiven all because of the cross!

JONATHAN DISMUKES: *17, Mobile, AL*
Redeemer Fellowship Church and Cottage Hill Christian Academy, Mobile, AL

IT'S REALLY APPEALING

"There is a way that seems right to a man, but its end is the way to death." —*Proverbs 14:12*

We've all heard that we shouldn't follow after the world's ways (music, clothes, etc.). But sometimes I get the feeling that when I'm supposed to not be worldly, that it means I'm supposed to think, Why would I ever desire to wear that, listen to that, or be like that. I get this feeling that I have to think the world's music sounds bad, and that their clothes are crazy, and they talk funny too. So I get to be a teen and I'm like, "It's not all that weird. It's cool and you can't resist this." My parents tell me "You cannot wear those jeans; they sit too low." At first I don't get it. I feel like, "Well they just like different clothes, why do I have to wear what they like?" But your parents know that some clothes are not modest or maybe they look like something a gangster would wear, even when they look good to us teens. Those jeans, they aren't as modest. They're OK, but let's shoot for the best. It's OK to have clothes that are in style, you don't have to wear plaid pants. It's our focus that becomes the problem. Some music creates attitudes of rebellion, lust, and a "me focus," which is just not good to be listening to all day. That's where a lot of our problems come in. So, as a teen, I can say that all this stuff looks good, and it sounds good, and it is definitely appealing. The Bible says that "Satan disguises himself as an angel of light" (2 Corinthians 11:14). Ever since Adam and Eve, he has been trying to make sin look good. Part of resisting the world is to say, "I know it's appealing, but it's not what I need in my life."

JOSHUA COOKSEY: *15, McMinnville, OR*
Valley Baptist Church, McMinnville, OR; Homeschooled

NATURE

"The heavens declare the glory of God, and the sky proclaims the work of His hands." —*Psalm 19:1*

Have you ever risen earlier than usual to see the sunrise or stayed up during the night to watch a meteor shower? If so, have you wondered why such beauty is included in the earth? Psalm 19:1 tells us that the purpose of creation is to declare the glory of God. How could such miraculous scenery be produced by an accident? God had a reason for each day of His creation and, at the end, He proclaimed that His work was good. Even if some people are not reached by the gospel, they are responsible for recognizing the existence of God through the nature around them. The majestic works of His hands serve another purpose also, to continually awe us as we live each day and remind us of the power of our Lord. So, do not lose sight of the creations of God, but rather realize the specific intention of each and how they work together to produce the world we live in. Take a silent walk through the woods or stare at the stars at night and remember the perfect intentions of the Creator to glorify Himself and bring us to salvation.

JONATHAN DISMUKES: *17, Mobile, AL*
Redeemer Fellowship Church and Cottage Hill Christian Academy, Mobile, AL

LOSING LOVED ONES

"Those who mourn are blessed, for they will be comforted."

—Matthew 5:4

It was a long, hard battle with spinal cerebella ataxia. But after eight years, on August 31, 2008, I lost my grandmother to the disease. I didn't handle it well: it is difficult to be joyful when you lose someone you have grown up loving, and it took time to find my source of joy. I struggled with depression for several years and was embarrassed to tell anyone because I was afraid of how people would react. I could fake happiness, and I tried to find satisfaction in family, friends, and personal achievements. While none of these are bad things, they didn't give me joy. I questioned God: Why would He take an incredible woman away, but let people who have no desire for God live such corrupt lives? This summer I felt God calling me to get into His Word. I didn't really want to listen, but on this particular night, I was unable to fall asleep. I opened my Bible for the first time in a long time, searching for a verse that I could relate to. Matthew 5:4 brought me comfort: "Those who mourn are blessed, for they will be comforted." I felt a peace that was overwhelming. I talked to my mother about my situation and my struggle with depression. We began to pray daily that the Lord would enable me to choose joy. When I struggle, I ask the Lord for His strength. God has also shown me ways my grandmother touched people's lives, giving me better understanding for her death. The Lord has given me comfort and hope when I thought it wasn't possible. He is my true source of joy.

CHANDLER SMITH: *16, Springdale, AR*
Cross Church Springdale Campus and Shiloh Christian School, Springdale, AR

THE CHURCH

"And let us be concerned about one another in order to promote love and good works, not staying away from our worship meetings, as some habitually do, but encouraging each other, and all the more as you see the day drawing near." —*Hebrews 10:24–25*

When my parents decided that our family needed to attend a different church, my reaction to the news was not good, and I struggled to control my desire to question my parents' decision. As the day approached, I became very nervous about this change. We visited a new church, and my parents decided to start going there. I gradually warmed up to the idea. Now I really don't want to leave this new church. I went from frustration and questioning to eagerness to join and make new friends. A variety of circumstances changed my mind; the major one was simply getting involved. Once I became involved, got into ministry, and immersed myself in activities with the church's youth group, I didn't want to leave. I made a decision that I was going to look for ways to help others in this new church as I got to know them. Hebrews 10:24–25 tells us that we are to encourage each other, to be concerned about one another, to spend time with one another, and to promote love and good works. I now understand that the church is not about me, and how it can make me feel good. The church is about believers worshipping with each other, and encouraging each other. That means that not only are we to be encouraged, but also we are to encourage others.

JOSIAH MCGEE: *15, Kansas City, MO*
Summit Woods Baptist Church, Lees Summit, MO; Homeschooled

FINDING YOUR PURPOSE

"For I know the plans I have for you-this is the Lord's declaration-'plans for your welfare, not for disaster, to give you a future and a hope.'"

—Jeremiah 29:11

Have you ever wondered what you want to do when you grow up, or even what God's plan for your life is? We all have. I have encountered this question a lot lately. I am a senior in high school. This is a big point in everyone's life. The choices we make can shape our paths in life. Deciding whether to go to college or straight into the workforce, and what to do when there are so many questions that need to be dealt with. For me, I've decided that I want to go to college so I can play soccer and continue my education. When applying, I came to a section where I had to choose a major. There were many choices listed, but none of them really stuck out to me. I didn't really have an idea of what I wanted to do after college. I knew I wanted to play soccer, but other than that, I really wasn't sure. At that point, I realized that I didn't have to know exactly what I want to do. All I had to do was pray to God about it, and let Him point me in the right direction. God knows what our purpose in life is. He is the one who created us. He tells us this in Jeremiah 29:11. Another thing God promises us in this verse is that His plans for us are "plans for your welfare, not for disaster, to give you a future and a hope." With this verse, I know that I can trust God and follow the path He lays out for my life.

JESSE NIEMAN: *18, Ocala, FL*
Church @ The Springs and Forest High School, Ocala, FL

WHY DO I?
(PART 1)

"There is nothing new under the sun." —*Ecclesiastes 1:9*

Have you ever asked yourself why? Why do I go to school? Why do I learn, do chores, or play? Why am I here? Why do we do all the things we do? What's the purpose of it all? I think it's a pretty safe assumption that you have, at the very least, asked these questions once. And hey, even if you haven't, I'm sure someone you know has. Are we to live just to make money, start a business, build an empire, or to become millionaires? Then, once we've become successful and rich, are we to then hand it all over to our successor for them to decide whether to waste it away or increase it even more? Or are we to live for pleasure, always wanting the next big thing no matter the cost, wanting to feel good all the time? Is it our goal to go to hell with a full stomach and an empty soul? I sure hope your answer is no to that last question. So then, why do we live? What is our true purpose? Like the verse for today says, everything has been done before. And, like it says later in Ecclesiastes, all is vanity. If all is vanity, then why do we keep going on the way that we are? Consider the question why? Now, ask yourself if you are doing what you do for a purpose—a purpose that has lasting, even eternal value.

JOSHUA JOHANSEN: *18, Shrewsbury, MA*
Bethlehem Bible Church, West Boylston, MA; Quinsigamond Community College, Worchester, MA

WHY DO I?
(PART 2)

"There is nothing new under the sun." —*Ecclesiastes 1:9*

As we considered the question of *why?* in yesterday's reading let's move on today. If all is vanity, then this would mean that it's all worthless; there is no point— right? I'd keep reading if I were you. By the end of the book, Solomon, the wisest fallen man to walk this earth, concluded that life was worthless without God as our focus. Our purpose here on the earth is to bring glory to the only true and living God. We can't do any thing without the power of the Holy Spirit. Without God as our focus, life has no meaning; all is vanity, a striving after wind, instead of following Him. For although we may die of hunger, we go to a place where we shall never hunger again. Though we may die with empty pockets, we go to mansions filled with plentiful riches, where we spend an eternity praising God. That is what we should live for, that is why we are here. Life is all about bringing glory to God. Now, the next question is: Are you doing that?

JOSHUA JOHANSEN: *18, Shrewsbury, MA*
Bethlehem Bible Church, West Boylston, MA; Quinsigamond Community College, Worchester, MA

TEMPTATION

"And do not bring us into temptation but deliver us from the evil one."

—*Matthew 6:13*

Temptation is something we all struggle with, no matter who you are. A big problem that a lot of people have is that when temptation enters their lives they try to deal with it by themselves. But temptations need to be dwelt with by the Holy Spirit. He is there to help us battle temptation. You might feel as if the temptation is gone, but without the Lord's help it can never fully be taken care of. Without praying to God about it or reading a lot of Scripture on temptation and how to deal with it, the problem will always be in your life. Let's see what God's Word has to say about temptation: "Stay awake and pray, so that you won't enter into temptation. The spirit is willing, but the flesh is weak" (Matthew 26:41). That verse is so right. Our flesh couldn't be weaker. It would give in to every temptation if it weren't for Christ who lives in us. Jesus lived a life filled with temptations but never sinned. That's what we should strive for. Never forget that Christ is always with you and can pull you through anything. Just call on Him in the day of trouble, and He will battle the temptations for you.

JOSH DANIEL: *14, Troy, OH*
Two Rivers Community Church, Vandalia, OH; Homeschooled

SEPTEMBER

My son, if you accept my words and store up my commands within you, listening closely to wisdom and directing your heart to understanding; furthermore, if you call out to insight and lift your voice to understanding, if you seek it like silver and search for it like hidden treasure, then you will understand the fear of the LORD and discover the knowledge of God. For the LORD gives wisdom; from His mouth come knowledge and understanding. He stores up success for the upright; He is a shield for those who live with integrity so that He may guard the paths of justice and protect the way of His loyal followers. Then you will understand righteousness, justice, and integrity—every good path. For wisdom will enter your mind, and knowledge will delight your heart. Discretion will watch over you, and understanding will guard you, rescuing you from the way of evil—from the one who says perverse things, from those who abandon the right paths to walk in ways of darkness, from those who enjoy doing evil and celebrate perversion, whose paths are crooked, and whose ways are devious. It will rescue you from a forbidden woman, from a stranger with her flattering talk, who abandons the companion of her youth and forgets the covenant of her God; for her house sinks down to death and her ways to the land of the departed spirits. None return who go to her; none reach the paths of life. So follow the way of good people, and keep to the paths of the righteous. For the upright will inhabit the land, and those of integrity will remain in it; but the wicked will be cut off from the land, and the treacherous uprooted from it. (Proverbs 2:1–22)

ANXIETY

"But He said to me, 'My grace is sufficient for you, for power is perfected in weakness. Therefore, I will most gladly boast all the more about my weaknesses, so that Christ's power may reside in me." —2 Corinthians 12:9

I wish I could tell you some amazing story about how God helped me conquer some great fear or did an amazing thing that inspired a lot of people. I wish I could say that I haven't been anxious ever since, and that all you have to do is such-and-such a thing, but I can't. I can't because I haven't. I'm not some superstar hero, able to overcome any obstacle. I'm someone who gets anxious a lot, scared, and afraid. But I can say that every day I see the strength of God working in my life. I see that God has a plan for me and everything works out; He does know what He's doing. He knows everything and causes it all to happen. God is sovereign over every little thing; over the test you take this week; over your homework; over who you marry and how you meet her. I know I'm not the strongest, or the smartest, the fastest, or the boldest, but I do know one thing: In my weakness, God is strong; in my anxiety, God is courageous. We need to remember that we didn't earn our salvation and we can't keep it on our own. He gives us the faith to believe, and He gives us the strength to carry on to our final glory. Ask Him for strength, through prayer, and He will give it. Perhaps our greatest strength isn't even ours to begin with, and our courage is that of God. For in our weakness God's power is perfected.

JOSHUA JOHANSEN: *18, Shrewsbury, MA*
Bethlehem Bible Church, West Boylston, MA; Quinsigamond Community College, Worchester, MA

BE BOLD

"Keep asking and it will be given to you. Keep searching and you will find. Keep knocking and the door will be opened to you."

—*Matthew 7:7*

There are many times when we want something, whether it is money, jewelry, or a new car. These things are not bad at all, but do we need them? Are these things that God wants us to have now or even in the future? Do we ever just sit back and trust God's plan for our lives? In Jeremiah 29:11 it says, "'For I know the plans that I have for you'—this is the LORD's declaration—'plans for welfare, not for disaster, to give you a future and a hope.'" So right there, we know that God has a plan for our lives. But what about everything else? One day I was at church and had lost the only key to my grandpa's tractor, and today's verse came to my mind. So I prayed and asked God to help me find it. Then I started looking all around the churchyard and I finally found it. This situation helped me to realize how God cares about even the small things. He knew where the key was all the time, but I needed to call on Him and trust Him to lead me to it. So when you are in need of something, ask God and then seek it out in your life. He has a plan and He tells us to know what that plan is. Do you know what God's plan is for your life? It would be a good idea to get started learning what it is!

KYLE SUTTON: *16, Pageland, SC*
First Baptist Church and South Pointe Christian School, Pageland, SC

FOR SUCH A TIME AS THIS

"If you keep silent at this time, liberation and deliverance will come to the Jewish people from another place, but you and your father's house will be destroyed. Who knows, perhaps you have come to your royal position for such a time as this." —*Esther 4:14*

Through His sovereignty, God deliberately puts us in situations at the right time. I didn't fully realize this until I came into contact with a new group of believers. Together, we have encouraged each other to grow in Christ and to be a light in a dark world. I needed the encouragement of some friends to follow Christ more passionately and, in return, I have encouraged them too. I can see how God placed me in that position. Esther was in the right situation at the right time. The king had just divorced his wife and had set out to find a beautiful young girl. He chose Esther, an orphan who was raised by her cousin. As the king's wife, Esther's cousin Mordecai tells her of a plot to kill all of the Jews. Esther knows there isn't much time. After waiting for three days, she gets the courage to approach the king. Approaching the king uninvited could result in death. Esther tells the king of the plot to kill the Jews. The king eventually hangs Haman, the conspirator. The Jews were saved by Esther's courage. God put Esther in the right place at the right time. You are where you are for a reason, you have certain friends for a reason; you are in your school, your church, and your community for a reason! You are here for such a time as this, so make it count!

LUKE PERSTROPE: *17, St. Peters, MO*
First Baptist Church of St. Charles, St. Charles, MO; Fort Zumwalt East High School, St. Peters, MO

FORGIVENESS

"But with You there is forgiveness, so that You may be revered."
—Psalm 130:4

Forgiveness is a very special thing. There would be no need for forgiveness if Adam and Eve had never sinned in the Garden of Eden. But because they did sin, God sent His only Son to die at Calvary so that we could know what His forgiveness is all about. We all owe Jesus a very big thank-you, because He forgave us and still forgives us today. Jesus gave His life just to say that even though we get mad at Him for whatever happens in our lives, that He forgives us for stuff we have done and things we will do. The Bible reminds us that we need to forgive our brothers as many as seventy times seven. That is something to think about! Many of us find it hard to forgive a friend even one time. Without forgiveness, we would never make up with our friends or families. Just think: Without forgiveness, people would carry anger for one another for a long time, which would create all sorts of bitter and even hateful feelings. God does not want us to live our lives hanging on to bitterness and hate. Forgiveness is a wonderful thing, and we should not take it for granted.

TANNER PEYTON: *13, Pageland, SC*
Charlotte Southern Baptist and South Point Christian School, Pageland, SC

HOW TO LOVE THE UNLOVABLE

"But God proves His own love for us in that while we were still sinners, Christ died for us!" —*Romans 5:8*

Have you ever known someone who is extremely weird? Maybe you know someone who is a complete jerk. There are people who seem unlovable, but Christ gives an example of true love lived out. Christ lived a sinless life. He was completely perfect. As 2 Corinthians 5:21 says, "He made the One who did not know sin to be sin for us, so that we might become the righteousness of God in Him." He knew no sin, yet He took our sins upon Himself. Sin goes completely against His character and what He stood for. His love for us was demonstrated on the cross. We were sinners, we were unlovable, and we were His enemies, but He showed His great compassion and loved us even when we were undeserving. Notice who Christ hung out with on the earth: tax collectors and fishermen. These weren't the most lovable people in that society. Tax collectors were especially hated because they made citizens pay more money than the government required and pocketed the spare change. Jesus loved them anyway. We love because we are loved. We have to remember that at one time we were the ones who were unlovable. Christ loved us, despite our sins and rebellion. Part of loving is forgiving. We were forgiven by Christ, and we are called to forgive others, which is rather tough for many of us to do. If we do not forgive, then we are not being good witnesses of Christ. If you are holding onto something, ask God to give you the strength to forgive and make a difference to those who seem unlovable. Pray Christ's love will shine through you today!

LUKE PERSTROPE: *17, St. Peters, MO*
First Baptist Church of St. Charles, St. Charles, MO; Fort Zumwalt East High School, St. Peters, MO

RESPECT

"You are to rise in the presence of the elderly and honor the old. Fear your God; I am Yahweh." —*Leviticus 19:32*

Parents and other older authorities give us instruction that doesn't always make sense to us. Because we don't understand the reasons, we sometimes get angry when they refuse to let us do things we want to do that seem fine in our own eyes. "Wisdom is found with the elderly, and understanding comes with long life" (Job 12:12). Our authorities have lived longer and they're experienced. They have solid reasons for telling us *no*. First Peter 5:5–6 says, "In the same way, you younger men, be subject to the elders. And all of you clothe yourselves with humility toward one another, because God resists the proud but gives grace to the humble. Humble yourselves, therefore, under the mighty hand of God, so that He may exalt you at the proper time." The Lord will give grace to the humble. Kids who listen will understand that parents are gifts to keep us from doing dumb stuff. And God says He'll resist the proud. God has commanded us to honor our parents, submitting to their better judgment. Proverbs 3:1–2 says, "My son, don't forget my teaching, but let your heart keep my commands; for they will bring you many days." When confronted with commands that don't make sense, try thinking of a Roman soldier obeying his general without hesitation. A good soldier never questions the reason behind a seemingly foolish command. And that's how we should respect and obey our God-given authorities. God has commanded it. Who are we to differ?

MATTHEW COOKSEY: *13, McMinnville, OR*
Valley Baptist Church, McMinnville, OR; Homeschooled

SERVANT LEADERSHIP

"And whoever wants to be first among you must be your slave; just as the Son of Man did not come to be served, but to serve, and to give His life-a ransom for many." —*Matthew 20:27–28*

Leaders are crucial to guide and direct people to use their talents to accomplish a task. They are able to unite a group and achieve success through their combined efforts. The most thriving leader promotes service to gain the respect of his followers. By serving others, he characterizes humility and demonstrates that he will do anything for the betterment of the group. Lao Tzu, a Chinese philosopher, said, "To lead people, walk behind them." The greatest example of a leader was Jesus Christ. He dedicated His short life on the earth to the ministry, serving those around Him, even washing the disciples' feet. Christ presents us with a perfect illustration of how we should act to gain respect and rightfully lead others. It is not done with force, but rather with love. If we first focus on obtaining a life of care and compassion for others, people will begin to seek guidance from you and look to you for leadership. Daily, we must look to the example of Christ and follow His portrayal of servant leadership, so that we can create a positive impact on those we have contact with.

JONATHAN DISMUKES: *17, Mobile, AL*
Redeemer Fellowship Church and Cottage Hill Christian Academy, Mobile, AL

NO TEMPTATION OVERTAKES

"No temptation has overtaken you except what is common to humanity. God is faithful, and He will not allow you to be tempted beyond what you are able, but with the temptation He will also provide a way of escape so that you are able to bear it." —*1 Corinthians 10:13*

Temptation can come in many different forms. Everyone is and will be tempted, as long as we are on this earth. We are fallible and Satan loves to tempt us, especially teenagers. But just because we are being tempted to sin does not mean that God has abandoned us. You see, God challenges us. Sometimes we might not even realize it! We need to remember that even Satan is under God's rule. We also need to remember that God is always with us, and He will not allow Satan to tempt us beyond what we can overcome with Him. Even though it is hard in that moment, Jesus also faced all of the things that we face today (plus many more), and still held His ground. Take a look through the Bible at all of the times Jesus was tempted. Once you give in to that sin, it's like you just forfeited the battle between you and temptation. But when we hold our ground, overcome the temptation, and stay true to God, we will have victory! And how amazing that victory will be! So stay strong, and God will see you through!

BRANDON CARROLL: *17, York, SC*
Hillcrest Baptist Church and York Comprehensive High School, York, SC

WHAT IS YOUR CALLING?

"Then He said to them, 'Go into all the world and preach the gospel to the whole creation.'" —Mark 16:15

This past summer, I went to a camp with my church in Kentucky. The speaker for the camp was Ed Newton. During one of the sessions, Ed told his story. He attended college at Clearwater Christian College in Florida and played basketball there. He thought he was being called to be a pastor, but then realized God had called him to be an evangelist. At that moment, I felt God stirring in me, telling me that He was calling me to be a pastor. Since that day, I have been anticipating the day when I will step up to the pulpit and preach my first sermon. My sister, Annalise, has always wanted to be a doctor or nurse. Last year, she went on a mission trip to Uganda, Africa, to help kids who were not able to have Christmas, and those kids touched her heart. This past November she went back to Uganda, and she has learned that her calling is to go to Africa to share the gospel and nurse people who are in need. Maybe you don't know what your specific calling is yet, but if you look at Mark 16:15, all of us are called as believers to go and preach the Word of God to the whole world. That is our calling, so we need to go and do it. If you spend time praying and seeking, God will tell you His specific plans for you. Mr. Ed's calling is to be an evangelist, mine is to be a pastor, and Annalise's is to be a missionary. What's yours? When you receive your calling, obey. Don't ignore God's perfect plan for you.

ANDREW CLEM: *13, Albany, GA*
Sherwood Baptist Church and Sherwood Christian Academy, Albany, GA

LOVING THE UNLOVABLE

"I give you a new command: Love one another.
Just as I have loved you, you must also love one another."
—John 13:34

In your school or youth group, is there someone who is often pushed to the side and ignored? There always seems to be that one person and, more times than not, they could use a little encouragement from a child of the King. It is very easy to stick with your friends and forget that a lonely person is even there; but the truth is, this is far from how God calls us to live. Our verse today makes it clear that God calls us to love those around as us He would, because He has loved us. It is extremely easy to love your friends and the people you hang out with, but loving those who aren't as cool or socially accepted is harder to live out. God calls us to love one another, and this clearly includes everyone. I often struggle with this in my own life. It is easy to love and include my group of friends, and it is all too easy to exclude those who really could use the encouragement of even a short conversation or an invitation to a party. After hearing a youth leader speak on this topic, I made a decision to do a better job at including others, and God has really blessed the effort. Even if it is just as simple as a high five in the hallway, small displays of Christlike love have more of an impact on my relationship with Christ than I ever expected. If you're willing to step out of your comfort zone and love the unlovable because Christ first loved you, I guarantee that your relationship with the Lord will be strengthened.

AUSTIN SOUTHERN: *18, Thailand and Mississippi*
Chiang Mai Christian Fellowship and Grace International School, Chiang Mai, Thailand

THEY ARE SO ANNOYING!

"And the King will answer them, 'I assure you: Whatever you did for one of the least of these brothers of Mine, you did for Me.'" —*Matthew 25:40*

Little brothers and little sisters are annoying a lot of the time, and if you have younger siblings, you know it's true. But that wasn't a mistake; God gave them to you for a reason. Sure they smash your stuff, they're gross, they lie, and everything else, but they're God's challenge for you. It's hard not to get angry with them. But really, they probably won't just stop—yet. When they get older they will mature. What you can do now is to really make them feel special. Don't ever let them think that you wish they weren't there. Also, if they know you value them, they will respect you more and want to treat your things better. Remember that you were probably the same way when you were a kid! If you don't think so, ask your parents. Your little siblings really won't be any different than your kids. And if you respond to your little siblings with anger, you will probably do the same thing to your own kids. Spend time with them, find something both of you like to do, and have fun. When you're riding in the car, instead of texting, sit next to them and have fun. When they do what's wrong, nicely tell them what's right. And seriously, little kids can be fun! God gave them to you; so don't waste the time you could be preparing to be a mom or dad. You can do this, and you will be rewarded in the end by those cute little siblings in your life and by God.

JOSHUA COOKSEY: *15, McMinnville, OR*
Valley Baptist Church, McMinnville, OR; Homeschooled

MONOPOLY

"Don't collect for yourselves treasures on earth, where moth and rust destroy and where thieves break in and steal. But collect for yourselves treasures in heaven, where neither moth nor rust destroys, and where thieves don't break in and steal. For where your treasure is, there your heart will be also." —Matthew 6:19–21

I have a deep love for the game of Monopoly, in which the main goal is to get rich and bankrupt your opponents by buying properties and charging rent. I love to beat my parents and my brothers in Monopoly by winning money and buying hotels and watching my opponents cash in their properties to pay rent after landing on a hotel that I own! It is awesome. However, for many people in this world, the game of Monopoly resembles their lives. They may not have lots of property and hotels, but they are consumed with money and possessions and having more stuff than others. Jesus teaches us that our lives should be the exact opposite. Jesus tells us that the material possessions we collect on the earth can be ruined by moths, rust, or be stolen. Instead, we should collect treasure in heaven that cannot be ruined or stolen. Teens rarely make much money, but we should do what we can to help others. Giving to others in the name of Jesus is one way to store up treasures in heaven.

MICAH PERSTROPE: *13, St. Peters, MO*
First Baptist Church of St. Charles, St. Charles, MO; Dubray Middle School, St. Peters, MO

ACCEPTANCE (PART 1)

"But the Lᴏʀᴅ said to Samuel, 'Do not look at his appearance or his stature, because I have rejected him. Man does not see what the Lᴏʀᴅ sees for man sees what is visible, but the Lᴏʀᴅ sees, the heart.'"

—*1 Samuel 16:7*

Regardless of fronts that all of us put up to protect ourselves or to prove ourselves, I think there is one thing that most everybody has a fundamental need for: acceptance. Popularity is extremely important to students and many other people in today's society—the need to be a part of the "in" group. I know that has been important for me, and I have seen it in others. The longing for acceptance and belonging leads to an evolution of one's personality, and sometimes a lapse in morals, in order to fit the mold of the group they wish to be a part of. There are some things to keep in mind concerning this pursuit. First, popularity is totally subjective. Athleticism, talent, possessions, and appearance are all factors that may contribute to one's superficial acceptance. However, we can see in the story of David that the Lord has a very different vantage point on these things. When Samuel comes to Jesse to look for the next king of Israel, he views all of David's brothers, always assuming the next one must be king because of his appearance or his height. Then the Lord speaks and says, "Man sees what is visible, but the Lᴏʀᴅ sees the heart." We also see the Lord in the book of Micah ask only three things of us: that we act justly, love mercy, and walk humbly with our God. Are you striving to live according to what God asked?

LUKE MERRICK: *15, Springdale, AR*
Immanuel Baptist Church and Shiloh Christian School, Springdale, AR

ACCEPTANCE
(PART 2)

"But the Lord said to Samuel, 'Do not look at his appearance or his stature, because I have rejected him. Man does not see what the Lord sees for man sees what is visible, but the Lord sees, the heart."

—*1 Samuel 16:7*

We can definitely be popular and be an awesome Christian at the same time. I am not trying to say popularity is a sin. However, for everyone who has ever longed to be popular or accepted, or for those who have lost sight of what true acceptance is, take this to heart. Our earthly bodies and all the things of this world will pass away, and the only thing that will last is the life we live for the Lord. It is our lives, our words, and our actions that affect others' lives. God wants you to be you, but to allow Him to work through you to minister for Him. God did not make you to be somebody else. You are special and can change the world in a way that no one else can, so live every day acting justly, loving mercy, and walking humbly with God. God has given us what we need in His Word to teach us and to help us to trust Him. Humility will come when we allow God to be more important in our lives than being popular. We are already accepted by God if we know Him as Lord and Savior, so what others think is not so important after all, is it? Remember, people see with eyes that are often worldly, but God sees the heart.

LUKE MERRICK: *15, Springdale, AR*
Immanuel Baptist Church and Shiloh Christian School, Springdale, AR

DOING THE WORD

"But be doers of the word and not hearers only, deceiving yourselves."
—James 1:22

What would the body of Christ look like if we all did what we know we should do? What would your life look like if you did what you knew was right? I think it's easy for us to let this become a problem in our lives. We love going to camps and conferences and Wednesday night youth groups to learn the Word. We may hear the speaker say some good stuff, come across some good advice, read a touching Bible verse, and we leave feeling good about ourselves. "Well, thank the Lord, He spoke to me today." We agree with it in our heads and maybe even feel spiritually pumped up in our hearts, but then we go out and get caught up in the real world without even knowing it, and never end up actually applying what we learned. The subtle barrier between hearing and doing isn't broken. But friend, the Bible says that a faith without works is dead! You see, when we don't settle for the satisfaction that comes from just knowing the Word, when we actually apply and do the Word, we get the satisfaction that comes from God Himself! God tells us that obedience is more beautiful to Him even than sacrifice, and when the God of the universe is pleased with you—it's pure, incredible joy! That moment we are filled with Him like we've never been before in our lives, when He showers all of His amazing love on us, will leave us never wanting anything else ever again! So choose Him, live His Word, and be amazed!

CONNOR HOWINGTON: *17, West Monroe, LA*
First Baptist West Monroe and Northeast Baptist School, West Monroe, LA

GUARD YOUR HEART

"Guard your heart above all else, for it is the source of life."
—*Proverbs 4:23*

When most people think of their hearts, they think one of two things. The first is the stereotypical Valentine's Day heart that represents love and all things romantic. Second, they think of your actual heart, which looks really gross and pumps blood. While it may be important to protect these "hearts," Solomon, the main writer of Proverbs, is not talking about either one of them in this verse. He is referring to your spiritual heart. The translation shown says that your heart is the source of life. In the NIV, it says that everything you do flows through it. In both versions it says that what you put into your heart is what you are going to get out of it. Many of us choose to fill it with sin and ungodly things of the world. The verse says you need to protect it from those things and instead fill it with things directly from God. One great defense God has given us is the Bible. If we fill ourselves with Scripture we will be prepared for every situation and our hearts will be properly guarded. Another thing that I find interesting about this verse is when it says "above all else." Solomon was the wisest man in the world, and Proverbs is considered to be a book people go to when in need of wisdom or advice. It's like in class when the teacher says if you only get one thing out of this lesson remember this, and every student writes it down so they can get at least one answer right on the test. Above all else, he wanted us to know that we need to protect our hearts no matter what happens. Unfortunately, we cannot hope to guard it properly ourselves. So my challenge to you is to ask God to guard it for you and be your protection.

CHRIS NATION: *15, Gallatin, TN*
The Fellowship at Two Rivers, Nashville, TN; Station Camp High School, Gallatin, TN

WORLDLINESS

"Do you not know that friendship with the world is hostility toward God?
So whoever wants to be the world's friend becomes God's enemy."

—James 4:4

God's enemy! So, why is it un-Christian to try to please and befriend the world? Mark 14:19 says, "But the worries of this age, the seduction of wealth, and the desires for other things enter in and choke the word, and it becomes unfruitful." Huh, so, worldly pleasures and desires will get in the way of our relationship with the Father. Why can't we just be like the world and then they would like us and come to our churches? Matthew 5:13 says, "You are the salt of the earth. But if the salt should lose its taste, how can it be made salty? It's no longer good for anything but to be thrown out and trampled on by men." So, it's like salt that's good for a wound, but if the salt loses its taste it won't have a healing effect. The next verse, Matthew 5:14, says, "You are the light of the world. A city situated on a hill cannot be hidden." So, we're supposed to stand out like a city on a hill that can't be hidden, so people can see a difference in our behavior. Others should see what we do for Christ, without us having to tell them. John 15:19 tells us, "If you were of the world, the world would love you as its own. However, because you are not of the world, but I have chosen you out of it, the world hates you." John 15:18 also reminds us that, "If the world hates you, understand that it hated Me before it hated you." Remember that Jesus died at the hand of the world. We should try to persevere for the awaiting promised prize that we will receive in heaven.

MATTHEW COOKSEY: *13, McMinnville, OR*
Valley Baptist Church, McMinnville, OR; Homeschooled

TRUST GOD FOR GUIDANCE

"I am able to do all things through Him who strengthens me."
—*Philippians 4:13*

Eighth grade was highlighted by having the same teacher I had in seventh, so I didn't have to learn a new teaching style. That year was all about making our last year in middle school memorable, with time to focus on high school. My mom says, "First we pray and ask God for wisdom." James 1:5 says, "Now if any of you lacks wisdom, he should ask God, who gives to all generously and without criticizing, and it will be given to him." We asked for suggestions about which high schools would be a good fit. My principle had all the info on high schools, and she knew I had done some acting, so she suggested we start there. Proverbs 15:22 tells us, "Plans fail when there is no counsel, but with many advisers they succeed." We started the application process for the Arts Conservatory for Louisiana and two others schools. The auditions would be a challenge, and I had no formal training. I visited the school several times before audition day, watching other students come and go with their instruments, practicing choreography, and singing, and I was amazed at their talent. My mind quickly turned to thoughts like, *A director said that I take instruction well and I listen,* and *I didn't put all my eggs in one basket,* even *God gives talent.* We had followed instructions to the letter, and the rest was in God's hands. Hebrews 11:1 says, "Now faith is the reality of what is hoped for, the proof of what is not seen." We prayed every step of the way. I aced the audition and, with God's favor, soon received an invitation to attend the workshop for students who would be attending the fall full-time arts and academic high school. Praise God!

PAUL CRAIG GALE: *14, New Orleans, LA*
Franklin Avenue Baptist Church and New Orleans Center for Creative Arts, New Orleans, LA

DATING

"Charm is deceptive and beauty is fleeting, but a woman who fears the Lord will be praised." —*Proverbs 31:30*

Dating is of major importance to us guys. We see that attractive girl, start talking to her, become friends, and sooner or later it could lead to a relationship. It all seems great, but is this girl a godly woman? Would God approve of this girl and this relationship? God has an idea of what kind of girl we should be looking for. He wants us to be with a woman who is dedicated to the family. She will work with the family and do what is right for it. She is well-known for her good works. She helps the needy whenever she can. And above all things, she is a godly woman. So when you are dating, do not be like most boys. Don't go after the most attractive girl in school; instead look for the girl who values her faith and relationship with Christ over everything else. Look for a girl who will be committed to the relationship. This goes the same for you as well. A godly woman will take the relationship seriously, and you should too. As the relationship goes on, you and the girl should move closer to God together as a result of the fellowship. So when out in the dating world, look for a girl filled with the Holy Spirit.

ZACH WATKINS: *16, Henderson, NV*
Highland Hills Baptist Church and Green Valley High School, Henderson, NV

TELLING OTHERS ABOUT GOD

"Haven't I commanded you: be strong and courageous? Do not be afraid or discouraged, for the LORD your God is with you wherever you go." —Joshua 1:9

We all know someone who hasn't accepted Jesus as his or her Savior. For some of us, these people are family members or close friends. These are people who we care about dearly and wouldn't want anything to happen to. Many times it can be hard to bring Jesus up in a conversation, and when we do it can get pretty awkward. A lot of people struggle with talking seriously to others about God, including myself. I used to be really shy but, as I've gotten older, I've become a lot more open to others. Still, sometimes I worry about what others will think of me if I bring God up in a conversation. Today's verse has helped me with this. God tells us to "be strong and courageous . . . for the LORD your God will be with you wherever you go." This promise gives me confidence in the fact that no matter what happens, and no matter what people think of me, God will always be there with me. God wants us to be strong and courageous. That's how He designed us. So the next time you want to talk to someone about God, be confident and just go with it. God will always be by your side in every situation. You can even shoot up a small prayer for help at any time. Know that nothing can stop you with the presence of God. "I am able to do all things through Him who strengthens me" (Philippians 4:13).

JESSE NIEMAN: *18, Ocala, FL*
Church @ The Springs and Forest High School, Ocala, FL

THE FATHER OF
THE STRAYING CHRISTIAN

"Accepting one another and forgiving one another if anyone has a complaint against another. Just as the Lord has forgiven you, so you must also forgive." —*Colossians 3:13*

As a young Christian, I have Christian role models who help me shape my life into the person God wants me to become. Each of these people treats everyone, no matter what background they come from, as the father in this parable treated his straying son (Luke 15:11–32). Even though the son neglected his entire family and spent all of his inheritance on worldly things, his father prepared the best and waited with his arms wide open when his son returned. This would be difficult for anyone that felt betrayed by a family member, friend, enemy, or stranger. Christians try to live like Christ throughout their entire lives. However, every Christian has strayed from Christ. We know we can't change past events, so we learn to leave them behind and forgive anyone that may have hurt us. The father in the parable forgave his son and welcomed him home, as if his son had never left. Jesus wants all of His followers to treat people this way, because it demonstrates His unending love for us. Looking at my role models, I expect them to not hold a grudge against those that may have hurt them, but to welcome them back into their lives to celebrate Christ's love for them.

BILLY RAMSEY: *17, Sharon, SC*
Faith Baptist Church, Clover, SC; York Comprehensive High School, York, SC

HIDDEN TREASURE

"The kingdom of heaven is like treasure, buried in a field, that a man found and reburied. Then, in his joy he goes and sells everything he has and buys that field." —*Matthew 13:44*

As we grow in faith and our future is shaped, the issue of how much value we put on the gospel arises. If we truly want to see the gospel move many people, we have to carefully balance our priorities between things of this world and things that are eternal. Today's passage provides instruction on how to live. The man in this passage had things, like us. However, he realized the value of what he had was far inferior to what he discovered in the field. The gospel and the materialism of today's culture do not mesh. Everything is rendered obsolete by the glory that is coming. The man realized that the things he once had didn't matter! Heaven is so much greater than anything on the earth. We should look forward to the future. When the man saw the absolute perfection and gorgeous treasure, he knew that everything else he owned was insignificant compared to what he now held in his hand. With joy, he gladly sold everything he had because he knew that the pearl was worth more than anything else he could have imagined in his wildest dreams. This passage applies to our lives too. We have to dedicate our lives to the kingdom that is coming! Things of this world will pass away, but the Word of the Lord and the souls of men are eternal. As Colossians 3:2 says, "Set your minds on what is above, not on what is on the earth." If we want to make an impact for eternity, we must shift our focus from things of the world to things that are above. We must invest our lives in things that will have eternal rewards.

LUKE PERSTROPE: *17, St. Peters, MO*
First Baptist Church of St. Charles, St. Charles, MO; Fort Zumwalt East High School, St. Peters, MO

GOVERNMENT

"Everyone must submit to the governing authorities, for there is no authority except from God, and those that exist are instituted by God."

—*Romans 13:1*

It is sometimes hard to respect and obey leaders who you think believe the wrong thing or have different opinions than you do. Yet, in the verse above, we are told to submit to their instruction because God has placed them in authority for a purpose. We might not understand God's reasoning but, as stated in Romans 8:28, "We know that all things work together for the good of those who love God: those who are called according to His purpose." Our Father would not place an obstacle in front of our lives if it did not serve a higher purpose. It is meant to help us grow and mature and ultimately rely on the Lord for direction. Take advantage of the chance to learn and expand your knowledge, even if it is not what you believe is correct. As you go about your day, be conscious of authorities in your life and realize that they are there to help you grow. If you have trouble submitting to authority, pray and ask God to grant obedience to your heart, so that you may follow the path laid before you.

JONATHAN DISMUKES: *17, Mobile, AL*
Redeemer Fellowship Church and Cottage Hill Christian Academy, Mobile, AL

WHY GOD ALLOWS TROUBLES IN OUR LIVES

"Consider it a great joy, my brothers, whenever you experience various trials, knowing that the testing of your faith produces endurance. But endurance must do its complete work, so that you may be mature and complete, lacking nothing." —*James 1:2–4*

James 1:12 says that "A man who endures trials is blessed, because when he passes the test he will receive the crown of life that God has promised to those who love Him." When you see someone going through a hard time in their life, you may say to yourself, "They are such a good person. Why is that happening to them?" You may even think that God is being unfair and unjust to that person. It may even be you who is struggling and wondering why. God doesn't allow us to go through hard times just for the fun of it. He has a perfect plan for everyone and He knows that whatever comes out of it will be for our good and His glory. As it states in James 1:12, "A man who endures trials is blessed." Trials can also be a test from God to see how you will handle the situation. Will you complain about it and make other people miserable, or will you be a light to others while going through your own trials? We are to be living examples of Jesus. Are you?

JACOB LAVALLEY: *16, Pageland, SC*
Mount Moriah Baptist Church and South Pointe Christian School, Pageland, SC

PAUL AND TIMOTHY

"A disciple is not above his teacher, but everyone who is fully trained will be like his teacher." —Luke 6:40

Each of us has a Paul, and everyone also has a Timothy. Paul was the teacher, and Timothy was the student. Our Paul is the one who mentors us, the one who shows us the true, pure, and right way to live our life. Mine is my brother. He led a discipleship group for me and my friends when I was in middle school, and he has always talked to me about following Christ and living my life by God's principles. He is my Paul, the man I look up to. You could say he is my role model. I was my brother's Timothy. I learned from him what I needed to know. He was my mentor. Now, I lead a discipleship for middle school boys. I am now the Paul in someone's life. I am no longer the student, Timothy; I am a Paul. I teach my Timothys how to live for Christ and, one day, my Timothy will become a Paul and lead. It is a constant spreading of God's Word from generation to generation. Let me challenge you: Who is your Paul? Who is your Timothy? If you don't have either, you're not going in the right direction.

KORD OFFENBACKER: *16, Springdale, AR*
Cross Church Springdale Campus and Shiloh Christian School, Springdale, AR

WORSHIP

"Our Lord and God, You are worthy to receive glory and honor and power, because You have created all things, and because of Your will they exist and were created." —Revelation 4:11

What is worship? Is it singing? Dancing? Praying? What is it? I've been thinking about this for the past few months, especially since I've started leading worship music in my youth group. I've been learning that worship is not so much an action as an attitude. We don't have to be in a certain place or doing a certain thing in order to worship God. First Corinthians 10:31 says, "Therefore, whether you eat or drink, or whatever you do, do everything for God's glory." We can worship God through whatever we do if we have the right attitude and are trying to do it for God's glory. Focus on where your heart is. What do you love? You will worship what you love the most. How much do we love God? Do we let Him be the steering wheel of our lives or just use Him as a spare tire when we need to? Our worship reflects our love for God. What about singing worship, though? That's what most people think of when they hear the word *worship*. Singing worship songs is a time where we can clear our minds of everything and focus on the cross and who God is. Sure, life gets crazy and both positive and negative things happen, but we get to let that all go and replace those worries with God—holy and awesome God! Some people say, "I don't really worship, I don't have a good voice." That doesn't give you an excuse to not join in. Skill does not make your worship more acceptable to God. It's about where your heart is. A. W. Tozer said, "If worship bores us, we are not ready for heaven" (A. W. Tozer, *The Pursuit of God*, Camp Hill, PA: Wingspread Publishers, 2009). Worshipping God in heaven will be the most amazing experience ever! I pray we all can't wait to be there!

AUSTIN CANFIELD: *18, Tulsa, OK*
Evergreen Baptist Church, Bixby, OK; Homeschooled

FAITH

"Now faith is the reality of what is hoped for, the proof of what is not seen. For our ancestors won God's approval by it. By faith we understand that the universe was created by God's command, so that what is seen has been made from things that are not visible." —*Hebrews 11:1–3*

Most Christians struggle with having faith or with having it when we feel we need it most. Do not feel as if you are the only one who faces doubts. The devil tries to make you feel like you are not saved, and he warps your thinking so that might believe you are too busy to do anything for the Lord. Once you are sure of your salvation, you need to read the Bible often, and study and meditate on what it says, so that you can see that your faith is strengthened. The stronger your faith is, the harder the devil will try to make you doubt your salvation. The Bible says that the Lord will not allow you to be tempted more than you can bear. Think about Job who lost everything and was tempted to curse God. He stayed strong, as you should, and he was blessed for what he did. God wants to use you for His work on the earth, but you need to know Him and know what He has in store for you. That takes the assurance of salvation and a commitment to study the Bible and to communicate with God in prayer.

DAVID ATKINSON: *14, Pageland, SC*
Mount Moriah Baptist Church, Marshville, NC; South Pointe Christian School, Pageland, SC

TOUGH PLAYER

"Search me, God, and know my heart; test me and know my concerns.
See if there is any offensive way in me; lead me in the everlasting way."
—*Psalm 139:23–24*

The verse above is one of the most beautiful passages in all of Scripture. David is asking God to search his heart and to clean out all of the junk so he can live his life in a manner that would glorify God. David acknowledges that only God can search and know what we hold deep in our hearts, and he asks God to rid him of the things in his life that God finds offensive. How humbling. These are the kind of prayers that get us into a deeper relationship with God. It's a tough prayer to pray! Asking God to look into your heart and see what is offensive can be painful, because there is so much filth in all of us. To pray this type of prayer, you have to realize that God's everlasting way is the best way, the only way. This prayer was prayed out of desperation for more of God in David's life; it wasn't lighthearted. David wanted to go deeper with God and to follow His way no matter what, even if it meant giving up things he enjoyed but he knew were not pleasing to God. If we ever want our relationship with God to reach the depths that David desired, then we must be willing to be humbled the same way and to pray the same type of prayers that will bring us closer to God the Father.

CLAY NORMAN: *18, Albany, GA*
Sherwood Baptist Church and Sherwood Christian Academy, Albany, GA

BECOMING A GOOD MAN

"When all has been heard, the conclusion of the matter is: fear God and keep His commands, because this is for all humanity."

—*Ecclesiastes 12:13*

The verse above contains simple instruction on how to become a better Christian. But, though simple, they are by no means easy tasks, especially for teen boys. In this context, *fear* means both to love and respect God. Loving and respecting God does not come easily to sinners like us. Along with respecting God, we must keep His commandments. We must grow close to God by staying in the Bible daily and by spending time with Him in prayer. We need to listen to Him and not do all the talking! We learn to fear God, not to make us afraid, but a fear that shows respect for who He is. We keep His commandments out of the love and respect that we have for Him. We will fail trying to do these things, but we must get back up with God's help. When we do these things, we will inevitably grow closer to God.

JACKSON REESE: *18, Pageland, SC*
South Pointe Fellowship and South Pointe Christian School, Pageland, SC

OCTOBER

Two Ways of Life

Listen, my son. Accept my words,

and you will live many years.

I am teaching you the way of wisdom;

I am guiding you on straight paths.

When you walk, your steps will not be hindered;

when you run, you will not stumble.

Hold on to instruction; don't let go.

Guard it, for it is your life.

Don't set foot on the path of the wicked;

don't proceed in the way of evil ones.

Avoid it; don't travel on it.

Turn away from it, and pass it by.

For they can't sleep unless they have done what is evil;

they are robbed of sleep unless they make someone stumble.

They eat the bread of wickedness and drink the wine of violence.

The path of the righteous is like the light of dawn,

shining brighter and brighter until midday.

But the way of the wicked is like the darkest gloom;

they don't know what makes them stumble. (Proverbs 4:10–19)

MOVING MOUNTAINS IS A GOD THING (PART 1)

"'Because of your faith..' He told them. 'For I assure you, if you have faith the size of a mustard seed, you will tell this mountain, "Move from here to there," and it will move. Nothing will be impossible for you.'"

—*Matthew 17:20*

So why aren't there mountain movers today? Do we really have faith that God could move a mountain through us? It just seems like such a big idea, yet it is just a small task for God. What mountains does God have for you to move in your life? How can we, teen boys, understand the kind of faith that can move mountains? Remember that we are referring to mountains figuratively speaking, although it is definitely possible for God to move the Swiss Alps if He chose to do so. We need to first realize that moving the mountains in our lives is not about the thing, the person, or the circumstance that is a hindrance to us, but it is all about God.

It is about trusting God, who is the only one able to do exceedingly abundantly above all that we can ask of Him, or even imagine in our finite minds. If God wants a mountain to be moved, whether physically or metaphorically, He will use a Christian who He knows will give Him all the glory. Do you have mountains in your life that need to be moved? Actually, we all do. This is not something that is only common to teens, but teens struggle with all sorts of stuff that is in the way of a solid relationship with God. Today could be the day that you make a major decision to give God a place of honor in your life and allow Him to move all the mountains. He is available, are you?

TREY SUEY: *16, Mt. Juliet, TN*
The Fellowship at Two Rivers, Nashville, TN; New Life Academy, Mt. Juliet, TN

MOVING MOUNTAINS IS A GOD THING (PART 2)

"'Because of your faith,' He told them, 'For I assure you, if you have faith the size of a mustard seed, you will tell this mountain, "Move from here to there," and it will move. Nothing will be impossible for you.'"

—*Matthew 17:20*

God is always available to move mountains, but you need to realize that God doesn't work on your time schedule. He is the master of all things, and everything will go according to the way He wants it to. To be a mountain mover you need to be in God's will, because He will never move a mountain that isn't a part of His plan for you. Sometimes things need to stay just like they are for a purpose that we cannot understand, but God's plan includes that thing and He will leave it there until we learn the lesson He has for us to learn. This shouldn't upset us, but it should show us how awesome and in control our God is. We need to rise up! It is time for a generation of mountain movers! We need to go into our schools, churches, jobs, and the world and let the people in each place know that our God is a mountain mover, and He works through us. Just let your friends know that if they are struggling with something in their lives that our God is in the business of moving mountains! Take some time to pray and ask God to raise you up to be a mountain mover for Him. Ask Him to work through you and to guide you in His will. Pray that He will use you to display His great power and love.

TREY SUEY: *16, Mt. Juliet, TN*
The Fellowship at Two Rivers, Nashville, TN; New Life Academy, Mt. Juliet, TN

DO MY THOUGHTS MATTER?

"Finally brothers, whatever is true, whatever is honorable, whatever is just, whatever is pure, whatever is lovely, whatever is commendable—if there is any moral excellence and if there is any praise—dwell on these things" —*Philippians 4:8*

Have you ever thought about whether it matters how you think? Many people believe that their thoughts have no lasting impact; therefore, it must be perfectly all right to think whatever they like as long as it doesn't hurt anybody. For instance, some people harbor deep hatred inside and justify doing so by claiming that as long as they don't act on it no one gets hurt. Thoughts do matter for two very important reasons. First, God commands us how to think. He tells us what our minds should be on in Philippians 4:8. We are told to think about just, honorable, pure, and true things. To deceive yourself without lying to anyone else is still sin. To harbor anger in your head is sin. This alone is a very good reason to watch how we think. The second reason is that it will affect our actions. If we believe the lies that we tell ourselves, we will begin to act as if we believe. If we harbor anger long enough, it will eventually show. We will become bitter, surly, and no fun to be around. If we allow ourselves to enjoy tempting thoughts, then we are weakening our ability to resist. By opening the door to enjoying thoughts, we are gradually lessening the severity of the crime and our memory of the consequences. God calls us to be holy like He is. We are blessed with the ability to think and reason like no other part of creation. We need to recognize this and keep our thoughts pure in order to honor God with them.

JOSIAH MCGEE: *15, Kansas City, MO*
Summit Woods Baptist Church, Lees Summit, MO; Homeschooled

ANOREXIA

"This is why I tell you: Don't worry about your life, what you eat or what you will drink; or about your body, what you will wear. Isn't life more than food and the body more than clothing?" —*Matthew 6:25*

Anorexia is spreading at alarming rates among both males and females, particularly among teenagers. They stop eating and try to become as perfect as they can. This is, of course, useless, because there was only one man who walked this earth who was perfect. Jesus fasted in the name of the Lord so that He would not become what the world wanted Him to be. He didn't worry what clothing made Him look the thinnest. He only wore what covered His body well enough to walk around outside. Matthew 6:25 tells us, "This is why I tell you: Don't worry about your life, what you eat or what you will drink; or about your body, what you will wear. Isn't life more than food and the body more than clothing?" In this verse, Jesus tells us not to worry about how others see us. He tells us to rest in the Lord and to let Him worry about us. In return for obeying Him and doing as He commands, we will be rewarded with the opportunity to do more for Him. If we worry about our clothing and our weight, how do we expect to have time for God? God designed us all to be unique, so why worry about becoming something else, something that is the opposite of His perfect design.

DAVID JOSEPH DALESANDRO: *14, York, SC*
Hillcrest Baptist Church and York Comprehensive High School, York, SC

THE WORLD OF SOCIAL NETWORKING

"To the pure, everything is pure, but to those who
are defiled and unbelieving nothing is pure; in fact,
both their mind and conscience are defiled." —*Titus 1:15*

Facebook, Twitter, Kik, Instagram—I'm sure you have at least one of these. Social networking has become the way the world communicates and it's usually about who has the most friends, or who tweets the most and generates the most likes. Now, don't get me wrong. I'm not saying that social networks are horrible and that we all need to just forget about them. In some ways they can be good. It all depends on how you use them, the time you spend on them, and who you associate with while using them. Usually people will accept requests to have others watch their site and communicate with them, or allow others to follow them, even if they don't know the person. There is often one person on one of your social media sites who will post profanity or crude and vulgar pictures, etc. This behavior often causes us to be dragged into the same thing. If we were to delete the friends that post all of this nonsense and gossip, and use the system for keeping in contact with our actual friends, that would be a good thing. That was a big issue for me. I deleted six hundred friends off of Facebook, which leaves me with the forty who I actually associate with in real life. I am also not on the site 24/7, so I have more time with my family. I encourage you to get your social media sites in order and only use them for the good that will glorify God.

BRANDON CARROLL: *17, York, SC*
Hillcrest Baptist Church and York Comprehensive High School, York, SC

CHARM

"Charm is deceptive and beauty is fleeting, but a woman who fears the Lord will be praised." —*Proverbs 31:30*

It is very easy for teenage guys to be attracted to a girl because of her outer appearance. While you do need to be attracted to a girl physically, it is much more important to be attracted to her desire for God. What we consider beauty when we are teen boys rarely lasts in the same way as the girl grows older. If a girl is just beautiful but has no desire to know and to be like God, what will happen when she is no longer beautiful? I believe we, as young men, often treat dating too much like a game. We see who can get the most attractive girl, and a lot of times we don't even care about her personality or her relationship with God. Pride certainly is an issue for us guys. We should never date anyone who we could not see ourselves marrying one day. We should strive for a girl who wants to please God more than she wants to please us. Seek God's highest in the girl you date as a potential wife, one who possesses the sweet aroma of Christ. Don't let lust get in your way of love. God wants so much more for our lives and the girl we date!

CHANDLER SMITH: *16, Springdale, AR*
Cross Church Springdale Campus and Shiloh Christian School, Springdale, AR

GOD HAS A PLAN FOR YOU

"'For I know the plans I have for you'—this is the LORD's declaration—'plans for your welfare, not for disaster, to give you a future and a hope.'"

—Jeremiah 29:11

Have you ever found yourself wondering what you are going to do with your life? Whether it's your career, what school or college to go to, or maybe what to eat for lunch. Our verse today tells us that God has a plan for every single one of our lives. So each and every day, God knows what is going to happen and He knows what is best for us. We can trust Him and know that His intentions are for our good and not to harm us. I know that even though we know that God has a plan for our futures, it can still be hard to see. God can be trusted. Proverbs 3:5 says to, "Trust in the LORD with all your heart and do not rely on your own understanding." So if you are trying to figure out what to do with your life, please know that you can trust that God's plan is best.

CLAYTON TEAL: *17, Pageland, SC*
Smyrna Baptist Church and South Pointe Christian School, Pageland, SC

FULFILLING THE GREAT COMMISSION

"Go, therefore, and make disciples of all nations, baptizing them in the name of the Father and of the Son and of the Holy Spirit, teaching them to observe everything I have commanded you. And remember, I am with you always, to the end of the age." —*Matthew 28:19–20*

If you look at the first word at the beginning of Matthew 28:19, it says, "Go." That wasn't a suggestion! Everywhere you go you should be preaching the Word of God and telling people about Jesus. Now does that mean you should go to a foreign country and be a missionary? Not necessarily. But it does mean that while you are going wherever you go and doing whatever you do, you should be witnessing to people about Christ. You might say, "Well, my calling isn't to be a pastor or a missionary, so that doesn't apply to me," but it does. It applies to every person who calls themselves a Christian. The second part of the verse says we must also "make disciples," which means we need to help people that accept Jesus grow in their Christian walk. I am involved in a small group Bible study at my school and have a high school mentor who challenges and encourages me. This is discipleship. Attending Sunday school and worship at my church also helps me grow. Finally, "baptizing them in the name of the Father and of the Son and of the Holy Spirit" shows our obedience to God's call. We are not going or doing it for our own benefit, but for the Lord. We go and we share Jesus to please Him and glorify His name.

ANDREW CLEM: *13, Albany, GA*
Sherwood Baptist Church and Sherwood Christian Academy, Albany, GA

RESISTING TEMPTATIONS AND BREAKING ADDICTIONS

"God is faithful, and He will not allow you to be tempted beyond what you are able, but with the temptation He will also provide a way of escape so that you are able to bear it." —*1 Corinthians 10:13*

Six steps to help eliminate addictions in your life:

1. Trust God! He says that you can handle any temptation thrown at you with Him, so believe it! Sometimes all it takes in the heat of the moment is to say, "God and I are perfectly able to defeat this!"

2. Control. Have a problem with lust? Develop the habit of bouncing your eyes away from temptation. Remember, there's always a way out, whether it's going into another room with other people, getting some work done, or whatever works for the situation.

3. Get filled with Him daily. Pray honestly and passionately, read the Word until you're full. It's important to spend time with God at the start of your day to prepare you for the struggles ahead. You can't fight your battles without your armor.

4. Do God's will. Know what God wants you to do in life and do it! If you're doing God's will, you won't even have a thought about pleasing your flesh. If you ask God, He'll show you His will through His Word.

5. Eliminate the obvious sources of temptation in your life. Obedience might take sacrifice. Need an Internet filter? Need to get rid of the TV or video games?

6. Be held accountable. If you know you're having trouble, get a godly Christian friend to encourage you. When you're free from guilt and living for God, you will be so glad you did!

CONNOR HOWINGTON: *17, West Monroe, LA*
First Baptist West Monroe and Northeast Baptist School, West Monroe, LA

DEPRESSION

"Why am I so depressed? Why this turmoil within me? Put your hope in God, for I will still praise Him, my Savior and my God." —*Psalm 42:11*

During my freshman and sophomore years in high school, I struggled with depression. I had completely stopped reading my Bible and praying. This is a huge reason why I had these problems. I didn't listen to anything that went on in church; I totally ignored it. I became angry and bitter, always fighting with my parents and siblings. One night, after I said some terrible things to my parents and was storming off to my room, my parents stopped me and told me they loved me. As I walked to my room, I was baffled. How could they love me after all the things I had said and done to them? Then it really hit me. How could God love me after all I had done to Him? The Bible says God can love us more than any human possibly can. I dropped to my knees and started crying. I couldn't thank God enough for His love! I didn't realize how selfish and prideful I was being. I had absolutely no reason to feel depressed when God had blessed me so much! My mistake was not turning to Christ when I started feeling unhappy; I blocked Him out. But He loves us and wants to help us. He wants to draw us closer to Him. We need to allow Him to do that. First Peter 5:6–7 says, "Humble yourselves, therefore, under the mighty hand of God, so that He may exalt you at the proper time, casting all your care on Him, because He cares about you." Whenever you're going through a rough time, turn to God. He loves you and wants to help you!

AUSTIN CANFIELD: *18, Tulsa, OK*
Evergreen Baptist Church, Bixby, OK; Homeschooled

WHERE IS YOUR HEART?

"For where your treasure is, there your heart will be also."
—*Matthew 6:21*

Where is your heart? What do you treasure most? The things we value the most show a lot about where our heart is. In Matthew 6:24, Jesus says, "No one can be a slave of two masters, since either he will hate one and love the other, or be devoted to one and despise the other. You cannot be slaves of God and of money." Jesus calls us to full devotion to Him. Not half of us or even 95 percent; He calls for the full 100 percent or none at all. In this passage, Jesus uses the example of money, but it can be anything. You can't serve both God and money, God and sports, God and relationships, or fill in the blank with anything else that is important in your life. In Matthew 19 Jesus describes a rich young ruler who says he had kept all the Ten Commandments. He asks Jesus what he lacks, and He tells the young man to sell all he has and give it to the poor. The man couldn't do it, and he walked away from God. The reason is because his money was his treasure; it was where his heart was. Until we get rid of the idols in our lives that we hold onto at as high a level as God, we can never serve Him fully.

CLAY NORMAN: *18, Albany, GA*
Sherwood Baptist Church and Sherwood Christian Academy, Albany, GA

PREPARING

"Rejoice, young man, while you are young, and let your heart be glad in the days of your youth. And walk in the ways of your heart and in the sight of your eyes; but know that for all of these things God will bring you to judgment." —*Ecclesiastes 11:9*

It's easy to think of your teen years as a time to basically have as much fun as possible until it's time to settle down and start a family. That's the picture promoted by most movies today. But, the biblical picture is that young men and women use their teenage years to prepare for adulthood. So, rather than marriage being the boring end to years of fun, it's the pinnacle of years of preparation. We have so much to look forward to! God gave us our teenage years so that we could mature, develop skills, and prepare for the day that we say "I do." One of the key ways to prepare for marriage is to learn to get along with your parents and siblings. Learning to treat your family well is one of the best ways to learn how to treat your spouse well. You can also prepare by saving your money; you will be so glad you did later on. Yet another way is to develop skills that will help you be a good parent or provide for your family. Learn a programming language, talk to people in your church who have skills like plumbing, architecture, etc. Help a family at church with their kids. This is so much more valuable than playing "Call of Duty" in your living room.

MICAH COOKSEY: *19, McMinnville, OR*
Valley Baptist Church, McMinnville, OR

GOD LOVES YOU!

"For God loved the world in this way: He gave His One and Only Son, so that everyone who believes in Him will not perish but have eternal life."

—John 3:16

God loves you, and He sent His only Son to come to this earth to die for us. Jesus' death on the cross paid the price for our sins, and all you have to do is accept this free gift of salvation. If you were to die tonight, would your soul end up in heaven or hell? Please think about it and know that Jesus will forgive you no matter what you've done. Salvation is a free gift; it's not something we work for. Remember that we are all sinners and that there is no sin too big for God to forgive. Romans 5:8 says, "But God proves His own love for us in that while we were still sinners, Christ died for us," and in Romans 6:23 we are told that, "The wages of sin is death, but the gift of God is eternal life in Christ Jesus our Lord." The Bible also says in Romans 10:9, "If you confess with your mouth, 'Jesus is Lord,' and believe in your heart that God raised Him from the dead you will be saved." The wages of sin is death, but the free gift of God is eternal life in Christ Jesus. Please think about the question asked earlier, and if you are not sure please pray the following prayer: *God, I admit that I am a sinner, and right now I accept Your free gift of salvation, I accept You as my Lord and Savior. I accept what You did on the cross. I confess Jesus is Lord, and believe in my heart that God raised Jesus from the dead. Thank You for saving me and forgiving me of all my sins. Amen.*

HANK F. GRIFFIN: *14, Pageland, SC*
White Plains Baptist Church, Jefferson, SC; South Pointe Christian School; Pageland, SC

PASSION

"For me, living is Christ and dying is gain." —*Philippians 1:21*

Today's verse is one of those verses that almost every Christian can quote but few actually live by. Paul had such a passionate love for Christ that he no doubt meant every word. For Paul, Christianity wasn't clinging to a prayer that he prayed when he was a kid; it was a true surrendering of his whole life to God and His purposes. Paul never held anything back. For Paul, his whole reason for living was to make Christ known to others, and he knew what lay ahead. He knew that death was a victory for him because it meant he finally got to stand face-to-face with the God he loved and lived his whole life for. He understood that no matter where he was, his job was to preach Christ, even if it got him thrown in jail. Paul's deep passion for Christ was because he was so grateful for what Christ had done in his life, and he realized what Christ had saved him from . . . a life spent in eternal damnation. We have no excuse for not having the same passion as Paul had. God has saved us, too, and the same Holy Spirit that lived inside Paul lives in every other Christian the world over. God hasn't changed; He will use us if we let Him. We need to pray for the same passion that Paul had to spread the gospel message and to give our whole lives to God. We need to be able to truly say that every second we live is for Christ, and if we die it is gain, because we will finally get to see Him face-to-face in all His glory!

CLAY NORMAN: *18, Albany, GA*
Sherwood Baptist Church and Sherwood Christian Academy, Albany, GA

BULLYING

"Do not take revenge or bear a grudge against members of your community, but love your neighbor as yourself; I am Yahweh."

—*Leviticus 19:18*

At some point, somewhere, we have all been bullied, but maybe it wasn't called by that term. Even friends will tell you, "Words can never hurt you," but the truth is they can and they often do. I understand what it means to be bullied. I lived a very sinful life for a long time and I was made a mockery with some hateful and vile words. The words hurt, and they cut me to my core. Leviticus 19:18 says, "Do not take revenge or bear a grudge against members of your community, but love your neighbor as yourself." The ones bullying you mean to hurt you, so because we are fallible we often try to hurt them back. Today's verse is for all of us who have said something hateful to someone. A lot of the times we don't realize we are bullying others, but as a result people cry, self-harm, and even commit suicide. We should love our bullies and pray God reaches them and try to help them come to know the Lord. And when we find ourselves bullying others, we should apologize and make amends with them. God wants us to see the damage caused by our words. We all say things that hurt others, but He wants us to pray for even our enemies, and to build up everyone. If we pray for the bullies, we won't have the time or the heart to want to get back at them. Something good to try, don't you agree?

DAVID JOSEPH DALESANDRO: *14, York, SC*
Hillcrest Baptist Church and York Comprehensive High School, York, SC

IS THAT AN IDOL?

"They served their idols, which became a snare to them."
—*Psalm 106:36*

In Old Testament times, an idol was a statue that people worshipped instead of God. I doubt that many Christians today worship statues. However, I would not be surprised if most Christians were to tell me that they struggle with an idol. I know that I do. An idol is anything you decide is just as important as God, or more so. It causes you to sin because you want it so badly. When I think about it, there are many things that could become an idol. Some examples are friends, popularity, and cell phones. Another example is social media. You may be asking how in the world social media can be an idol. It becomes an idol when it takes the place of God. I have completely ignored the need for time with God and personal devotions because I struggle to resist the desire to connect with my friends. When checking e-mail, seeing what my friends are up to, or communicating with them is more important to me than communicating with God, I have allowed an idol to appear in my life. Social media can also present itself as an idol when it causes me to sin. Have you ever snapped at a sibling when on Facebook? Have you ever ignored and disobeyed your parents in order to stay on Twitter? These acts of disrespect are examples of sin that comes from idolizing social media. Media is not an idol unless you allow it to be by misusing it and making it more important than God's commands. Social media is not bad. However, if we ignore the need to connect with God in order to connect with friends, if we treat others badly when we are online, if we ignore God's command to treat others respectfully, then we have made media an idol.

JOSIAH MCGEE: *15, Kansas City, MO*
Summit Woods Baptist Church, Lees Summit, MO; Homeschooled

IF DEATH IS BAD, WHY DOES GOD ALLOW IT?

"But you will receive power when the Holy Spirit has come on you, and you will be My witnesses in Jerusalem, in all Judea and Samaria, and to the ends of the earth." —*Acts 1:8*

"One does not simply walk into Mordor!" Similarly, expressing what you believe in and sharing your testimony with others is no easy thing. Most of the time we wait for opportunities to arise and then sometimes don't act on them, because we're afraid of what others might think of us. There are opportunities for sharing God's Word all the time, but I often notice that we are either too blind to notice them, or too stubborn to act on them. Once when I was at school, the subject of death was brought up and a girl addressed a group of about four people and asked, "If death is so bad, why does God put us through it?" I recognized an opportunity instantly and decided to jump on it. I told the small group that I was a Christian and was pleased to see that there was another in the group. I asked the four if it was all right if I shared my religious answer. Everyone was fine with it. I told the girl that death isn't bad, it's a part of life, and you don't need to fear it if you've received Jesus Christ as your Savior. That night I prayed that she would think about what I had said. Now I guarantee you that I've missed many opportunities for sharing the gospel over the years that I've been a Christian, whether I just didn't notice them or didn't act on them. When I shared my religious faith with that group of four, I was surprised at how willingly they listened. If you share your beliefs with others, I'll bet you'll be surprised too. God can use you to do marvelous things, and He will. With the Lord on your lips, you may change the hearts of the people you least expect.

JASON MCKEE: *15, Anchorage, AK*
First Baptist Church of Anchorage and Service High School, Anchorage, AK

FISHING

"'Follow Me,' He told them, 'and I will make you fish for people!'"
—*Matthew 4:19*

One summer I went fishing with my grandpa. It was exciting because it was the first time I would be fishing in a boat going down the river. I caught some fish, and even surprised myself at my casting skills. We had a great day. Peter and his brother Andrew were fishermen before they became Christ followers. When they met Jesus, He called them to be fishers of men. When they changed from fishermen to fishers of men, they took a different approach to life: no more nets thrown out and no more selling fish. Instead, they caught the people with the Word of Christ, the gospel. We should constantly be fishing for the kingdom, trying to tell people about Jesus and leading them to the most important decision of their lives. Fishing for people will be challenging, but just like being out in the boat and casting time after time in the water, you will need to be persistent. Most people don't receive Jesus Christ the first time they hear about Him. It often takes many times of sharing the message of Jesus before someone actually becomes convicted of their sin and convinced about Jesus. Fishing for men might be harder than fishing for fish, but the rewards are so much sweeter. You can lead someone to receive eternal life. Most of the time when you fish it's just for the fun of it. Sharing the message of Jesus is to be exciting and fun. It's fun to fish for people!

MICAH PERSTROPE: *13, St. Peters, MO*
First Baptist Church of St. Charles, St. Charles, MO; Dubray Middle School, St. Peters, MO

FAILURE

"I am writing you these things so that you may not sin.
But if anyone does sin, we have an advocate with the Father. . . .
He Himself is the propitiation for our sins, and not only for ours,
but also for those of the whole world." —*1 John 2:1–2*

It happened again. I gave in to that one type of sin that I have wanted to stop in the past. What should I do? What do I say? I love the Lord and want to do the right thing, but Satan causes the wrong to look so deceitfully good. Christians still sin, though we are saved. Salvation is not a magic potion that causes sinful desires and actions to disappear. That is what makes it beautiful. Though we are eternally saved, salvation is also an everyday thing. Every day we discover that we desperately need our Savior. Every day we can know that He is the only way to live. Every day we know that Jesus is standing in the gap, interceding for us in the heavenly court. When we sin, instead of focusing on our guilt (I didn't say not feeling guilty, just not focusing on it), we ask for forgiveness and know that Jesus covers our sins. After confessing, we should focus on not giving into sin again. The world is filled with sin, and Satan can make sin look awesome. It takes hard work to turn around and walk the other way. As a reference when dealing with temptation, remember a representation you have seen of Jesus on the cross. Think of the cross and that should cause you to think twice before giving into sin. Pray that God will deliver you. Go and live the victorious life God wants you to live!

LUKE MERRICK: *15, Springdale, AR*
Immanuel Baptist Church and Shiloh Christian School, Springdale, AR

SERVING GOD

"We know that all things work together for the good of those who love God; those who are called according to His purpose."
—*Romans 8:28*

Do you sometimes, think, *Oh, well I don't know what my friend will think,* or *I don't want them to not like me,* or, *So I just will let someone else serve God in this way,* or *will let another do this, and so-and-so do this, and so on.* There are times when we all want to let others do the will of the Lord while we engage in things that are not so pleasing to God, or that provide pleasure for us and have little to do with serving Him. If we read what God's Word says to us in today's verse, we understand that He has everything under His control, and even when we don't do what we are supposed to do for Him, He is not surprised and certainly not caught lacking when it comes to having others do what He requires. So, friend, do you love God? Are you willing to serve Him, in whatever He wants you to do? Are you also willing to do what He asks of you right now, without waiting for others to do their part and yours? God gives us a choice, and it would be the right thing to do to act on His call on our lives. Think about it!

HANK F. GRIFFIN: *14, Pageland, SC*
White Plains Baptist Church, Jefferson, SC; South Pointe Christian School, Pageland, SC

WALK IN LOVE, THE LOVE OF JESUS

"And this is love: that we walk according to His commands. This is the command as you have heard it from the beginning: you must walk in love." —2 John 6

So often we look at love as a feeling or emotion but, truthfully, it is so much more complex. We are all very good at loving the people who benefit us, but how often do we go out of our way to love the helpless? Jesus did not just love the rich; He loved the weak, the downtrodden, and the poor. If this were not the case, why would God love us? Does He really benefit from our existence? His love is not based on conditions, but on the fact that He wanted people, made in His own image, that He could fellowship with and grow with through the intimacy and depth of relationships. God loves us despite our flaws. How would we feel if God judged us the way we judge others? Would we be encouraged by God, or would we feel unwanted? Would we want to run to the Lord, or would we want to flee from Him? We, as Christians, may be the only representative of Jesus that people we know ever see, and we want their experience to be positive. Let's walk in love, the love of Christ Jesus, before a lost and dying world!

CHANDLER SMITH: *16, Springdale, AR*
Cross Church Springdale Campus and Shiloh Christian School, Springdale, AR

FIND YOUR PLACE

"Now you are the body of Christ, and individual members of it."

—*1 Corinthians 12:27*

Let me tell you a story about two teenage boys. One Sunday morning they decided to go to church, but when they walked in, they had trouble finding a seat. After a few moments of searching, the two young men started to walk out and head back home. Before they were able to exit, an usher stopped them. He asked if they were looking for a seat. They said yes and were escorted to a few open seats in the church. Later in that service, both of the boys committed their lives to follow Jesus. One of these young men was named Billy Graham. Now, if you don't know Billy Graham, he is one of the most famous and influential Christian men in the world. He was a spiritual mentor to several US Presidents and even worked with Reverend Martin Luther King Jr. This isn't the important part of the story though. What's important is the man who stopped Billy and his friend from leaving that church service and showed them to some open seats. This man may have only seen himself helping a couple of teenagers find seats, but in that moment, he helped to change the course of history forever. We can all be just like this man. First Corinthians 12:27 says that we "are the body of Christ, and individual members of it." We are all a necessary part of the plan God has for the world, and there is not one of us that God does not want to use for the good of mankind. God has even given us all special gifts, and He wants us to use them to serve each other, just like the man served Billy and his friend (1 Peter 4:10). So keep this story in mind. The small things you do now may turn into life changes later.

JESSE NIEMAN: *18, Ocala, FL*
Church @ The Springs and Forest High School, Ocala, FL

HEARTBREAK AND DESPAIR (PART 1)

"My flesh and my heart may fail, but God is the strength of my heart, my portion forever." —*Psalm 73:26*

We guys like to present the image of the tough guy, like we are somehow better than everyone else by acting like we do not get hurt. When we get scratches or cuts we tough it out, saying, "Put some dirt on it"; and we walk away tougher than before, at least on the outside. Most guys refuse to talk about it when their feelings and heart get hurt. I know that I don't have any idea what to do when my heart gets broken. It would help to be free to open up with someone who might help me walk through the pain. It seems as if our culture can't imagine the difference between hurt and heartbreak, almost like heartbreak is not allowed but anger is OK and almost expected. Guys hate to admit it, but they give their hearts away a lot. I know, because I have done so in the past and, of course, without even meaning to. Whether the heart is given to sports, our dreams and aspirations for the future, or the most difficult to handle—girls! The only thing I've found healing in the midst of heartbreak has been the love and grace of Jesus Christ. The Bible tells us in 2 Corinthians 12:9, "'My grace is sufficient for you, for power is perfected in weakness.' Therefore, I will most gladly boast all the more about my weaknesses, so that Christ's power may reside in me." This wonderful verse seems to be in the Bible for teenagers. It is one you might want to know well. When you experience heartbreak and despair, remember that God's grace is sufficient!

PATRICK STANFORD: *18, Albany, GA*
Sherwood Baptist Church and Sherwood Christian Academy, Albany, GA

HEARTBREAK AND DESPAIR (PART 2)

"My flesh and my heart may fail, but God is the strength of my heart, my portion forever." —Psalm 73:26

When we think about how seemingly important it is for teen boys to come across as being the tough guy, it is even more important that we consider God's Word, like what we find in the verse above. Take my example: I really liked this girl. She was smart, funny, pretty, and was everything guys want in a girl. I was ready to go ahead and give my heart to her just because we were dating. Unfortunately, I did, and a few months later we were done and I thought I was dying! I know you have felt something similar. I couldn't find comfort in anything or in what people said to me. As a matter of fact, much of what people said actually made me just plain miserable. Then finally I came across this passage in Psalms. It hit me like a ton of bricks: Why not put my heart somewhere that can't fail me? Since then, this way of thinking has never let me down. When I give all my heart, even the part related to girl problems, to God, I'm more than confident He won't hurt me. He will love and comfort me through the whole relationship, even if there is a painful breakup. He can do the same for you! All you need to do is cry out to God in prayer, then trust Him through the reading and understanding of His Word! He longs to hear from His children. Try it! God never fails us.

PATRICK STANFORD: *18, Albany, GA*
Sherwood Baptist Church and Sherwood Christian Academy, Albany, GA

DOES GOD WANT TO TALK WITH ME?

"Pray constantly." —*1 Thessalonians 5:17*

I know a lot of people who find it very difficult to pray, especially in public. Many people consider it weird, frightening, unnecessary, or noneffective. Some teens are very self-conscious when it comes to praying, and they worry about how they sound or appear. Some people don't feel that it will help them and would rather work things out on their own, without consulting God. Prayer is conversation with God. I believe that it is very important that teens pray. First, we are commanded to, as seen in 1 Thessalonians 5:17. Second, prayer is necessary to maintain the fellowship we have with God. If you had a friend and never communicated with him, how long would he remain a close friend, rather than just somebody you know? Third, we are commanded not to worry, but instead we are supposed to make our requests of God. To do that is a special gift that brings much peace. It is important that we develop the ability to communicate with God, because that is a sign that our relationships with God are genuine and not something we do because everyone else does. If we have no desire to become personal with God by expressing weaknesses, needs, and even desires, then there is a problem. If we have no desire to thank God for what He has given us, then we are taking far too much for granted and not giving God the acknowledgment He deserves. Through Jesus, God has made a way for us to talk to Him and He calls on us to approach His throne with confidence. We should not waste such an opportunity.

JOSIAH MCGEE: *15, Kansas City, MO*
Summit Woods Baptist Church, Lees Summit, MO; Homeschooled

KINDNESS

"The one who despises his neighbor sins, but whoever shows kindness to the poor will be happy." —*Proverbs 14:21*

Don't you love being around people who are always friendly and make you feel like you are important? I know that I do! Kindness toward others dissolves any prior tension and can create a long-lasting friendship. It might be a smile, an act of encouragement, or a simple compliment, but it could be the difference that someone needs on that day at that very moment. In a world full of technology, people have lost the ability to act when we are face-to-face with one another. Everyone is in a rush and, therefore, we are short when we might need to engage in conversation. Instead of being so focused on something else, like your cell phone, try being more attentive to those around you and add some happiness to their lives. And, by all means, be aware of opportunities to shine God's light through your actions. Who knows, it might eventually lead to sharing the gospel and seeing a soul won to Christ. How much better our world would be if everyone performed just one kind act for someone else each day. Be that person to stop and help, despite what other things you need to do. You are glorifying your Father and spreading His love without saying a word. I challenge you to search for a way to help today, and bring a smile to someone's face.

JONATHAN DISMUKES: *17, Mobile, AL*
Redeemer Fellowship Church and Cottage Hill Christian Academy, Mobile, AL

THE GREAT COMMISSION

"Go, therefore, and make disciples of all nations, baptizing
them in the name of the Father and of the Son and of the Holy Spirit,
teaching them to observe everything I have commanded you.
And remember, I am with you always, to the end of the age."

—Matthew 28:19–20

Before Jesus left this earth, He commanded His disciples to spread the gospel with the help of the Holy Spirit. As believers who have been saved through the blood of Christ, we should have a desire to bring others to a saving relationship with the Lord. We are not to take a complacent attitude toward this task, but instead we should be focused and intentional on teaching others the good news. We should be reassured that we do not solely bear this whole weight, but we have the help of God to rightfully proclaim His grace and mercy to sinners. Yet, we must delve into the Bible and strengthen ourselves with the Truth so that we may defend the Word and its teachings. Ephesians 6:10–18 tells us of the armor of God we receive when gaining wisdom from the Bible. This is a fight not for the weak but for those who stand ready to defend their faith. Each day, we should return with our armor worn from the attacks of Satan, unhindered due to the protective power of God upon our lives. As you go out today, be prepared to share the gospel with those you meet, and pray for ease of mind and heart so that you might clearly relate the joy of salvation.

JONATHAN DISMUKES: *17, Mobile, AL*
Redeemer Fellowship Church and Cottage Hill Christian Academy, Mobile, AL

VANITY

"The words of the Teacher, son of David, king in Jerusalem. 'Absolute futility,' says the Teacher. 'Absolute futility. Everything is futile.' What does a man gain for all his efforts that he labors at under the sun?"

—*Ecclesiastes 1:1–3*

Most people's goal in life is to become successful beyond compare. They strive for wealth and position so that they may live comfortably for only a few decades. Yet, Solomon tells us of the worthlessness of earthly possessions after death. Nothing will be brought into eternity along with our soul. No name, no power, nor riches. Would it not be better to store your riches in heaven while on the earth, so that you might live eternally in the joy of the Lord? However, many do not realize the sad truth that will befall them after death. They will be unable to rely on what they had for future promise. Their status will be forgotten and they will be no more. On the other hand, those faithful to the Lord will be blessed beyond measure with the glory of the saints as they benefit from a life dedicated to serving God, our Creator. They will be spared from hell due to the sacrifice of Christ on the cross. They will emerge onto streets of gold with radiant faces and be filled with the purity of God. How much better does a plentiful and eternal life sound than a short, meaningless existence on the earth? Hopefully, you will recognize the vanity of worldly riches and honor and seek the wholesome, lasting glory of God.

JONATHAN DISMUKES: *17, Mobile, AL*
Redeemer Fellowship Church and Cottage Hill Christian Academy, Mobile, AL

FORGETTING THE PAST

"Brothers, I do not consider myself to have taken hold of it. But one thing I do: Forgetting what is behind and reaching forward to what is ahead."
—*Philippians 3:13*

We all have something we want to forget about from our past. Generally the older we get, the more of our past that we would like to forget. Even though I am only fourteen, I have things that I wish I could forget. The question is how we forget something that is hard to forget. Whether we can't seem to forget or we aren't sure we want to, it's still hard to do. Today's verse, Philippians 3:13, is inspiring to me. We get so caught up in what happened last month and last year that we don't look at what God has in store for us in the now and in the future. Paul had a horrible past; but when he got saved he learned to lay down everything, including his past, for his new life in Christ. Sometimes we can forget things from the past, but when we can't because others remind us or the circumstances continue to follow us around, all we have to do is look at what God has waiting for us. The Bible will tell us what His future plans are for us. When God forgives, He also forgets.

DAVID JOSEPH DALESANDRO: *14, York, SC*
Hillcrest Baptist Church and York Comprehensive High School, York, SC

DISCOURAGEMENT

"Haven't I commanded you: be strong and courageous?
Do not be afraid or discouraged, for the LORD your God
is with you wherever you go." —*Joshua 1:9*

How many times have you ever been scared or discouraged? In today's verse, God was telling the Israelites to trust in His power and to not be scared or worried that they wouldn't be able to take out Jericho. What is our Jericho in life? What do we face from day to day that makes us feel uncomfortable, discouraged, or, in serious circumstances, scared? God wasn't just telling them in this verse that it is a good idea to be courageous; He *commanded* them to be strong, courageous, and to not be discouraged. So, take on life knowing that God is always by your side and that you can be confident in His strength. Discouragement is something that is like a sickness in teens. We are told we aren't good enough, then we pass our low self-esteem off to everybody else. But as Christians, we are filled with the power of the Holy Spirit. So no matter what people say, you are always good enough, and our awesome God has an amazing plan for you. Take some time to pray and ask God to lead and guide you, and to remind you that He is always there for you and that nothing can keep you from the help of His power and strength.

TREY SUEY: *16, Mt. Juliet, TN*
The Fellowship at Two Rivers, Nashville, TN; New Life Academy, Mt. Juliet, TN

NOVEMBER

Wisdom calls out in the street; she raises her voice in the public squares. She cries out above the commotion; she speaks at the entrance of the city gates:

"How long, foolish ones, will you love ignorance?

How long will you mockers enjoy mocking and you fools hate knowledge?

If you respond to my warning, then I will pour out my spirit on you and teach you my words. Since I called out and you refused, extended my hand and no one paid attention, since you neglected all my counsel and did not accept my correction, I, in turn, will laugh at your calamity.

I will mock when terror strikes you, when terror strikes you like a storm and your calamity comes like a whirlwind,

when trouble and stress overcome you.

Then they will call me, but I won't answer; they will search for me, but won't find me.

Because they hated knowledge, didn't choose to fear the Lord, were not interested in my counsel, and rejected all my correction, they will eat the fruit of their way

and be glutted with their own schemes. For the turning away of the inexperienced will kill them,

and the complacency of fools will destroy them. But whoever listens to me will live securely

and be free from the fear of danger." (Proverbs 1:20–33)

WHY?

"Who is this who obscures My counsel with ignorant words?"
—*Job 38:2*

There are times in life when we are like Job: faced with hard times, we are quick to ask God why. Maybe a loved one died, we failed a test, or we didn't make the team. Sometimes we just need to hear what God told Job in this verse. We ask God questions, but we are being ignorant. We don't know what we are talking about because God has a plan. If anyone had a right to ask God why, it would've been Job with all the things that had happened to him. However, when Job went to ask God why, God began asking Job questions to show him who was in control. Some important facts we need to remember when we start to ask God why are that God's ways are higher than ours, He is all knowing, and He loves us and wants the best for us. It's a human tendency to want to know why certain things happen to us, but we have to have faith in God in these tough times. Some other great verses to remember are Jeremiah 29:11 and Romans 8:28. Jeremiah 29:11 says, "'For I know the plans I have for you'—this is the Lord's declaration—'plans for your welfare, not for disaster, to give you a future and a hope.'" And Romans 8:28 reminds us, "that all things work together for the good of those who love God: those who are called according to His purpose." In your times of suffering, remember to cling to God and know that He has a plan for you; and that if you love Him and are called according to His purpose, then He is working all things together for good. We may not understand it now, but we learn a lot of good lessons through hard times.

CLAY NORMAN: *18, Albany, GA*
Sherwood Baptist Church and Sherwood Christian Academy, Albany, GA

THE KING'S TABLE

"So Mephibosheth ate at David's table just like one of the king's sons."

—*2 Samuel 9:11*

In 2 Samuel 9 the story of David searching for Mephibosheth and adopting him is told. In the beginning of the chapter, David, the king of Israel, seeks out any children of his old friend Jonathan. He learns that there is a young man living in the poor town of Lo-debar who was crippled in both feet. David then brings this broken man to his castle. Now, even though Mephibosheth was the son of David's friend Jonathan, he was also the grandson of Saul. Saul was the old king of Israel and had tried to kill David because he knew David would one day take over his kingdom. With him being in the family of Saul, Mephibosheth was always fed lies about David—that he was the evil man who destroyed his family—so he was very frightened when he learned that David had summoned him. He could have expected for King David to take his life, but David instead made him like a son to him and allowed him to eat at the king's table. This amazing story is not only the story of two men who lived many years ago but is also the story of us. We are crippled by sin and live in horrible conditions because of this, but God, our King, takes us in and calls us His children. In this story, Mephibosheth could have just as easily said no and turned down David's offer to come and live in his castle and gone back to his crummy home. This is what many people do. Even when we have this extraordinary offer, we still choose sin. Why would we not want to live with the King and dine where only the most important and privileged stay? The King has offered His home to you, will you accept it?

CHRIS NATION: *15, Gallatin, TN*
The Fellowship at Two Rivers, Nashville, TN; and Station Camp High School, Gallatin, TN

BELIEFS AND FACTS

"Happy is a man who finds wisdom and who acquires understanding."
—*Proverbs 3:13*

When I was younger, I memorized Bible verses for rewards, and I read the Bible because I was supposed to. As I got older, I read it for knowledge and, now, I add to that guidance. When reading because I was supposed to, I rarely tried to understand the meaning of what the Bible was saying or how it applied to my life. There were occasions that I gained understanding, but it wasn't until I started to read the Bible for its teaching messages that I began to learn. I began in the New Testament then went on to Old Testament books—in particular, Proverbs, which is what I was searching for. I wanted guidance for my daily life as a male teen. For the most part, Proverbs is basic rules and wisdom to live your life by. I continued to read Proverbs and other books in the Bible for several years, until the summer of my junior year when I was changed drastically. While reading these rules and lifestyles, I kept seeing where I was faltering and prayed for help and guidance. After a time, God answered, instilling peace in me and showing me a new way of learning. Instead of reading out of obligation, He gave me a desire to learn about Him and His promises. It was great! To read the Bible and other books pertaining to it was relaxing, enjoyable, and fulfilling. God nurtured me, even when I doubted earlier that summer, showing me answers through His Word and other literature. It is imperative that modern-day Christians study the Bible and learn its truths, especially in a world that doubts. It is God who gives us the wisdom, knowledge, and understanding that leads to love, peace, and joy.

ROBBY D. LAND: *18, Gatlinburg, TN*
First Baptist Church and Gatlinburg-Pittman High School, Gatlinburg, TN

BEING AN EXAMPLE TO THE BELIEVERS (PART 1)

"Let no one despise your youth; instead, you should be an example to the believers in speech, in conduct, in love, in faith, in purity." —*1 Timothy 4:12*

Probably like you, I have heard the phrase "boys will be boys" repeated many times throughout my life. While at first I agreed with the statement, I later realized what an incorrect statement this is. This statement seems to be saying that we are given a free pass to be stupid and unconcerned because of our youth. While the world gives its youth a free pass, the Bible gives us a different picture and the Bible teaches us that being responsible and accountable is vitally important. In our verse for today we find Paul is writing to Timothy. While we do not know Timothy's exact age, we can conclude from the passage that he was a young pastor. He faced the challenges of being an example to other believers. We might be looked down upon by teachers, parents, or other adults because of our young age, but it is our responsibility to be held accountable and to be an example instead of making excuses. Excuses might give us a reprieve for a moment in life, but solid results with eternal benefits from the things that we speak, and do, and share with others is what matters. "Boys will be boys" might sound cute and might even be what the world expects, but if we want to live for Christ and set examples of His Word, then we need to act like mighty men of God.

LUKE PERSTROPE: *17, St. Peters, MO*
First Baptist Church of St. Charles, St. Charles, MO; Fort Zumwalt East High School, St. Peters, MO

BEING AN EXAMPLE TO THE BELIEVERS (PART 2)

"Let no one despise your youth; instead, you should be an example to the believers in speech, in conduct, in love, in faith, in purity." —*1 Timothy 4:12*

"Boys will be boys" might fit some even as they grow into adulthood, and others still act like boys when they are well into mid-life. The best example is to be like Christ, which offers lasting value. I have a friend who wasn't born into a Christian home. However, he started to come to church and soon learned about salvation. By the working of the Holy Spirit in his life, he prayed to receive Christ and was baptized. His parents and his friends said they could tell a difference between my friend's pre-Christ life and his current life. My friend is being an example to his lost parents. Recently, one of his close friends also decided to follow Christ. We should aim to be examples not only to other believers, but to the lost world. The world should see a difference in us. Our speech, behavior, and the expressions of our love should be completely different from what we hear in the halls of our schools every day. On a couple of occasions, I have been completely surprised when someone told me that he or she was a Christian. These people didn't live out a life that exemplified a relationship with Christ. We must demonstrate our relationship with Christ to the world and be an example to fellow believers.

LUKE PERSTROPE: *17, St. Peters, MO*
First Baptist Church of St. Charles, St. Charles, MO; Fort Zumwalt East High School, St. Peters, MO

DREAMS

"Brothers, I do not consider myself to have taken hold of it. But one thing I do: Forgetting what is behind and reaching forward to what is ahead, I pursue as my goal the prize promised by God's heavenly call in Christ Jesus." —*Philippians 3:13–14*

I set goals. I strive for things bigger and better until I reach them. I am a Christian, and to the outside world I am one of the many people representing Christ. I should be the best I can be at all I do. I'm an athlete, and if I don't set goals, I will never reach the pinnacle of my abilities. It is often hard to press on, especially if I don't have a goal or a dream. Dreams are my motivation for everything. They represent the realization of what I can be. I strive for greatness and do so with a desire to represent Christ in a way that honors Him. In a song by Christian rap artist, Lecrae, titled "Dream" he sings about the life that God gave us. We only have this one life so we need to make right decisions. Teens are often torn between what the Lord wants and what the world offers. Lecrae sings about the faith that he is going to live his life for Jesus however God wants to use him. The artist encourages us to dream big and to allow God to do His wonderful work in and through us. Let's dream to do big things with our lives for God's glory!

DAVID WOODY: *16, Greencastle, PA*
Greencastle Baptist Church and Greencastle-Antrim High School, Greencastle, PA

GOD'S PRESENCE IN OUR LIVES

"No one will be able to stand against you as long as you live. I will be with you, just as I was with Moses. I will not leave you or forsake you."

—*Joshua 1:5*

Have you ever been somewhere by yourself? I remember some of my first experiences when I was alone in the midst of a crowd. The security of parents, family, and friends was gone. Though I may have been alone, I know that God never left me. In this verse, God promises Joshua that He will never leave or forsake him. This is a great promise to us! A promise such as this should bring us great joy! If God will never leave us, then where is He? Well, Deuteronomy 31:8 gives us the picture that the Lord is before us. He leads us to where we are going! He is behind us in Isaiah 30:21. Not only are we protected from the front, but He protects our blind side. Psalm 139:5 says that the Lord encircles us. He is around us. He is above us in Matthew 6:9. His residence in heaven is above us. Deuteronomy 33:27 reminds us that He is below us. Finally, He is within us, 2 Corinthians 6:16. The Holy Spirit comes and lives inside of us and makes us new creatures! You may feel lonely, but remember that God is with us everywhere and all the time! We cannot escape from Him. This presence should bring us great comfort, knowing that God is with us all the time. When we face the trials of life, it brings us much comfort to know that the God of the universe is with us. However, we should feel a sense of conviction knowing that God is always around us. Our attempts to hide things from God are unsuccessful. He knows our hearts and knows us better than we know ourselves. When you walk into today, know that the Lord your God is with you wherever you are.

LUKE PERSTROPE: *17, St. Peters, MO*
First Baptist Church of St. Charles, St. Charles, MO; Fort Zumwalt East High School, St. Peters, MO

GOD'S STRENGTH TO BE GIANT SLAYERS (PART 1)

"David said to the Philistine: 'You come against me with a dagger, spear, and sword, but I come against you in the name of Yahweh of Hosts, the God of Israel's armies—you have defied Him. . . . Today I'll strike you down, cut your head off, and give the corpses of the Philistine camp to the birds of the sky and the creatures of the earth. Then all the world will know that Israel has a God, and this whole assembly will know that it is not by sword or by spear that the LORD saves, for the battle is the LORD's. He will hand you over to us.'" —1 Samuel 17:45–47

In order to be a giant slayer like David was, I know that I need to trust in God to protect me and to give me strength for the battle. I need Him just as much to protect me when I want to spread the gospel, so that I would be able to reach many people without being scared. I also know that I can do all, not just a few, but "all" things through Christ who strengthens me, as Philippians 4:13 encourages me to know and to apply to everyday situations. You and I will probably never face a real giant and be asked to kill him but, just like me, you will face all sorts of giants in your life. They come in the form of temptation, sin, choices, whether to respect authority or not, and even deciding to follow Jesus. Life is not always easy. If you are in a situation in which you need physical or mental strength, ask God for help. I know He will deliver you, and He is always available to do so.

TERRELL STRAIN: *13, Spokane, WA*
Airway Heights Baptist Church, Spokane, WA; Medical Lake Middle School, Medical Lake, WA

GOD'S STRENGTH TO BE GIANT SLAYERS (PART 2)

"David said to the Philistine: 'You come against me with a dagger, spear, and sword, but I come against you in the name of Yahweh of Hosts, the God of Israel's armies—you have defied Him. . . . Today I'll strike you down, cut your head off, and give the corpses of the Philistine camp to the birds of the sky and the creatures of the earth. Then all the world will know that Israel has a God, and this whole assembly will know that it is not by sword or by spear that the LORD saves, for the battle is the LORD's. He will hand you over to us.'" —1 Samuel 17:45–47

In the above passage are the words David spoke before he went into battle against Goliath, the Philistine giant. He was probably no more than thirteen or fourteen years old, but he still trusted God 100 percent. He didn't back away from the nine-foot-tall giant that stood before him. Instead, he looked Goliath straight in the eye and told him that God would allow David to strike him down. David was able to get this strength from God by trusting in Him. Imagine how many lost could be won to Christ if every one of us trusted in God like that. Strength is not always how strong you are physically; it can also be, and most often is for men of God, how strong you are mentally. One of the main reasons I don't share God's Word with my friends or those I don't know is that I'm scared. I am afraid of being hurt or laughed at, sometimes even getting beat up. God can take the fear away and we can be giant slayers too!

TERRELL STRAIN: *13, Spokane, WA*
Airway Heights Baptist Church, Airway Heights, WA; Medical Lake Middle School, Medical Lake, WA

HOLY BATTLE

"But honor the Messiah as Lord in your hearts. Always be ready to give a defense to anyone who asks you for a reason for the hope that is in you."

—*1 Peter 3:15*

We live in a world in which Christianity is being shoved out of society. Even in America, a Christian nation, Christianity is slowly but surely being undermined. Christians must be ready to face persecution and to defend and advance the faith. Recently Congress's Defense of Marriage Act was struck down. It is amazing that we even have to defend the sanctity of marriage, one of God's most beautiful creations. To have that defense struck down shows the need for a revolution of well-equipped Christians who will not sway with the whims of the world but will stand fast in the truth. Christians must seize every opportunity to do good and to make God known. The majority of Christians today know little to nothing about theology, God, Christian philosophy, or Christian science besides "God is good" and "Jesus died for me." In order for God to continue to affect and bless our country, Christians, especially as teens on whom so much of the burden lies to decide the future, must be well-versed in all aspects of Christianity. Continuing trends of recent years will mean that we will witness the decline of Christianity in society and the destruction of morality as a whole. We cannot afford to sit idly by and accept scientific theories that contradict the Bible when there is ample evidence to support the Bible's authority, or allow "tolerance" to skew our perception of right and wrong. Christians must have a thirst for knowledge that comes from God, and we must continually equip ourselves with the Scripture, godly wisdom, and with truth to combat the decay of morality and Christianity.

CODY BRANDON: *17, Mt. Juliet, TN*
The Fellowship at Two Rivers, Nashville, TN; Mt. Juliet High School, Mt. Juliet, TN

WHAT MATTERS MOST

"'For I know the plans I have for you'-this is the Lord's declaration-'plans for your welfare, not for disaster, to give you a future and a hope.'"

—Jeremiah 29:11

The summer of my junior year in high school was a tough one because I had been sinning quite a bit and had not tried to correct it. Reading the Bible and praying was generally a ritualistic task rather than spending time with God. I wasn't doing drugs or partying, but I had become more accustomed to and complacent with worldly practices. I might try to work on an area of my life, but I would quickly fall back into the same habits. It concerned me. When I read 1 John about "walking in the light," it actually scared me. I saw so many similarities between those words and my life. I felt that I had been saved, but something was wrong! I was putting all my thoughts and emphasis on physical appearance, social standing, academic achievements, and sports performance. Summer break found me still running on the nervous excitement of the school year. My concern about how I appeared was obvious in my relationship with my girlfriend, and I was nervous around her. Doubting and anxieties about my spiritual life caused my stomach to hurt, and I felt crushed under the stress. I prayed for help, forgiveness, peace, and another chance. I realized what mattered to me: family, forgiveness, peace, love, those things God provides. A simple life with God and with family is quite good. God was working. I talked to my youth pastor who offered help and finally a display of Jesus Christ, my God, became real and that is undeniable. He is available to help you, too, to give you a future and a hope!

ROBBY D. LAND: *18, Gatlinburg, TN*
First Baptist Church and Gatlinburg-Pittman High School, Gatlinburg, TN

WORSHIP

"Therefore, brothers, by the mercies of God, I urge you to present your bodies as a living sacrifice, holy and pleasing to God; this is your spiritual worship." —Romans 12:1

Worship: All Christians have an idea of what worship is. When some think of worship, they think of their worship band playing songs on Sunday morning with the church clapping along, singing, and some might even have their hands held up to God. Others think that worship is very subdued music, with only an organ and a piano playing as the choir sings old hymns. And others see worship as quiet moments alone with God, seeking Him as they read the Scriptures and pray. In Romans, Paul tells us that worship is "to present your bodies as a living sacrifice." This means that worship doesn't stop at the songs. We are to live our lives in worship. In everything we do, we are to be a living testimony to the glory of God. It can be anything from playing your favorite sport to hanging out with your friends. In Matt Redman's song, "The Heart of Worship," he sings, "For a song in itself/Is not what You have required, I'm coming back to the heart of worship/And it's all about You." Worship isn't just the songs we sing; it is the action of giving our lives to God for His will.

ZACH WATKINS: *16, Henderson, NV*
Highland Hills Baptist Church and Green Valley High School, Henderson, NV

SUFFERING FOR CHRIST

"Dear friends, don't be surprised when the fiery ordeal comes among you to test you as if something unusual were happening to you. Instead, rejoice as you share in the sufferings of the Messiah, so that you may also rejoice with great joy at the revelation of His glory."

—1 Peter 4:12–13

Having faith in Christ means that we have to accept the fact that we will have trouble and trials for those beliefs. First Peter 4:12–13 says: "Dear friends, don't be surprised when the fiery ordeal comes among you to test you as if something unusual were happening to you. Instead, rejoice as you share in the sufferings of the Messiah, so that you may also rejoice with great joy at the revelation of His glory." Now this is not something that I have experienced personally, but I do know that we will all have to suffer for the name of Christ. When we share God's Word with others, we are often rejected; yet, as Christians, we should not be surprised, but rejoice in the face of it. We shouldn't be caught off guard. In fact, Jesus promised it to us. Acts 9:16 says: "I will show him how much he must suffer for My name!" God promises trials, so we should expect it, and be glad for it! In fact, as 1 Peter 4:14 says, "If you are ridiculed for the name of Christ, you are blessed, because the Spirit and glory of God rests on you." Does this not make you anticipate ridicule and look forward to opportunities to share Christ? If it means that God will rest His Spirit upon me, I greatly anticipate it! So in those times of trouble for Christ's name, we need to rejoice! We can expect persecution for the Lord, but that does not mean that we cower away when the time comes for us to stand up for Him. Bottom line: expect suffering. God promised it, so don't be afraid to share your faith with others.

JESSE D. SANDO: 13, Pleasant Hill, OH
First Baptist Church, Vandalia, OH; Homeschooled

GOD LAUGHS AT FEAR (PART 1)

"He laughs at fear, since he is afraid of nothing; he does not run from the sword." —Job 39:22

Fear is defined by the Collins English Dictionary as "a feeling of distress, apprehension, or alarm caused by impending danger, pain, etc." We fear if we are going to lose a loved one, or if we stand up for something we believe in, or if there is danger approaching, or we feel that there is no hope for rescue. This is fear: invisible, yet undeniable; irrational, yet debilitating. When I say irrational, I do not mean to downplay fear, for I myself am fearful of many things. By irrational, I wonder how we can fear when we serve a God who laughs at fear, and confronts evil, hardship, and hurt head-on. This is the same God who says that He will never leave us or forsake us (Deuteronomy 31:6)! Satan wants to strip us of our dreams, our spiritual armor, and our threat to the kingdom of hell. He wants to turn the army of God into a motley crew of those who just did not want to take the risk. Men of God, let us throw off fear and put on our armor!

LUKE MERRICK: *15, Springdale, AR*
Immanuel Baptist Church and Shiloh Christian School, Springdale, AR

GOD LAUGHS AT FEAR (PART 2)

"He laughs at fear, since he is afraid of nothing; he does not run from the sword." —*Job 39:22*

The God who scattered the enemies of the Israelites is the same God who stands steadfast as our vanguard today. So live your lives to the fullest for God! If you have dreams that honor God, shoot for the stars (Philippians 1:6)! You don't have to have dreams to change the world, but at least strive to transform the lives of those around you. We all need to remember to live our lives as children of God, because people are watching us. So the next time you want to do something, but you just don't have the strength or bravery, remember that God has the ability. When we are weak, He is strong (2 Corinthians 12:9)! So as our God does not run from the sword, let us neither turn away. Let us confront strongholds of sin, regret, and loss, or whatever is holding us down with the weapons of Christ drawn and ready! God wants us to climb high mountains for Him! After all, I why else would Paul say, "I can do all things in Christ who gives me strength" (Philippians 4:13)?

LUKE MERRICK: *15, Springdale, AR*
Immanuel Baptist Church and Shiloh Christian School, Springdale, AR

REFUGE IN GOD

"God—His way is perfect; the word of the LORD is pure. He is a shield to all who take refuge in Him." —Psalm 18:30

God is our perfect provider and He will do whatever is best for us. Knowing this, we have nothing to fear or stress about. If we are in a hard time, we can go to God in our prayer and He will comfort us. We can take refuge in Him in all situations. As the verse above says, God and His ways are infallible and we will always have comfort in Him. No matter what tragedy or circumstance, God will always be there to provide for our needs. God is like a good friend; no matter how you treat Him or how long you ignore Him, He will always listen and be there for you. You could be the biggest sinner in the world and could ignore God for most of your life, but if you repent of your sins God will forgive you and take you in as one of His own. In your times of need God will nurture and care for you. The key to God being our shield is taking refuge in Him. God is always available, but you have to take the initiative. Matthew 7:7 says "Keep asking, and it will be given to you. Keep seeking, and you will find. Keep searching, and the door will be opened to you." So if you knock on God's door, He will open it and you can take refuge in Him. If you are upset about something, just pray and ask God for comfort, and you will get that comfort. If you are not sure about what to do, you can ask God for His input and you will get it. So the next time you are down or need help, just remember that God is always there for you.

MICHAEL LOWE: *15, Pageland, SC*
Wolf Pond Baptist Church and South Pointe Christian School, Pageland, SC

FORGIVENESS IS A CHOICE!

"Therefore I tell you, her many sins have been forgiven."
—Luke 7:47

What many people do not understand about sin is the way God sees it. In our minds, we rank sin. There's little white lies, then there's petty theft or misdemeanors, and then there's grand theft or homicide. And that system of ranking sins kind of works for our society in terms of justice for each other. But God sees sin in an entirely different light. God set right and wrong in the Ten Commandments and many other places in the Bible and conveys that to us through the Holy Spirit, so that we are fully aware of when we sin. So when we sin, God doesn't see us "just fibbing a little bit." He sees a rebel who has denied His love saying, "I know You are an all-powerful God who has sacrificed everything for me and has told me what is right and wrong. However, I think I know more than You do, and I am better than You and too good to live under Your law." Every time we sin we are placing ourselves above God, yet God constantly forgives us. That not only shows the infinite love He has for us, but sets an example for how we should forgive. The next time you think, *Well that was the last strike, I just can't forgive that person,* remember how many and how great your offenses are against the God that will always forgive you.

"Then Peter came to Him and said, 'Lord, how many times could my brother sin against me and I forgive him? As many as seven times?' 'I tell you, not as many as seven,' Jesus said to him, 'but 70 times seven'" (Matthew 18:21–22).

CODY BRANDON: *17, Mt. Juliet, TN*
The Fellowship at Two Rivers, Nashville, TN; Mt. Juliet High School, Mt. Juliet, TN

FAITH AND DOUBT

"I assure you: If you have faith and do not doubt, you will not only do what was done to the fig tree, but even if you tell this mountain, 'Be lifted up and thrown into the sea,' it will be done." —*Matthew 21:21*

It's a certainty that all Christians will experience doubt in their faith, especially during the teen years. Doubt is a natural obstacle to faith because it is, biblically speaking, the enemy of faith. We must ask: Why do we doubt and how do we deal with doubt? At some point in my walk with Christ, I began to doubt if my faith was good enough and began trying to prove myself a Christian. Since the Bible says grace through faith saves me, not my works, it became difficult to prove anything. I became ineffective as a messenger for Christ, and evil was winning the battle. My soul was already won for Christ, just as all Christians are, but now a different battle was raging. A wise man told me that once you are Christ's He will never let you go, and the devil knows he has lost your soul. The only thing left for the devil to do is to keep you from rescuing others' souls. He deploys fears and temptations, and his biggest weapon is doubt. Doubt chains Christians, ruining our power to witness. Christ says if we will release our doubts, we will be able to do the seemingly impossible with His power. Don't be surprised by doubt. The best way to deal with doubt is to have wiser, more mature Christians who have gone through something similar to talk to. Always bring it to God and ask His peace; and remember who you serve and that He will lift you through anything and everything because you are His child. The doubt will pass away as your faith grows to cast it out. "I am sure of this, that He who started a good work in you will carry it on to completion until the day of Christ Jesus" (Philippians 1:6).

CODY BRANDON: *17, Mt. Juliet, TN*
The Fellowship at Two Rivers, Nashville, TN; Mt. Juliet High School, Mt. Juliet, TN

CRUCIFIXION

"As soon as the chief priests and their officials saw Him, they shouted, 'Crucify! Crucify'" —*John 19:6*

Jesus and His disciples made a triumphal entry into Jerusalem, and a week later Jesus went to the Mount of Olives with the disciples. Jesus asked His disciples, Peter, James, and John, to pray. Jesus prayed asking His heavenly Father if there was any way to take this burden off of Him. If not, He would do as His Father commanded. Jesus went back to find Peter, James, and John sleeping. This scenario was repeated three times and finally, after the third time, Jesus gathered all the disciples, for He knew His time was coming to an end. Judas and the Roman soldiers came, and Judas kissed Jesus to signal that this is the one they were to take. Jesus did not fight but went with them to be tried by Pilate and the Roman people. Since it was a Jewish holiday and Pilate could not find fault in Jesus, he asked if they would like to release Jesus. The people said no; they wanted Barabbas released and Jesus punished. Pilate sent Jesus to the chief priests to see if *they* could find fault in Him, but they could not. Jesus was returned to Pilate who asked again what the people wanted him to do with Jesus. The people shouted, "Crucify Him! Crucify Him!" Pilate ordered Him crucified. Beaten and spit on, Jesus, even in death, said, "Father, forgive them, because they do not know what they are doing" (Luke 23:34). Jesus says the same thing about us today. And the cross is a reminder of His love for us and His forgiveness of our sins. We need to think about the price He paid for our sins.

TANNER PEYTON: *13, Pageland, SC*
Charlotte Southern Baptist and South Pointe Christian School, Pageland, SC

TEMPTATIONS AND A WAY OF ESCAPE (PART 1)

"No temptation has overtaken you except what is common to humanity. God is faithful, and He will not allow you to be tempted beyond what you are able, but with the temptation He will also provide a way of escape so that you are able to bear it." —1 Corinthians 10:13

Being tempted is horrible and Satan knows just what to tempt us with. Temptation is everywhere in your everyday life. People you know, sometimes even your best friends, might tempt you with drugs, sex, or theft. You might say it doesn't hurt to take one illegal pill; or drink one alcoholic beverage down; or say, "No one will see us" as you engage in something sinful. But there is one person that does: God. He sees what you do and wants to change you. He wants to guide you down a road of success, not of addiction and failure. I have faced many temptations like the ones I just listed. You might not have a parent or anyone who wants you to do well in life or even care for you. There is one person: Jesus. He made you and He wants you to do well in life, in everything you do. He wants you to succeed and prosper. You might say, "Well, you don't know what I'm going through." And you might be right, to a point. I might not know exactly what you are going through, but Jesus Christ, our Lord and Savior, does know, and He wants to help. Remember that He is the One who promises to make a way of escape for us.

HUNTER TREMBLAY: *14, Pageland, SC*
South Pointe Fellowship and South Pointe Christian School, Pageland, SC

TEMPTATIONS AND A WAY OF ESCAPE (PART 2)

"No temptation has overtaken you except what is common to humanity. God is faithful, and He will not allow you to be tempted beyond what you are able, but with the temptation He will also provide a way of escape so that you are able to bear it." —*1 Corinthians 10:13*

Temptations will always be in our way as Christians, but we have to trust Jesus Christ to show us His way of escape and never take steps backward. Most of you guys reading this are probably thinking, *Well, I've heard this a million times, don't do sex out of marriage, don't steal, don't do drugs, and loosen up, I get it!* However, if you aren't staying out of those things, then do you really know? You might say, "You don't understand how hard it is for me to stop," or, "No way, I can't stop, it's too late." Let me tell you, it is *never* too late! You can always stop right then and there with the power God gives you. Maybe you don't have a church to go to in the area and it's too far for you to drive. Or you might make up other excuses to keep you from stopping the sin that has you entangled. Well, maybe God is calling you to get some friends involved. God can do anything. So, don't yield to temptation. God gives you a way to escape all temptation!

HUNTER TREMBLAY: *14, Pageland, SC*
South Pointe Fellowship and South Pointe Christian School, Pageland, SC

STRENGTH AND PROTECTION IN GOD

"God is our refuge and strength, a helper who is always found in times of trouble. Therefore we will not be afraid, though the earth trembles and the mountains topple into the depths of the seas." —*Psalm 46:1–2*

"LORD, my strength and my stronghold, my refuge in a time of distress, the nations will come to You from the ends of the earth, and they will say, 'Our fathers inherited only lies, worthless idols of no benefit at all'" (Jeremiah 16:19). The Christian life is not an easy one. Christians face daily opposition from the world and the temptations of the devil. Sometimes it seems that the pressures of being a Christian are too much to handle. We are constantly attacked by the world and cannot seem to get away from Satan's arrows that he constantly fires upon us. Then, unfortunately, many of us lose our faith in God, for we believe that He is not here for us. Thankfully, God is always near, and He is waiting for us to find refuge in Him. He is right beside us, waiting for our return to Him. The Bible says that God is our refuge and strength. No matter what trials we face, God offers His protection to us. Psalm 18:30 says, "God—His way is perfect; the word of the LORD is pure. He is a shield to all who take refuge in Him." The Bible also assures us that no matter how weak we become, we can find new strength in God. Psalm 94:22 says, "But the LORD is my refuge; my God is the rock of my protection." Over and over again the Bible proclaims to us that we can seek God's protection no matter what situation we are facing. So when you are facing the feeling of defeat, remember that there is strength and protection in the Lord.

KYLE RAPE: *15, Wingate, NC*
Mountain Springs Baptist Church and South Pointe Christian School, Pageland, SC

GRATITUDE

"Let the message about the Messiah dwell richly among you, teaching and admonishing one another in all wisdom, and singing psalms, hymns, and spiritual songs, with gratitude in your hearts to God." —*Colossians 3:16*

The Lord Jesus wants us to be grateful and to show our gratitude. Sometimes we need to sit back and reflect on the many blessings we have that we never even realize or think about. We often forget to give God thanks for the small things, which many others will never have. Many people are not able to go home to a house or even a family that loves them. So don't take anything for granted. Love others and proceed to do all you can to help and take care of the many needs of others who are hurt and lost. God has blessed us beyond measure. One dear friend constantly reminds me of how precious life is and how I don't deserve anything, but God loves me and wants to bless us and make us happy. That person always reminds me to be thankful for everything I have, and to enjoy the life I've been given: to enjoy every step, every breath, every moment of life. God has blessed me beyond measure. Give thanks for what you've been given. Don't wish your life away. Enjoy what you have. Help others enjoy their lives. But never forget to give God thanks for the blessings only He can give. After all, we are commanded to be grateful in 1 Timothy 4:3: "They forbid marriage and demand abstinence from foods that God created to be received with gratitude by those who believe and know the truth."

LUKE HUMANIK: *15, Jefferson, SC*
Mt. Olive Baptist Church, Marshville, NC; South Pointe Christian School, Pageland, SC

INVOLVEMENT IN CHRISTIAN ORGANIZATIONS

"But if we walk in the light as He Himself is in the light, we have fellowship with one another, and the blood of Jesus His Son cleanses us from all sin." —*1 John 1:7*

Have you ever attempted a task too great for one person to handle? You can't do it, right? However, as soon as you asked for help, the problem was relieved. We all understand that situation. Sometimes our walk with Christ can reach this point. We strive to follow Him by knowing His Word, but doing it ourselves without the help of some much wiser than we are makes it seem impossible. How much easier it becomes when we surround ourselves with others who are focused on the same goal. We can rely on them for support and to help hold us accountable to remain steady on the narrow path of righteousness. This is why it is beneficial to join groups such as The Fellowship of Christian Athletes at your school. Not only do you find a common ground with other students, but you will also find that you will grow in your faith along with peers who are in the same situation. Also, you hear the Word preached in such a way that it is applicable to your teenage life. It is easy to get caught up in the monotonous school setting and avoid time spent with God in prayer and Bible study. But when you attend meetings focused on the gospel, you are able to reset your heart and your mind on Christ and live your life for Him.

JONATHAN DISMUKES: *17, Mobile, AL*
Redeemer Fellowship Church and Cottage Hill Christian Academy, Mobile, AL

TRUSTING IN THE LORD

"Trust in the LORD with all your heart, and do not rely on your own understanding; think about Him in all your ways, and He will guide you on the right paths." —*Proverbs 3:5–6*

Do you trust God? It's a very big thing and it's not always easy. Say you have a situation in your life, such as your friend wants you to smoke, or drink, but you know that God says, "Don't you know that your body is a sanctuary of the Holy Spirit who is in you, whom you have from God? You are not your own, for you were bought at a price. Therefore glorify God in your body" (1 Corinthians 6:19–20). You don't want to tell your friends no, but you don't want to damage your body either. What do you do? So, I want to ask you the question again: Do you trust God? God will provide for you, just trust in Him. Genesis 15:6 tells us that, "Abram believed the LORD, and He credited it to him as righteousness." So, do you trust in the Lord? Well, maybe you trust Him on some things, but not on others. God wants you to trust Him in everything, not just some things! The verse today says "Trust in the LORD with all your heart." It doesn't say half of your heart; it says all of your heart! Will you do that today?

HANK F. GRIFFIN: *14, Pageland, SC*
White Plains Baptist Church, Jefferson, SC; South Pointe Christian School, Pageland, SC

THAT ONE HAIR IS STICKING UP!
(PART 1)

"Be angry and do not sin. Don't let the sun go down on your anger."
—*Ephesians 4:26*

First off, I want to say, yes, it's a weird title; but trust me, it works for the message for today. I picked this title because I noticed a friend of mine was playing with her hair for literally a straight half hour! When I asked her what she was doing she said, "There is this one hair that is sticking straight up and it's been driving me crazy all day." Honestly, I looked at her like she was nuts, but I said, "Seriously, it's one hair!" But I get it. There are small things, one after another, and we focus on them until we blow up, often leaving people with hurt feelings and full of misunderstanding about us! So my advice is this: When something small happens, don't worry about it. It's small. Discard it if you can, or at least put it into perspective. If you can't let it go or put it in some order that you can manage, another bad thing might happen that you pile on top of the last thing that you refused to deal with and you can't let go of that thing either. If you can deal with your problems as they arise, there will be nothing for the new problem to sit on top of and cause pressure. No boiling, no building, and no exploding. Your life will be more calm and you will be able to press on!

DANIEL BAEHR: *17, Manassas, VA*
Emmanuel Baptist Church Youth Group and Emmanuel Christian School, Manassas, VA

THAT ONE HAIR IS STICKING UP! (PART 2)

"Be angry and do not sin. Don't let the sun go down on your anger."
—*Ephesians 4:26*

Recently I noticed that a friend of mine was getting really angry over what seemed like nothing. Like most teens, I didn't even notice a single thing that would make him feel that way. Soon after, I did notice that there were issues going on that would make him mad. However, I thought, *These things are so small. Why is he getting this mad?* When I asked him, I learned there was a bunch of small things that had piled up, and he was not dealing with them as they came. When the load got too heavy, he would blow his top. After considering what was happening in my friend's life, I realized that I do this a lot as well. In fact, many people do not deal with problems in their lives until they are so burdened that they blow up. So how should we deal with this problem? I know this is a popular saying, but seriously: "Don't sweat the small stuff." Even as teens, we need to learn to give all of life's issues to God. He cares about us. We need to deal with issues as they come up and not wait until they fester and get so huge that we blow up from the stress. By letting go of things that are small you will find more time to focus on things that do matter. And you will be able to hear God's voice clearly. So, relax!

DANIEL BAEHR: *17, Manassas, VA*
Emmanuel Baptist Church Youth Group and Emmanuel Christian School, Manassas, VA

TEMPTATION

"No temptation has overtaken you except what is common to humanity. God is faithful and will not allow you to be tempted beyond what you are able. He will also provide a way of escape so that you are able to bear it." —*1 Corinthians 10:13*

Let's be honest, guys. Everyone faces temptation. Even Jesus was tempted. Say you are at school and your friend tries to get you to smoke, drink, or do something else that is wrong. You have two options: Do it or don't do it. If you do it, you will definitely regret it eventually. Whether you grew up in church or not, everyone can tell the difference between right and wrong. It's just like a baby bird knows how to fly when it is thrown out of its nest. If you don't give into temptation, it will be easier to resist the next time. A lot of people try to justify their sins by saying, "Well, my friends do it, and they do it a lot more than I do." You know the story. Always remember that when you are faced with temptation, God is there to help you through it. God created everything, so He knows how to deal with everything. If your computer broke down you would not call a plumber, would you? You would call a computer technician, an expert on the matter. In the case of temptation, God is the expert. So, when you need help facing temptation, call on God. He will be happy to help.

DAVID ATKINSON: *14, Pageland, SC*
Mount Moriah Baptist Church, Marshville, NC; South Pointe Christian School, Pageland, SC

THE POWER OF THE WORD OF GOD

"For the word of God is living and effective and sharper than any double-edged sword, penetrating as far as the separation of soul and spirit, joints and marrow. It is able to judge the ideas and thoughts of the heart." —*Hebrews 4:12*

Having God's Word nearby and memorized in your heart can be so encouraging and uplifting. Whenever you are feeling down, or whenever you are having a bad day, you can always turn to the Word of God to enlighten you. I am a freshman and recently moved to a new state. I started at a new school, not knowing anyone but my brother, Luke, and a very sweet girl named Sara. With baseball season approaching, I decided that I would try out for the team. I felt nervous about trying out because it had been a couple of years since I had played on a team. During try-outs, I broke out my old baseball cap that had Bible verses written on the inside bill. Looking at those verses reminded me that God was always with me. The key verse on my bill was Philippians 4:13, which says, "I am able to do all things through Him who strengthens me." The tryouts went well. I felt like I was doing well in the field, but hitting was a challenge. The last day of tryouts, when the coach made final cuts, was nerve-racking. After practice, the coach had a short meeting with every player who tried out. My name was called third. "Congratulations," and then he said to be at school the next morning at 9:00. Walking out to the car I took my hat off and looked at the verses I had written on it. I then looked up and thanked God who was with me at the tryouts, and I knew it. God's Word is so uplifting and powerful. I have already begun to write verses in my new baseball cap.

JOEL PERSTROPE: *15, St. Peters, MO*
First Baptist Church of St. Charles, St. Charles, MO; Fort Zumwalt East High School, St. Peters, MO

DECEMBER

Faith Triumphs

Therefore, since we have been declared righteous by faith, we have peace with God through our Lord Jesus Christ. We have also obtained access through Him by faith into this grace in which we stand, and we rejoice in the hope of the glory of God. And not only that, but we also rejoice in our afflictions, because we know that affliction produces endurance, endurance produces proven character, and proven character produces hope. This hope will not disappoint us, because God's love has been poured out in our hearts through the Holy Spirit who was given to us.

Those Declared Righteous Are Reconciled

For while we were still helpless, at the appointed moment, Christ died for the ungodly. For rarely will someone die for a just person—though for a good person perhaps someone might even dare to die. But God proves His own love for us in that while we were still sinners, Christ died for us! Much more then, since we have now been declared righteous by His blood, we will be saved through Him from wrath. For if, while we were enemies, we were reconciled to God through the death of His Son, then how much more, having been reconciled, will we be saved by His life! And not only that, but we also rejoice in God through our Lord Jesus Christ. We have now received this reconciliation through Him. (Romans 5:1–11)

FOLLOWING CHRIST THROUGH THE STORM

"This is how we know that we remain in Him and He in us:
He has given assurance to us from His spirit." —*1 John 4:13*

Many storms come into our Christian lives that make us wonder about our faith in Christ. I know that I have backed off on my faith by not dedicating my life fully to the Lord at times and by being more concerned with what I wanted instead of what God wanted for me. It is hard to come out of a slump like this, but I knew that God was always there for me and that He would guide me to the end. I would just have to listen. Trials will come into our lives to test our faith. We don't know why things happen the way they do, and we often question God about them. I know I was like this when my parents got divorced. I kept asking God why He'd allow my family to be separated and why He'd let them argue so much. I was reading my Bible one night and came across James 1:12: "A man who endures trials is blessed, because when he passes the test he will receive the crown of life that God has promised to those who love Him." God puts trials in our lives to strengthen our faith. All we have to do is listen to what He tells us to do and we will make it through any storm. God will never forsake His children and will never leave any of us in any hard situation.

BILLY RAMSEY: *17, Sharon, SC*
Faith Baptist Church, Clover, SC; York Comprehensive High School, York, SC

PRAYER

"Therefore, you should pray like this: Our Father in heaven, Your name be honored as holy. Your kingdom come. Your will be done on earth as it is in heaven. Give us today our daily bread. And forgive us our debts, as we also have forgiven our debtors. And do not bring us into temptation, but deliver us from the evil one. For Yours is the kingdom and the power and the glory forever. Amen." —*Matthew 6:9–13*

This is the Lord's Prayer and it is recited by Christians all over the world. I think it is great that it is one of the most memorized verses, but I don't think it is just a ritualistic prayer. It is an actual guideline for prayer: 1) we are to start off as recognizing God as who He is, our Holy Father, and glorify His name; 2) we are to pray for His will to be carried out, that we are a part of His plan for the universe; 3) we are to ask for our needs. Daily bread is not just food, it can be anything. God knows what we want and need, but we still need to ask, and; 4) we must ask for forgiveness. We sin every day, and every day we need God's grace and forgiveness. We must also ask Him to give us the ability to forgive the people who sin against us, which is a hard thing to do. Only through God's power in us can we truly forgive someone who has wronged us. We must pray for the day ahead, that we can stay close to God and far away from sin. Pray to keep from succumbing to temptation, but to be able to fight off Satan's attacks. Our conversations with God need to be more than just asking for our wants and expecting to get them, like some sort of vending machine. This is a conversation with a friend.

ZACH WATKINS: *16, Henderson, NV*
Highland Hills Baptist Church and Green Valley High School, Henderson, NV

NOT OF THIS WORLD

"They are not of the world, as I am not of the world."
—*John 17:16*

Christians are not to be "of the world." Most people consider being "of the world" something that only people who commit sins like murder or adultery are a part of. Most Christians, especially teens, find it hard to distinguish between godly people and worldly people. I'm friends with a lot of people from different backgrounds, but I couldn't truly tell you the spiritual condition of each of my friends, because that's not exactly a topic of frequent discussion. I also have my church youth group that I hang out with every Sunday and Wednesday, and just about every other day of the week. I say all of this to ask a tough question: Should we not associate with someone because they are "of the world"? I hate to admit it, but I have asked myself this question. Now I have a better understanding of how to handle the situation. It should matter to you if someone is saved or not but, as the old saying goes, "You can lead a horse to water but you cannot make it drink." Just because someone isn't a Christian doesn't mean you should shun them like they are some kind of diseased animal or something. I believe simply hanging out with the unchurched is the best form of fellowship one can take part in. There is a difference between being friends with someone and partaking in the same worldly actions they do. In fact, denying opportunities to do things that you know are not biblical or godly can make you stand out even more for the sake of God's glory. Although it may not be easy, being "not of this world" is something God calls us to do, and He can help us whenever we struggle.

BRADY FOWLKES: *16, Tuscaloosa, AL*
Valley View Baptist Church and Hillcrest High School, Tuscaloosa, AL

MOUTH HEART CONNECTION

"May the words of my mouth and the meditation of my heart be acceptable to You, Lord, my rock and my Redeemer." —*Psalm 19:14*

Making mistakes is all part of growing up, so I'm told. I attended summer camp a few summers ago. All the rules were given to us ahead of time, and I agreed to them in writing. One rule was that no cell phones were to be used during camp. Another camper asked me to hold something while he went to play basketball. While he was jumping around and I was sitting still, it seemed reasonable for me to hold his cell phone! Not thinking, I took it just to hold. Well, one of the counselors saw me. I tried to explain, but she didn't want to hear it. By the time my mom came to pick me up, the issue had grown. She called my mentor, who came over immediately. He drew on his years of experience to help me understand what I had been pulled into. I recalled a prayer before the consequences of my mistakes, by the grace of God, because I couldn't think right with all that was going on. It's become one of my most used and favorite prayers. Psalm 19:14, "May the words of my mouth and the meditation of my heart be acceptable to You, Lord, my rock and my Redeemer." I tried to explain, it didn't work, so I kept my mouth closed and listened. Now here's where it gets tricky! Most of the time I can control my mouth but my thoughts, well, that's another story and one I'm sure you can relate to. I thank God continually that what goes through my mind doesn't come out of my mouth. The result of this process is that I'm continually thanking God. That's got to be a good thing.

PAUL CRAIG GALE: *14, New Orleans, LA*
Franklin Avenue Baptist Church and New Orleans Center for Creative Arts, New Orleans, LA

UNCLEAN
(PART 1)

"Finally brothers, whatever is true, whatever is honorable, whatever is just, whatever is pure, whatever is lovely, whatever is commendable–if there is any moral excellence and if there is any praise–dwell on these things." —*Philippians 4:8*

Although Paul is writing this letter to the church of Philippi, I want us to look at how it applies to us today. Teenagers these days, including me, focus on many things completely out of these categories. Take video games, for example; teens are constantly committing murder on a screen, yet they feel no concern and have no regrets for doing so. Instead, we rationalize that behavior and say things such as, "It's only a video game. It's not even real." Or, the most common one, "It's not like I would ever do this." Shootings throughout the country are almost always linked to these games. And since when was manslaughter amusing? Let me give you an example that might change your view on violence in video games: Say you were sitting in school one day. The day seems to drag on forever and you wonder if it will ever end. Suddenly, bursting through the door, a man appears holding a gun. He begins to shoot at random. Is this now entertaining? My hope is that you said no! Now this doesn't only apply to video games, but also to the television programs we watch on a daily basis. If we fail to follow the instruction found in God's Word, we may be ignoring how wrong and dangerous these things are and how they hurt the cause of Jesus.

JESSE D. SANDO: *13, Pleasant Hill, OH*
First Baptist Church, Vandalia, OH; Homeschooled

UNCLEAN
(PART 2)

"Finally brothers, whatever is true, whatever is honorable, whatever is just, whatever is pure, whatever is lovely, whatever is commendable—if there is any moral excellence and if there is any praise—dwell on these things." —*Philippians 4:8*

I'm sure you've noticed that you have the same problem I do when it comes to not always obeying God, especially when trying to apply the verse above to our own lives. I really want to emphasize this for everyone's benefit and to show everyone the problems surrounding it. Think about your absolute favorite movie or television show. Now read through Philippians 4:8 and see if it meets any expectations God has for you. Most likely, it didn't pass a single one of them. That should surprise you. After all, you are a Christian; you are reading your Bible on a regular basis. That meets all of the categories, doesn't it? Yes, indeed it does. But even though we obey this command occasionally, we are called to follow His commands constantly. Those things we focus on and find entertainment in influence our hearts greatly. And, what is in our hearts will reflect in our actions. As Jesus tells us in Matthew 15:18–19, "But what comes out of the mouth comes from the heart, and this defiles a man. For from the heart come evil thoughts, murders, adulteries, sexual immoralities, thefts, false testimonies, blasphemies." So next time you go to turn on the box, be hesitant and recite Philippians 4:8 to yourself. You'll be surprised at the number of shows that are unclean.

JESSE D. SANDO: *13, Pleasant Hill, OH*
First Baptist Church, Vandalia, OH; Homeschooled

AN AREA OF MINISTRY

"Go, therefore, and make disciples of all nations, baptizing
them in the name of the Father and of the Son and of the Holy Spirit,
teaching them to observe everything I have commanded you.
And remember, I am with you always, to the end of the age."

—*Matthew 28:19–20*

Every one of us has some talent. We just need to recognize what it is, then find out how God wants to use our talent in ministry. When God puts us in the place where He can use our talent, that is a great position to be in. God has given me a musical talent. I see this as a great way to minister to people. Unfortunately, a lot of musicians today, even some who call themselves Christians, don't set a godly or even a good example. I feel that God has given me this talent to help reach out to people in a more positive way, because I can express and share God's Word through my music. Maybe you have a talent or are in a place where God has put you for ministering purposes. I encourage you to use these opportunities. If you refuse to let God use you, your talent could become a stumbling block to others, but if you allow God to use your talent, I promise you one thing: Someone will hear what you have to say or to play, and that one person might be someone who you help to come to know Jesus!

BRANDON CARROLL: *17, York, SC*
Hillcrest Baptist Church and York Comprehensive High School, York, SC

LIVING OUT THE TEN COMMANDMENTS

"Then God spoke all these words." —*Exodus 20:1*

The Ten Commandments are the basis of all Christian and Jewish morality and provide a clear definition of what God expects from us. They tell us how to live our lives and provide guidelines around which we mold our societies. They are, however, more than just a set of rules. If you look at the Bible, you know God does everything He does for a good reason, even the order in which He does or says things is very important, like creating light and water before plants, so that the plants could live. So it is important that we study the order in which some of the most essential precepts in Christianity are presented.

The first five commandments deal with our actions toward God. God needs to be the priority in our lives. He places Himself first because He is the most important and everything we do should be for Him. If we keep Him first, then chances are the rest of the commandments will come easily. The next commandment God separates a special group of people to be honored above all others, the family. God puts this commandment here to emphasize the importance of family in our lives and ensure that we honor the people who will influence us the most on this earth and will usually play a huge role in our faith. The last four deal with our relationships with the rest of the world. These are the laws that bind our societies together with strings of morality and allow us to function and glorify God both individually and collectively.

So by taking the Ten Commandments as a whole, we see not only how we are supposed to live, but the progression of love for humanity. God should always remain our number one priority and we should love Him with everything we have. In doing that, He will allow us to partake in His infinite love and share it with our families and the entire world, turning more people to Him.

CODY BRANDON: *17, Mt. Juliet, TN*
The Fellowship at Two Rivers, Nashville, TN; Mt. Juliet High School, Mt. Juliet, TN

LOOKING INWARD
(PART 1)

"Your beauty should not consist of outward things like elaborate hairstyles and the wearing of gold ornaments or fine clothes. Instead, it should consist of what is inside the heart with the imperishable quality of a gentle and quiet spirit, which is very valuable in God's eyes." —1 Peter 3:3–4

As teenage guys, we are hammered by everything anti-1 Peter 3:3–4 in today's culture. The average conversation you hear when guys are talking about girls is not, "Oh man, she just has such a sweet spirit and loves the Lord so much!" No, our entire culture is geared toward outer visual enjoyment for men. Pornography is rampant. Appearance is more important than ever, and social status can often be determined by the brand of somebody's clothing. This infatuation is stripping us of God's design for marriage, attraction, and relationship. Don't take what I am saying wrong. God definitely designed women to be beautiful and for men to be attracted to them, but this is not what the relationship should consist of entirely. As young men, we should be looking out for young Christian women who are quality. The foundation we are building now will exist for the rest of our lives, so start now settling for only the best, which will always be God's highest in everything, especially in choosing your wife.

LUKE MERRICK: *15, Springdale, AR*
Immanuel Baptist Church and Shiloh Christian School, Springdale, AR

LOOKING INWARD (PART 2)

"Your beauty should not consist of outward things like elaborate hairstyles and the wearing of gold ornaments or fine clothes. Instead, it should consist of what is inside the heart with the imperishable quality of a gentle and quiet spirit, which is very valuable in God's eyes." —*1 Peter 3:3–4*

As young men of God, we should be developing our own attitudes and lives to be examples of godliness. We should set our eyes only upon what is honoring to God (Job 31:1), we should be considerate in everything we do (Philippians 4:5), and "Let no one despise our youth: instead, we should be an example to the believers in speech, in conduct, in love, in faith, and in purity" (1 Timothy 4:12). If we do these things and seek after God, I firmly believe that He will provide us with the perfect mate someday. We need to remember as teenagers, though, that while we are definitely grown-up compared to when we were six, we are nowhere close to being able to make major life decisions such as marriage. So, if you do date, let it be with someone you think you would be interested in marrying, and remember it is totally all right to not date at all. However, always try to notice girls who are exceptionally beautiful in godliness and a gentle and quiet spirit!

LUKE MERRICK: *15, Springdale, AR*
Immanuel Baptist Church and Shiloh Christian School, Springdale, AR

LIVING SACRIFICES

"Therefore, brothers, by the mercies of God, I urge you to present your bodies as a living sacrifice, holy and pleasing to God; this is your spiritual worship." —Romans 12:1

What does Paul mean when he says to present our bodies as a living sacrifice? Aren't sacrifices usually killed? I've been thinking about this verse a lot lately. It is true that people used to sacrifice animals because they had sinned, and sin demanded punishment. The sacrificed animal represented God's willingness to accept a substitute for the punishment. The people could be continually forgiven in this way. Jesus's death on the cross takes the place of blood sacrifices.

Paul is talking about something different. When he says present your bodies, he doesn't really mean your actual body and appearance. Instead, it means how you act, what your body does. Our actions need to reflect God's love and mercy. That's what He showed us when He forgave us!

What about the "living" part of that verse? Our lives should be filled with visible behavior that shows Christ through us. We need to make it clear through our actions that God is the most important thing in our lives. This is how we can worship Him! But, no matter how hard we try, none of us can be perfect in this. I heard one man say, "We are living sacrifices. Living sacrifices don't stay on the altar, they crawl off." When we realize we've done this, we need to get back on the altar as living sacrifices. Imagine how much our lives would change if we woke up each morning and said, "God, I'm getting back on the altar today. My life is Yours to use as You want. Let everything I do today reflect You and show I'm a living sacrifice." When we worship in this way, we will please God and encourage change in the lives of those around us!

AUSTIN CANFIELD: *18, Tulsa, OK*
Evergreen Baptist Church, Bixby, OK; Homeschooled

FORGIVE SEVENTY TIMES SEVEN!

"'Lord, how many times could my brother sin against me and I forgive him? As many as seven times?' 'I tell you, not as many as seven,' Jesus said to him, 'but 70 times seven.'" —Matthew 18:21–22

"Be on your guard. If your brother sins, rebuke him, and if he repents, forgive him. And if he sins against you seven times in a day, and comes back to you seven times, saying, 'I repent,' you must forgive him" (Luke 17:3–4). Forgiveness is probably the most difficult and most necessary thing we must apply to our lives. For when we are hurt, we do not think the one who has wronged deserves our forgiveness; but Christ commands us to forgive and love the ones who have hurt us as many as seventy times seven. When Christ spoke these words, He did not mean the literal product of seventy times seven, but that we should forgive time and time again without the slightest bit of hesitation, even to the point of death. Christ demonstrated this on the cross in Luke 23:34 when He said, "Father, forgive them, because they do not know what they are doing." Although He was mocked, beaten, spit upon, and crucified, Christ still forgave each person involved. The parable of the Prodigal Son (Luke 15) shows us the perfect example of forgiveness. An ungrateful son leaves home and squanders his inheritance and ends up eating pigs' food. The son later returns home to beg for his father's forgiveness. While the son was still far from home, the father saw him, ran to him, threw his hands around his neck, and kissed him. The father completely forgave his son of all the wrong that he had done. Therefore, we should also forgive, no matter what the situation.

KYLE RAPE: *15, Wingate, NC*
Mountain Springs Baptist Church and South Pointe Christian School, Pageland, SC

FEAR

"What then are we to say about these things?
If God is for us, who is against us?" —*Romans 8:31*

Fear is a very intense word that can describe a lot of situations in our lives. It can also determine multiple factors about the way we live our lives. I think a good example is the gut feeling I get while playing football when I receive a kickoff. If I let the fear of these huge guys running at me full speed take over, the play would be a disaster. Instead, I have faith in my coach, my teammates, and myself. In the end, it works out. Many times we, the youth of today, let fear decide what we do. This sad fact is displayed in how we live our lives. We don't witness like we should because we're afraid of what people will say or do if we talk about God. We fail to lead our friends to Christ because of fear. We don't ask the Lord to bless our food at lunch or talk to the outcast kid who needs a friend because of fear. Summed up, we don't live the way God wants us to simply because of fear. Whatever happened to having faith in the all-powerful God that lives within us? Block out your fears today and pursue what God wants. You'll find, as I have found, that life gets a lot more enjoyable when you do. I get my motivation from Psalm 91. Look it up. Read it, and see what you think.

DAVID WOODY: *16, Greencastle, PA*
Greencastle Baptist Church and Greencastle-Antrim High School, Greencastle, PA

MOUNT EVEREST

"His master said to him, 'Well done, good and faithful slave!'"
—*Matthew 25:21*

Often we look at something, and if it seems to be too hard we tend to give up. Everyone has done it. I do it, you do it, and probably everyone you know has experienced the same thing about something in their life. But if something is truly worth having or achieving, it is worth hard work, don't you agree? So the next time you see something that might be rather hard to accomplish, ask yourself, "Is this really worth having?" If you work for something by giving it your full effort, you get that wonderful sense of achievement. God tells us in the Bible that we will be rewarded for the good that we do, although we don't get saved to be rewarded. My favorite quote comes from Matthew 25:21; it says that God will look at us and say, "Well done my good and faithful slave." Today's verse is one of my favorites. Thinking about these words gives me chills. God, the Creator of the universe, will tell me that I did a good job and that He is proud of me. That is just so surreal; it's going to be amazing. Serving Him, no matter how hard a task may be, will be worth it when we get to heaven. Now, that's something to look forward to!

DANIEL BAEHR: *17, Manassas, VA*
Emmanuel Baptist Church Youth Group and Emmanuel Christian School, Manassas, VA

BEING CONTENT

"I don't say this out of need, for I have learned to be content in whatever circumstances I am." —*Philippians 4:11*

What many people do not know is that Paul wrote the letter to the church of Philippi while he was being held in prison! Imagine writing this sentence about being content in the setting of being without a bed, without light, without much food, and sleeping on a dirt floor? We fail to be content when we don't have the latest mobile device! The truth is, we don't have a reason to be discontent, since most of us have much more than we need and are extravagantly blessed. The rich man may turn away something he doesn't like, but a poor man will accept it. We need to learn to accept the things that are given to us and take them as gifts from God. God always gives us what we need, and often gives us the things we want. Just remember that God may give one more than another because He knows what that one will do with it, wise or unwise. He knows whether or not they will be good stewards of His possessions. One may take the gifts of God and squander them according to his will, but another may take it and put it to the Lord's work. Which one are you? The one who squanders or the one God can trust to use what He gives for His kingdom?

JESSE D. SANDO: *13, Pleasant Hill, OH*
First Baptist Church, Vandalia, OH; Homeschooled

FORGIVE US OUR DEBTS

"And forgive our debts as we also have forgiven our debtors."
—*Matthew 6:12*

In the verse above, the Bible talks about when we ask for our debts to be forgiven, but are we also showing mercy by forgiving our own debtors? If we can't get up the courage to forgive the people who owe us money, or are in debt to us in any other way, then why would the people we are in debt to have any reason to forgive us? In Matthew 18:24–35 we are told about the man who was in debt to another man for a little, but the man didn't want to forgive him. That man was in debt to yet another man for a lot more, and he was forgiven every penny of it. So, if I owe a lot to someone and they forgive me, why would I demand that the person who owes me a little pay me in full or I will mistreat them? I know that our human nature wants what it wants. But as Christians, and particularly as teens trying to learn solid life lessons, we are to act better than those who do not know Jesus. I think we are to set the examples, don't you?

GABRIEL PLYLER: *14, Pageland, SC*
Greater Vision Baptist Church and South Pointe Christian School, Pageland, SC

A JOB WELL DONE

"His master said to him, 'Well done, good and faithful slave! You were faithful over a few things; I will put you in charge of many things. Share your master's joy!'" —*Matthew 25:23*

What will people say about you when you die? Will they come to your funeral? Would you be a respected man or woman? Well, that's up to you. Let me tell you a story about a man who was probably the most well-respected man I know. He had numerous health issues in his later years. He was in and out of the hospital and never really felt well. However, guess how many times I heard him complain about his circumstances? He never complained—about anything! This man could've gotten mad at God or just said forget it, but he chose to be joyful no matter what. That was who he was; a man of strong character, honor, and integrity. That man passed away not long ago; he was my granddad. Everyone who knew him respected him, and everyone could agree that his life was a job well done. Look at yourself. What will people say about you when you die? Would you be a respected man or woman? Did you live a life worthy to be called a job well done? Well, it's up to you. Your life is a blank sheet of paper, waiting for something to be written on it.

KORD OFFENBACKER: *16, Springdale, AR*
Cross Church Springdale Campus and Shiloh Christian School, Springdale, AR

MOVING

"'For I know the plans I have for you'-this is the LORD's declaration-'plans for your welfare, not for disaster, to give you a future and a hope.'"

—*Jeremiah 29:11*

Being the new kid is never fun. You're forced out of your comfort zone into a place that is full of unfamiliar people and surroundings. You are probably wishing you were somewhere else, anywhere else, but there. Ironically, you were meant to be there at that exact time and place. God has a purpose for everything, and His goal is only to benefit you (Jeremiah 29:11). Being an Air Force brat, I find myself constantly being the new kid on the block. I'm continually being thrown into new places and situations that make me uncomfortable and unsure of myself. Jumping from state to state, house to house, church to church isn't exactly what a teenager would call fun. But I know God has a plan for me and won't let me down. As humans, we live in the present, seeing only what is happening now and living in the moment. God sees not only the present, but also the future. He knows the experiences you're going to have, the friends you're going to make, the ups and downs, everything. Every single moment in your life has already been planned. You can't change it. But what you can change is how you react to it. Moving allows you to meet new people, make new friends, experience new feelings, and grow more as an individual. God has a reason for you being where you are. He isn't trying to ruin your life or make things miserable for you. He loves you and is opening a new chapter in your life that will be full of happiness and joy. The only question is, are you willing to read it?

NICHOLAS BERGER: *15, Fairchild Air Force Base, Airway Heights, WA Airway Heights Baptist Church, Airway Heights, WA; Homeschooled*

LEAVING BAGGAGE BEHIND

"Stop your fighting—and know that I am God, exalted among the nations, exalted on the earth." —*Psalm 46:10*

Have you ever had to carry something really heavy for a long period of time? Did you notice that the longer you held that thing, the heavier it seemed to get? Emotional baggage has the same effect on us. But unlike a physical object, emotional baggage can be hard to let go of. That is, without the help of God. I learned this lesson through a really good relationship I had that ended in a pretty emotional breakup. The breakup left me with some bitterness, confusion, and, at times, a little anger. It haunted me for a month or so, leaving me tired of the situation. I didn't know what to do. All I knew was that the only thing I could think about was the relationship we had. Then, one weekend at church, our pastor preached a message on baggage. Throughout the entire service, I felt as if God was talking directly to me. The pastor explained how emotional baggage is only bringing us down, and that the only way to get rid of it was to give it to God. This is the part that hit me. I need to stop worrying about what I was holding onto and let it go. I needed to trust that God had it all under control, because He really does. God doesn't want us to hold on to our guilt, or regret, or any other kind of baggage that we are carrying along. He tells us in Psalm 46:10 to, "Stop your fighting—and know that I am God." God can handle it. That's why He's God.

JESSE NIEMAN: *18, Ocala, FL*
Church @ The Springs and Forest High School, Ocala, FL

TALENT

"Based on the gift each one has received, use it to serve others, as good managers of the varied grace of God. If anyone speaks, it should be as one who speaks God's words; if anyone serves, it should be from the strength God provides, so that God may be glorified through Jesus Christ in everything. To Him belong the glory and the power forever and ever. Amen." —*1 Peter 4:10–11*

We all have different talents. We may be good at sports, art, music, speaking, or serving others. As Christians, we are meant to use our talents to glorify God. For example, I play the trombone. I can play Christian music for people who are not saved. After I finish playing the music, I can tell the audience my motivation and life story. Another example is my dad. He is an amazing and outgoing pastor. He preaches because God tells him to. My dad has a burning passion to serve the Lord through his words and actions. One final example is my mom. My mom has many, many health problems. Even with the many things wrong with her, she puts others first. She prays for everyone, and I mean everyone. She will go and pray with people personally. She is also good at serving others. She receives this inner strength from God. She tries to serve Him in any way possible. She is a model Christian. So we all have talents, and what one Christian lacks, another Christian makes up for. Take Moses and Aaron. Moses was chosen by God to lead and Aaron was chosen to speak. Only through their combined efforts and faith in God were they able to succeed in their duty to free the enslaved Israelites. They could not have done it without God. As you can see, God gave us all talents for us to use in His name. Pray that God will show you your talents.

TERRELL STRAIN: *13, Spokane, WA*
Airway Heights Baptist Church, Airway Heights, WA; Medical Lake Middle School, Medical Lake, WA

EFFORT

"Whatever you do, do it enthusiastically, as something done for the Lord and not for men." —Colossians 3:23

All my life I have been involved in sports. Whether baseball, basketball, volleyball, cross-country, track, or football, each one required me to dedicate my time and effort to practice and competitions. The more time I practiced, the better I did in the games. As with anything in life, you only get out what you put in. I bet you did not know that Benjamin Franklin was the creator of the phrase "No gain without pain." And since the colonial age of America, nothing has changed. We must still devote our fullest energy to each task that we set out to do. It has been said that 90 percent of success comes from effort and only 10 percent from skill. If you set your mind to something and do not give in before its completion, you can do anything! Also, effort is easily seen by anyone watching. Sometimes people give up after only a few failures. Wouldn't you rather have a worker that, even though he might fail at first, returns to his duty with even more determination than before? So, next time you find yourself facing a large task, whether it is school work, a job, or your sport, remind yourself to never give up and try your best. You never know, this might be your time to shine!

JONATHAN DISMUKES: *17, Mobile, AL*
Redeemer Fellowship Church and Cottage Hill Christian Academy, Mobile, AL

GOD'S WORD
(PART 1)

"I have treasured Your word in my heart so that I may not sin against You." —*Psalm 119:11*

What do you really believe about the Word of God? Do you think of the Bible as a book full of good ideas, or do you think of it as God's holy inspired Word? Do you think of the Bible as something that God gave to us in order that we could have the life He has planned for us? Many times teenagers will say with our lips that we consider the Bible to be God's Word, but we treat it just like a self-help book that we read to improve our lives, void of any relationship with its author. If we believe that the Bible is truly the inspired, infallible, and inerrant Word of God, we would treat it much more reverently than we do. It is hard to believe, but there are people in other countries who do not have the Bible translated into their own languages. Other people groups have only parts of the Bible written in their languages, or they have to learn another language in order to read the Bible. When they do get the Bible in their own language, it is a day of great excitement and celebration because the Word of God means something important. In my own life, I do not feel that I have the same longing for God's Word, partly because it is so accessible; I see it everywhere, and I, like many others, have come to take it for granted. Sometimes my quiet time is hurt by that, and I do not enjoy reading the Bible like I should. Sort of like when salt loses its flavor. When this happens, I have to pray and ask God to restore my thirst for His Word. When I do this I can then enjoy and appreciate spending time in the Word again.

WILLIAM DAVID ORR: *17, Albany, GA*
Sherwood Baptist Church and Sherwood Christian Academy, Albany, GA

GOD'S WORD
(PART 2)

"I have treasured Your word in my heart so that I may not sin against You." —*Psalm 119:11*

The question from yesterday remains: What do you really think about the Word of God? As we answer that question, it is important that we realize that the Bible is like a manual for us to live the Christian life by. Like those people groups that get excited and then celebrate the reality of owning a Bible, we should look at the truth in the Bible as the greatest gift we can receive, second only to our salvation. Joshua 1:8 says, "This book of instruction must not depart from your mouth; you are to recite it day and night so that you may carefully observe everything written in it. For then you will prosper and succeed in whatever you do." So, we need to remember that God gave us the Bible for important reasons and that we should not take it for granted. We need to want to read it and to learn from it. We also need to share with others what the Bible says to do, so that they can come to know Jesus as well. We need to have the same excitement every time we read the Bible as the first time we read it and it meant something special to us. We need God to be real and we need to ask Him today, without wasting a minute, to give us a hunger and a thirst for His Word.

WILLIAM DAVID ORR: *17, Albany, GA*
Sherwood Baptist Church and Sherwood Christian Academy, Albany, GA

AND THE ANGELS SANG, GLORY TO GOD!

"But the angel said to them, 'Don't be afraid, for look, I proclaim to you good news of great joy that will be for all the people: Today a Savior, who is Messiah the Lord, was born for you in the city of David.'"

—Luke 2:10–11

Christmas is one of the most celebrated and busiest times of the year. Commercials kick in earlier, lights go up brighter, and presents get bigger with each passing year. The night of Jesus' birth, not one, not two, but a host of heavenly beings, wrapped in God's glory and singing His praises, got so excited that God was coming to the earth that they came down from heaven and told the story! Their excitement for us caused them to be unable to contain their joy as they spread the good news. Fast-forwarding to a Monday morning: We wake up and take care of our morning business before rushing off to school, often failing to realize that God comes to the earth every morning to see us wake up and to walk beside us that day. The angels got excited about God coming to a small portion of a country and they sang His praises. We have God with us every day, and most of the time all we give Him is an, "Oh, cool." When we have such a miraculous event happening every day in our lives, how is it that we rarely recognize it? Maybe we lose focus and start worrying about the world. Maybe we just don't really understand how spectacular it is. But let's try, not just Christmas but every day, to remember the Savior's heralded coming to our humble world and appreciate His presence. Then we will find that great joy that the angels spoke of years ago and, perhaps, in our glorious celebration we will spread it to others.

CODY BRANDON: 17, Old Hickory, TN
The Fellowship at Two Rivers, Nashville, TN; Mt. Juliet High School, Mt. Juliet, TN

CHRISTMAS

"'This will be the sign for you: You will find a baby wrapped snugly in cloth and lying in a feeding trough.' Suddenly there was a multitude of the heavenly host with the angel, praising God and saying: 'Glory to God.'"

—*Luke 2:12–14*

As Christmas time rolls around, our minds are often on gifts, family, and the break from school, and we disregard little sayings such as, "Jesus is the reason for the season." Yet, have you ever really stopped and thought about the truth of this cliché? Why do we have a holiday dedicated to a little baby boy? The reason is simple. Without Christ coming to the earth in the form of a man and living a sinless life, we would have no chance of salvation from our sins or hope after death. We would be destined to a self-righteous lifestyle in which nothing else matters but our own success. However, because this gracious gift of the Lord provides a means of escape, we are able to have true meaning in life. We are here to glorify God and honor the privilege of being His children. We have the chance to share our story with those we have contact with through verbal testimony and our example in the way we conduct ourselves. The whole gospel revolves around Christ and the ultimate sacrifice on the cross. Therefore, we must remain thankful and remember the reason we celebrate such a holiday.

JONATHAN DISMUKES: *17, Mobile, AL*
Redeemer Fellowship Church and Cottage Hill Christian Academy, Mobile, AL

JESUS' ENTRANCE TO THE WORLD

"Today a Savior, who is Messiah the Lord, was born for you in the city of David. This will be the sign for you: You will find a baby wrapped snugly in cloth and lying in a feeding trough." —Luke 2:11–12

At Christmas, my mom always brings out nativity scenes and puts them around our house. We often have a nativity on the foyer table, on the piano, and under the Christmas tree. Some can be played with and some are very delicate and ornate. It gives such a pretty picture of the birth of Christ. However, the scene in Luke 2 is very different from what we would expect. Instead of an ornate scene, Mary and Joseph were sent to the stable because there was no room for them at the inn. Though our nativity scenes are clean and beautiful, this was not a beautiful place. Instead of having the comforts of a palace, Jesus was born in the rough environment of a cave. The animals smelled. The feeding trough would not have been your ideal baby bed. However, the young couple was overjoyed at the birth of Jesus. From the Fall of Man in Genesis 3, humanity has been plagued by the sin that entangles us. We were captive to sin. We all fall short of the mark God has set for us. Because God is perfect and we are sinful, we cannot enter into heaven. To bridge the gap between God and humanity, Jesus came to the earth; not to rule over an earthly kingdom or defeat mighty armies, but to be a sacrifice for all of humanity. The angel told Joseph in Matthew 1:21, "She will give birth to a son, and you are to name Him Jesus, because He will save His people from their sins." Today, remember the reason to celebrate Christmas is because of Jesus' birth.

LUKE PERSTROPE: 17, St. Peters, MO
First Baptist Church of St. Charles, St. Charles, MO; Fort Zumwalt East High School, St. Peters, MO

END OF THE YEAR

"Therefore, if anyone is in Christ, he is a new creation;
old things have passed away, and look, new things have come."
—*2 Corinthians 5:17*

The end of the year is a time for reflection upon the former year, as well as the renewal of mind for the next. It's a time to recognize mistakes and focus on ways to avoid them later; to realize what may be holding you back and replace it with something to support your future goals; and to forget the hurt while remembering all the happiness, peace, and love received. Even though we cannot change what we've done, we may alter the way we are heading. We must rely on the Word of God to guide us to the correct path and have faith in the strength of the Lord to refrain from all that hinders along the way. Nothing is impossible with the help of God, and He promises to never set in place an obstacle to hinder our progress. As long as we are set upon the will of the Lord for our life, we will be blessed and see fruitfulness in everything we do. Despite the regret, we must not ever wish to change what we have done because it has brought us to the point we are today. We are told in Jeremiah 29:11 that the Lord has plans "to give you a future and a hope." So, as the year passes and we are faced with a new one, remember your mistakes but do not dwell on them. Instead, use the experience to guide your future steps and abstain from common errors that so easily entangle.

JONATHAN DISMUKES: *17, Mobile, AL*
Redeemer Fellowship Church and Cottage Hill Christian Academy, Mobile, AL

NEW YEAR, NEW CREATION

"For I will create a new heaven and a new earth; the past events will not be remembered or come to mind." —Isaiah 65:17

You've heard all the statistics on New Year's resolutions. One study says only 8 percent of people are successful in achieving their resolutions! So why do we even try? Why set ourselves up for failure? And if we can't reform ourselves at the beginning of a new year, how would we ever do it any other time of the year? Let's look at another statistic. There is one man who has never failed, never missed an appointment or let other people down. He has never had a coffee addiction or procrastinated. This man hits the mark 100 percent of the time. In fact, He has never had to make resolutions because He is God and is perfect to begin with. Why does this matter? Because the God who created the entirety of our universe and everything in it, and who will reform heaven and earth, is the same God whose company we enjoy every day. He can speak things into existence and form galaxies with simple thoughts. If such a powerful God is behind us, then absolutely nothing can get in the way of dieting a little or reading the Bible more often. All we have to do is allow Him to work in our lives. He gives us a promise that all the sins, all the mess-ups, and all the other junk we have weighing us down will be forgotten, not even popping back into His head, so there is no need for us to allow them to disturb us. He is ready and willing to transform us into better heirs to His throne and into the people we need and want to be. Let Him take your life and make it into something you never dreamed it could be. "I am able to do all things through Him who strengthens me" (Philippians 4:13).

CODY BRANDON: *17, Old Hickory, TN*
The Fellowship at Two Rivers, Nashville, TN; Mt. Juliet High School, Mt. Juliet, TN

NEW YEAR'S

"Be diligent to present yourself approved to God, a worker
who doesn't need to be ashamed, correctly teaching the word of truth."
—2 Timothy 2:15

As we come to the end of the year, at our house we typically watch a lot of college football, eat a lot of snack food, play a lot of video games, and enjoy some family time. It is nice to relax a little bit at the end of the year. However, it is also a time to think about the next year. For New Year's, a lot of people make goals to improve themselves. Some people say they want to work out, get better grades, or get a job. Most of the time, the goals go down the drain in about a week. This year, my middle school Sunday school class has made a commitment to read the Bible in a year. It has been pretty hard, but so worth it. I have found that reading the Bible keeps you focused on God and helps give you a more positive attitude in life. This verse tells you to be diligent and prepared so you can stand before God and not be ashamed. At school, you prepare for tests so that you are not ashamed to bring your grade home to your parents. I challenge you to make a spiritual resolution for yourself. Your resolution could be to read the Bible in a year, or it could be to read the New Testament. Make some kind of spiritual goal to aim for. Don't give up on your goal, but push yourself all throughout the year. Then you can be a diligent worker who is not ashamed and you will hear God say, "Well done, good and faithful servant." Have a great New Year!

MICAH PERSTROPE: *13, St. Peters, MO*
First Baptist Church of St. Charles, St. Charles, MO; Dubray Middle School, St. Peters, MO

A PRAYER FOR THE NEW YEAR

Let my cry reach You, LORD;

give me understanding according to Your word.

Let my plea reach You;

rescue me according to Your promise.

My lips pour out praise,

for You teach me Your statutes.

My tongue sings about Your promise,

for all Your commands are righteous.

May Your hand be ready to help me,

for I have chosen Your precepts.

I long for Your salvation, LORD,

and Your instruction is my delight.

Let me live, and I will praise You;

may Your judgments help me. I wander like a lost sheep;

seek Your servant,

for I do not forget Your commands.

(Psalm 119:169–176)

BIOGRAPHIES

LUKE ABENDROTH: 16, Lancaster, MA; Bethlehem Bible Church and Bethlehem Bible Church Homeschool Co-op, West Boylston, MA; Parents: Pastor Mike/Kim Abendroth; two siblings; homeschooled; likes to read, surf with my family, snowboard, and exercise; teaches snowboarding and skiing at a local ski resort; is a certified lifeguard; serves as usher and greeter at church; plans to join military after school to serve his country; favorite verse, Ephesians 1:4–6.

IFE AKINBOYO: 15, Seymour, TN; male; Sevier Heights Baptist Church, Knoxville, TN; The King's Academy, Seymour, TN; Parents: Samuel/Gbemisola Akinboyo; three siblings; likes to play basketball, or be with friends; on The King's Academy basketball team; wants to be a professional athlete, or be engaged in helping with sports; favorite verse, 2 Corinthians 5:17.

DAVID ATKINSON: 14, Pageland, SC; Mount Moriah Baptist Church, Marshville, NC; South Pointe Christian School, Pageland SC; Parents: Randy/Eileen Atkinson; three identical triplet brothers and one sister; loves to play soccer; participates in soccer, baseball, basketball, church activities, and fine arts; considering sports and ministry as careers; favorite verse, 2 Chronicles 16:9.

DANIEL BAEHR: 17, Manassas, VA; Emmanuel Baptist Church Youth Group and Emmanuel Christian School, Manassas, VA; Parents: Paul/Lisa Baehr; one sibling; passion is music; enjoys playing the guitar and singing; involved with drama productions and sings in the school choir; leader in church youth group and youth band; plans include becoming a professional musician or a youth pastor; favorite verse, Matthew 25:21.

CHRISTOPHER COLEMAN BAILEY: 17, Albany, GA; Greater Second Mt. Olive Baptist Church and Sherwood Christian Academy, Albany, GA; Parents: Xavier/Sonya Bailey; one sibling; likes to dance, sing, play sports, eat, draw, travel, and have fun with friends; ushers at church; in a leadership group called G.P.S.; leads middle school Bible study; runs cross-country, plays basketball and soccer; plans to go to Georgia Southwestern for a business degree then to University of Georgia for graduate degree; plans to start a family and own a business or advance in the corporate world; favorite verse, Galatians 2:20.

NICHOLAS BERGER: 15, Fairchild Air Force Base, Airway Heights, WA; Airway Heights Baptist Church, Airway Heights, WA; Homeschooled; Parents Joshua/Laura Berger; three siblings; enjoys sports, reading, camping, and boating; on the swim team and participates in as many youth events as possible; hopes to become a youth minister; favorite verse, Jeremiah 29:11.

BRANDON BOHN: 16, Springdale, AR; Cross Church Springdale Campus and Shiloh Christian School, Springdale, AR; Parent: Jeanne Bohn; likes to listen to music, read books, and occasionally play video games; after college want to go into the media arts, specifically graphic design and three dimensional modeling; favorite verse, James 3:6.

CODY BRANDON: 17, Old Hickory, TN; The Fellowship at Two Rivers, Nashville, TN; Mount Juliet High School, Mt. Juliet, TN; Parents: Elvis/Lori Brandon; two siblings; likes to play football; is a Fellowship of Christian Athletes Officer on Varsity Football; plans to attend Carson-Newman University, and maybe run for president; favorite verse, James 2:14.

DUSTIN BRECHT: 17, Lancaster, SC; Spring Hill Baptist Church, Lancaster, SC; South Pointe Christian School, Pageland, SC; Parents: Lynn/Vickie Brecht; two siblings; likes to work out, play soccer, track and field, and golf; plans to major in agriculture business and start a farm; favorite verse, Matthew 4:4.

ZACH M. BYRD: 15, Jefferson, SC; Bethlehem Baptist Church, Buford SC; South Point Christian School, Pageland SC; Parents: Joey/Pamela Byrd; one sister; like to hunts; favorite activity is basketball; after graduation from high school would like to attend college and get a job in the field of fabrication; favorite verse is Philippians 4:13

AUSTIN CANFIELD: 18, Tulsa, OK; Evergreen Baptist Church, Bixby, OK; Homeschooled; Parents: Byron/Carolyn Canfield; four siblings; plays tennis competitively and loves playing guitar, recording music and leading worship; member of The NOAH homeschool tennis team, and the National Technical Honors Society; plans to become a pediatric anesthesiologist; favorite verse, Galatians 2:20.

BRANDON CARROLL: 17, York, SC; Hillcrest Baptist Church and York Comprehensive High School, York, SC; Parents: Jimmy/Alisa Carroll; loves living his life for God; loves music and plans to major in Music Education; loves working with younger children; member of the York Cougar Marching Band, and Concert Band; accepted to Winthrop University to major in music education and minor in religious studies; favorite verse, Psalm 23:4.

RHETT CHAPMAN: 15, Pageland, SC; South Pointe Fellowship and South Pointe Christian School, Pageland, SC; Parents: Eugene/Lynn Chapman; two siblings; likes to play sports; active in youth group, soccer, and baseball; wants to be a game warden; favorite verse, Psalm 23.

WYATT CHAPMAN: 17, Pageland, SC; South Pointe Fellowship and South Pointe Christian School, Pageland, SC; Parents: Eugene/Lynn Chapman; two siblings; likes to play guitar, play sports, ride four-wheelers, and go to the lake; participates in cross-country, soccer, baseball, praise band; plans to go to college; favorite verse, Psalm 18:16–19.

ANDREW CLEM: 13, Albany, GA; Sherwood Baptist Church and Sherwood Christian Academy, Albany, GA; Parents: Ted/Stacey Clem; two siblings; loves to play basketball and soccer; involved in SCA's Musical Theater program; participates in church youth group, the Relevate worship team, and leads a middle school boys' Bible study; after college and seminary wants to be a pastor; favorite verse, 1 Timothy 4:12.

JOSHUA COOKSEY: 15, McMinnville, OR; Valley Baptist Church, McMinnville, OR; Homeschooled; Parents: Pastor Ronny/Kathy Cooksey; seven siblings; mows lawns and hangs Christmas lights for home businesses; likes to read and play basketball; plays piano for our church's nursing home ministry; planning to play viola in our church's instrumental ensemble; plans to be a missionary; grew up as missionary kid; favorite verse, 1 Peter 5:9.

MATTHEW COOKSEY: 13, McMinnville, OR; Valley Baptist Church, McMinnville, OR, Homeschooled; Parents: Pastor Ronny/Kathy Cooksey; seven siblings; likes to draw, write and camp; sings tenor in church choir; wants to be a graphic designer; favorite verse, James 4:17.

MICAH COOKSEY: 19, McMinnville, OR; Valley Baptist Church, McMinnville, OR; Parents: Pastor Ronny/Kathy Cooksey; seven siblings; Web designer and entrepreneur living and working in greater Portland, OR; enjoys singing in choir, running, writing, and woodworking, among other things; enjoys spending time with friends and family; favorite verse, Ezekiel 33:8–9.

DAVID JOSEPH DALESANDRO: 14, York, SC; Hillcrest Baptist Church and York Comprehensive High School, York, SC; Parents: James J./Lisa A. Dalesandro; likes to play video games, writing, reading; member of schools DECA Club and Boy Scouts of America; wants to be an archeologist; favorite verse, Leviticus 18:22.

JOSH DANIEL: 14, Troy, OH; Two Rivers Community Church, Vandalia, OH; Homeschooled; Parents: Jesse/Tina Daniel; three brothers; likes to play basketball; participates in On the Rock Homeschooled Co-op; would like to be a United States Marine, basketball player, or pastor; favorite verse, Philippians 4:13.

JONATHAN DISMUKES: 17, Mobile, AL; Redeemer Fellowship Church and Cottage Hill Christian Academy, Mobile, AL; Parents: Edward/Leigh Ann Dismukes; two siblings; likes to run cross-country and track, performs community service, and does well in school; member of various school organizations/clubs (Key Club, Scholar's Bowl, Mu Alpha Theta, National Honor's Society, Fellowship of Christian Athletes) and the local Ronald McDonald House's Red Shoe Krewe (volunteer group of 50 high school students); would like to be a biomedical engineer or doctor; favorite verse, Romans 12:1–2.

BRADY FOWLKES: 16, Tuscaloosa, AL; Valley View Baptist Church and Hillcrest High School, Tuscaloosa, AL; Parents: Brent/Mandi Fowlkes; three siblings; likes to play guitar, watch Alabama Crimson Tide football; watch the Atlanta Braves; read, play video games; speak Spanish, play church league basketball, church youth group, youth leadership team; favorite verse, Philippians 1:20–21.

PAUL CRAIG GALE: 14, New Orleans, LA; Franklin Avenue Baptist Church and New Orleans Center for Creative Arts, New Orleans, LA; Parents: Paul Craig Sr. (Deceased)/Mary

S. Gale; one sibling; member Student Leadership Team at Franklin Avenue Baptist Church; enjoy spending time and learning the will of God with team members on field trips, hosting/participating in sporting activities, and visiting other youth-focused events; on production team called "The Avenue"; arts discipline is Drama; member of mentoring ministry at church; plans to pursue a career in law or acting or a lawyer that specializes in representing artists; favorite verse, Philippians 4:13.

HANK F. GRIFFIN: 14, Pageland, SC; White Plains Baptist Church, Jefferson, SC; South Pointe Christian School; Pageland, SC; Parents: Chuck/Tonya Griffin; no siblings; likes to study God's Word, serve God, fellowship; is a Prayer Team Director, home-missionary; may like to become a principal; favorite verse, Psalm 23.

AUSTIN HARGETT: 15, Marshville, NC; Bethel Baptist Church, Marshville, NC; South Pointe Christian School, Pageland, SC; Parent: James Hargett; one sibling; likes to hunt and fish. After graduation wants to come alongside his uncle and farm; favorite verse, John 3:16.

CONNOR HOWINGTON: 17, West Monroe, LA; First Baptist West Monroe and Northeast Baptist School, West Monroe, LA; Parents: Dwain/Karen Howington; one sibling; loves serving God, studying the Word, ministering, listening to great Christian music, singing, reading, playing guitar; participates in school choir, First West "Adoration Choir" background vocalists; desired career: engineering, or ministry, but servant of the Lord; favorite verse, Psalm 23:1.

LUKE HUMANIK: 15; Jefferson, SC; Mt. Olive Baptist Church, Marshville, NC; South Pointe Christian School, Pageland, SC; Parents: Tim Humanik/Angel Quick; four siblings; loves to play sports and absolutely loves to hunt and fish; pitches for school baseball and on golf team; part of my school's golf team; would love to join the military, be a game warden, be a hunting guide, or become a policeman or SWAT; favorite verse, Isaiah 54:10.

DREW G. JENKINS: 13, Pageland, SC; Grace Baptist Church and South Pointe Christian School, Pageland, SC; Parents: Deanna/Donald Jenkins; two siblings; likes to play baseball and soccer; unsure of career plans; favorite verse, Philippians 4:13.

JOSHUA JOHANSEN: 18, Shrewsbury, MA; Bethlehem Bible Church, West Boylston, MA; Quinsigamond Community College, Worcester, MA; Parents: Erik/Tracy Johansen; two siblings; likes playing piano, writing, and studying the Bible; active in college/career group Bible study at church and serve in the Moving ministry; hopes to continue education in engineering; favorite verse, Romans 5:10.

ELI JONES: 15, Tulsa, OK; Evergreen Baptist Church, Bixby, OK; Mingo Valley Christian School, Tulsa, OK; Parents: John/Donna Jones; three siblings; likes to play soccer; doesn't yet know what career path he will take; favorite verse, Psalm 23.

DYLAN KNOLES: 13, Jefferson, SC; South Pointe Fellowship and South Pointe Christian School, Pageland, SC; Guardian: Mrs. Oliver; enjoys playing video games on the weekends and watching television; after graduation plans to go to college; favorite verse, John 3:16.

ROBBY D. LAND: 18, Gatlinburg, TN; First Baptist Church and Gatlinburg-Pittman High School, Gatlinburg, TN; Parents: Steve/Casey Land enjoys hiking in the mountains, playing in the creeks; has taken up local Blue Grass, Gospel, Old Time, and Celtic music by playing the fiddle; generally loves being outdoors; busy with studies, varsity swim team, church, and the social life; favorite verse, Jeremiah 29:11.

JACOB LAVALLEY: 16, Pageland, SC; Mount Moriah Baptist Church and South Pointe Christian School, Pageland, SC; Parents: Jerod LaValley/Jessica Leaird; eight siblings; likes to play basketball, baseball, and cross-country; plans to join the Marine Corps; favorite verse, Psalm 23.

MICHAEL LOWE: 15, Pageland, SC; Wolf Pond Baptist Church and South Pointe Christian School, Pageland, SC; Parents: Ray/Robin Lowe; one sibling; plays baseball, basketball, soccer and golf; Beta Club member and in FCA; wants to be a youth minister after college; favorite verse, Romans 8:38–39.

DAVID MARTIN: 15, Pageland, SC; Mount Moriah Baptist Church, Marshville, NC; South Pointe Christian School, Pageland, SC; Parents: Kelly Martin/Heather Davis; three siblings; enjoys going to the beach, drag racing, and helping others; likes to volunteer; wants to be an RN; favorite verse, Psalm 23.

NOLAN MARTIN: 16, Marshville, NC; Mount Moriah Baptist Church, Marshville, NC; South Pointe Christian School, Pageland, SC; Parents: David/Teresa Martin; one sibling; likes to play basketball and soccer; wants to be a Physicians Assistant; favorite verse, Philippians 4:13.

JOSIAH MCGEE: 15, Kansas City, MO; Summit Woods Baptist Church, Lees Summit, MO; Homeschooled; Parents: John/Carole McGee; three siblings; member of Grounded Student Ministries; enjoys playing the keyboard in the youth group praise band, playing piano, and debating competitively; also enjoys memorizing Scripture and studying it with an AWANA curriculum, reading, watching sports, and listening to music; hopes to attend Patrick Henry College to study foreign policy, and use what he is learning to fight for God's values in our government; favorite verse, Matthew 5:16.

JASON MCKEE: 15, Anchorage, AK; First Baptist Church of Anchorage and Service High School, Anchorage, AK; Parents: Pastor Jae/Carole McKee; one sibling; likes filming movies, sports (running and skiing), hanging out with friends; active in youth group, after-school sports; plans to go to college; favorite verse, Psalm 100.

LUKE MERRICK: 15, Springdale, AR; Immanuel Baptist Church and Shiloh Christian School, Springdale, AR; Parents: Pastor Mickey/Vicky Merrick; one sibling; interests include music, photography, academics, and criminal justice; primary job will probably be a criminal justice-related profession such as being a lawyer, or a homeland security officer while actively involved as worship pastor or a sound tech; favorite verse, Romans 8:31.

CHRIS NATION: 15, Gallatin, TN; The Fellowship at Two Rivers, Nashville, TN; Station Camp High School, Gallatin, TN; Parents: Philip/Angie Nation; one sibling; likes to hang out with friends, play guitar, stay active; member of student council, DECA, FCA, tennis team; wants to go into ministry; favorite verse, Proverbs 12:3.

JESSE NIEMAN: 18, Ocala, FL; Church @ The Springs and Forest High School, Ocala, FL; Parents: Larry/Christine Nieman; two siblings; loves to play soccer, along with brother and dad, plays on school varsity soccer team and a competitive team; volunteers at church; plans to play soccer in college and pursue whatever God's calling is; favorite verse, Joshua 1:9.

CLAY NORMAN: 18, Albany, GA; Sherwood Baptist Church and Sherwood Christian Academy, Albany, GA; Parents: Alan/Beth Norman; one sibling; likes to play baseball (currently school's varsity team); plans to major in business or theological studies; wants to be a missionary and to win the lost to Christ; favorite verse, Psalm 139:23–24.

KORD OFFENBACKER: 16, Springdale, AR; Cross Church Springdale Campus and Shiloh Christian School, Springdale, AR; Parents: Eric/Kerry Offenbacker; plays baseball and golf; plans to pursue one of them in my college education; plans to work in public relations and speaking; favorite verse, 1 Timothy 4:12.

WILLIAM DAVID ORR: 17, Albany, GA; Sherwood Baptist Church and Sherwood Christian Academy, Albany, GA; Parents: David/Catherine Orr; serves as a middle school discipleship leader; plays soccer, football, and runs track; plans to attend college next year and hopes to play soccer; undecided on major; favorite verse, Proverbs 3:5–6.

RAJ PATEL: 15, Jefferson, SC; South Pointe Fellowship and South Pointe Christian School, Pageland, SC; Parents: Narendra/Bhavna Patel; one sibling; enjoys school, watching television; plays basketball, baseball and soccer; plans to be heart surgeon; favorite verse, Proverbs 16:3.

CALEB PAYNE: 18, White House, TN; Long Hollow Baptist Church, Hendersonville, TN; Volunteer State Community College, Gallatin, TN; Parents: Mitchell Payne/Lori Wortham; four siblings; enjoys helping at church and being in God's Word; called to full-time pastoral ministry; Jeremiah 29:11.

JOEL PERSTROPE: 15, St. Peters, MO; First Baptist Church of St. Charles, St. Charles, MO; Fort Zumwalt East High School, St. Peters, MO; Parents: Pastor Buddy/Juli Perstrope; three siblings; loves music and sings in the choir at school: plays keyboard in the youth praise band at church; plays guitar and trumpet; loves sports; on high school baseball team; active in church and Monday Night Guys' Bible study; plans to go to college and possibly study education; favorite verse, Philippians 4:13.

LUKE PERSTROPE: 17, St. Peters, MO; First Baptist Church of St. Charles, St. Charles, MO; Fort Zumwalt East High School, St. Peters, MO; Parents: Pastor Buddy/Juli Perstrope; three siblings; enjoys playing music, watching sports and reading books; in school choir, leads youth praise band, helps lead a high school guys' small group, and speaks on occasion; plans to attend college and then seminary; believes is called to be a pastor; favorite verse, 2 Corinthians 5:21.

MICAH PERSTROPE: 13, St. Peters, MO; First Baptist Church of St. Charles, St. Charles, MO; Dubray Middle School, Saint Peters, MO; Parents: Pastor Buddy/Juli Perstrope; three siblings: plays trumpet, drums, and learning piano; in school band; recently played in district honor band; active in church and Monday Night Guys' Bible study; plans to go to college and seminary to become a pastor; favorite verse, Matthew 5:13–14.

TANNER PEYTON: 13, Pageland, SC; Charlotte Southern Baptist and South Pointe Christian School, Pageland, SC; Parents: Harry/Kim Peyton; one sibling; likes to play video games; participates in sports; wants to create video games when he completes school; favorite verse, John 3:16.

GABRIEL PLYLER: 14, Pageland, SC; Greater Vision Baptist Church and South Pointe Christian School, Pageland SC; Parents: Mark/Sandra Plyler; likes hunting and fishing; participates in sports and church events; plans to go to college; favorite verse, Acts 2:38.

BILLY RAMSEY: 17, Sharon, SC; Faith Baptist Church, Clover, SC; York Comprehensive High School, York, SC; Parents: Rusty Ramsey/April Hamrick; three siblings; loves to make music and play the piano; member of YCHS Cougar Band; wants to become a music composer/educator with a minor in performing arts; favorite verse, Philippians 4:13.

KYLE RAPE: 15, Wingate, NC, Mountain Springs Baptist Church and South Point Christian School, Pageland, SC; Parents: Eric/Sharon Rape; two siblings; enjoys listening to music, singing, and participating in sports; in schools Fine Arts program, Beta Club, FCA, cross country, soccer, basketball, and track and field; plans to become a civil engineer or join the USMC; favorite verse, Revelation 21:4.

JACKSON REESE: 18, Pageland, SC; South Pointe Fellowship and South Pointe Christian School, Pageland, SC; Parents: Brett/Donna Reese; loves sports and shooting; plans to join the military after college; favorite verse, Psalm 56:10–11.

REED REYNOLDS: 15, Albany, GA: Sherwood Baptist Church and Sherwood Christian Academy, Albany, GA; Parents: Mike/Kendyl White; four siblings; enjoys playing basketball, singing, and participating in Musical Theater; member of Relevate Student Worship Ministry, active in youth group, and serves on student leadership team; would like to attend Mississippi State for college and continue with my singing; favorite verse, Romans 12:2.

PAUL RICHARDSON: 17, Huntsville, AL; Whitesburg Baptist Church and Whitesburg Christian Academy, Huntsville, AL; Parents: Eddie/Susan Richardson; two siblings; likes to play basketball and go hiking; is on basketball team and track team; member of National Honor Society; plans to go to a university and pursue a degree; favorite verse, 1 Timothy 4:12.

JESSE D. SANDO: 13, Pleasant Hill, OH; First Baptist Church, Vandalia, OH; Homeschooled; Parents: Dave/Heidi Sando; six siblings; likes to do: mechanics, Bible study, car shows, writing, reading lengthy books; plans to work in mechanics; favorite verses, Jeremiah 29:11 and Matthew 5:29.

COLLIN MICHAEL SEELEN: 18, Itami, Hyogo, Japan; Emmanuel Baptist Church and Kansai Homeschooled Network, Itami, Hyogo, Japan; Parents: Missionaries Charles/Teresa Seelen; one sibling; enjoys traveling, sports, and spending time with my friends; developed a desire to share Christ with the Japanese while growing up in Japan; serves with parents in street evangelism and ministry; after completing university hopes to use this experience to become a Christian leader encouraging and supporting others to be involved in missions; favorite verse, Jeremiah 29:11.

CHANDLER SMITH: 16, Springdale, AR; Cross Church Springdale Campus and Shiloh Christian School, Springdale, AR; Parents: Clint/Ashley Smith; likes to read; play football and run track; wants to be an orthopedic surgeon when he finishes school; favorite verse, Isaiah 40:31.

CHRISTIAN SMITH: 17, New Orleans, LA; Franklin Avenue Baptist Church and New Orleans Charter Science and Mathematics High School, New Orleans, LA; Parents: Huey/Jacqueline Smith; seven siblings; loves to play video games and record/edit videos; participates in the Senior Council at school and the Youth Ministry at church; wants to be a filmmaker/actor; favorite verse, Philippians 4:13.

AUSTIN SOUTHERN: 18, Thailand and Mississippi; Chiang Mai Fellowship and Grace International School, Chiang Mai, Thailand; Parents: Jerry/Kelly Southern; one sibling; enjoys writing, weight lifting, spending time with friends as well as other pastimes; involved in a local church youth group; actively involved in his parents' ministry to the Shan migrant worker population of Chiang Mai; plans to enter medical field with the dream of using medicine to minister to the sick and hurting of the world; favorite verse, Romans 12:1.

PATRICK STANFORD: 18, Albany, GA; Sherwood Baptist Church and Sherwood Christian Academy, Albany, GA; Parents: Bobby/Cindy Stanford; one sibling; love to play basketball and hang out with friends; involved in SBC youth group called Elevate; would love to coach basketball one day and influence guys to be leaders on and off the court and play to glorify Christ; favorite verse, Psalm 16:1–2.

TERRELL STRAIN: 13, Spokane, WA; Airway Heights Baptist Church, Airway Heights, WA; Medical Lake Middle School, Medical Lake, WA; Parents: Leroy/Francee Strain; one sibling; participates in sports; enjoys reading, video games, trombone, tuba, piano; active in cross-country, basketball, track, jazz-band, ASB, NJHS, youth group, AWANA, choir, and assists at banquets at church; wants to be some sort of technologist after school; favorite verse, Isaiah 40:31

TREY SUEY: 16, Mt. Juliet, TN; The Fellowship at Two Rivers, Nashville, TN; New Life Academy, Mt. Juliet, TN; Parents: Eddie/Amanda Suey; two siblings; likes music and ministry; leads worship in the youth band; wants to be a worship minister; favorite verse, Joshua 1:9.

KYLE SUTTON: 16, Pageland, SC; First Baptist Church and South Pointe Christian School, Pageland, SC; Parents: Carlyle/Janan Sutton; two siblings; likes to hunt, fish, and play golf, cross- country, and to serve in ministry; wants to be a youth minister; favorite verse, Jeremiah 29:11.

CLAYTON TEAL: 17, Pageland, SC; Smyrna Baptist Church and South Pointe Christian School, Pageland, SC; Parents: James William Teal/Carolyn Arant Teal; one sibling; likes sports and fishing; participates in soccer, cross country, basketball, and track; active in Beta club and American Christian Honor Society; wants to go into law after college; favorite verse, Joshua 1:9

AARON THOMPSON: 13, Tiger, GA; Clayton Baptist Church and Rabun County Middle School, Clayton, GA; Pastor Joey/Marla Thompson; three siblings; likes football, hunting, fishing, shooting, camping, working on cars with Dad, video games, playing with my dogs; member of FFA; aspires to be what God plans for his life; favorite verse, Isaiah 12:5.

HUNTER TREMBLAY: 14, Pageland, SC; South Pointe Fellowship and South Pointe Christian School, Pageland, SC; Parents: Heath/Sheri Tremblay; one sibling; plays baseball, soccer, a little bit of golf, and a little bit of basketball; enjoys hunting, fishing, and shooting; plans for a mechanical engineering degree then join the U.S. Army; favorite verse, Proverbs 17:1.

ZACHARY TREMBLAY: 13, Pageland, SC; South Pointe Fellowship and South Pointe Christian School, Pageland, SC; Parents: Heath/Sheri Tremblay; one sibling; likes to play guitar; involved in sports and youth group; would like to be a professional golfer after college; favorite verse, Philippians 4:13.

ZACH WATKINS: 16, Henderson, NV; Highland Hills Baptist Church and Green Valley High School, Henderson, NV; Parents: Tobie/Shawn Watkins; plays baseball and football; actively involved in church, with youth group, help out with band; loves playing guitar and ukulele; favorite sports are baseball and rock climbing; desires to be a missionary to unreached people to share the gospel; favorite verse, Matthew 28:19–20.

DAVID WOODY: 16, Greencastle, PA; Greencastle Baptist Church and Greencastle-Antrim High School, Greencastle, PA; Parents: Pastor Donald/Sarah Woody; two siblings; enjoys playing sports, especially football; loves playing the guitar and hanging out with friends; participates in high school art, sports, and weight lifting; plays guitar for praise band, helps with the welcome center, helps lead the youth group in Bible studies and games; considering a career in construction; favorite verse, Psalm 91.

PARENT
Connection
B&H KIDS

THE BIG PICTURE

MAKING GOD THE MAIN FOCUS OF YOUR LIFE

THE GOSPEL PROJECT

HAYLEY & MICHAEL DiMARCO

What if the focus of your life wasn't about you?

The Big Picture is a gospel-centered book for teenagers and young adults that tells the story of the God who has always been with man and, through his Son and Spirit, always will.

THE GOSPEL PROJECT
FOR STUDENTS

B&H KIDS
EVERY *little* WORD MATTERS®
BHKidsBuzz.com

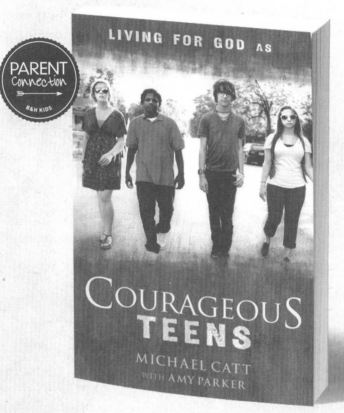